SERVICE MANUAL

FOR
MAC (SPRING FRAME) MODEL
350 c.c.

VELOCE LIMITED
: HALL GREEN WORKS :
YORK RD., HALL GREEN
BIRMINGHAM, 28

TELEphone : SPRingfield 1145/6/7
TELEgrams : "Veloce, Birmingham."

PAGE NUMBERS

The total number of pages in this manual is 128. However, both the 'Service Manual' and the illustrated 'Parts List' have their own individual index and page numbers. Consequently, the 'Parts List' begins immediately after page 88 of the 'Service Manual'.

INTRODUCTION

Welcome to the world of digital publishing ~ the book you now hold in your hand was printed using the latest state of the art digital technology. The advent of print-on-demand has forever changed the publishing process, never has information been so accessible and it is our hope that this book serves your informational needs for years to come. If this is your first exposure to digital publishing, we hope that you are pleased with the results. Many more titles of interest to the classic automobile and motorcycle enthusiast, collector and restorer are available via our website at www.VelocePress.com. We hope that you find this title as interesting as we do.

NOTE FROM THE PUBLISHER

The information presented is true and complete to the best of our knowledge. All recommendations are made without any guarantees on the part of the author or the publisher, who also disclaim all liability incurred with the use of this information.

TRADEMARKS

We recognize that some words, model names and designations, for example, mentioned herein are the property of the trademark holder. We use them for identification purposes only. This is not an official publication.

INFORMATION ON THE USE OF THIS PUBLICATION

This manual is an invaluable resource for those interested in performing their own maintenance. However, in today's information age we are constantly subject to changes in common practice, new technology, availability of improved materials and increased awareness of chemical toxicity. As such, it is advised that the user consult with an experienced professional prior to undertaking any procedure described herein. While every care has been taken to ensure correctness of information, it is obviously not possible to guarantee complete freedom from errors or omissions or to accept liability arising from such errors or omissions. Therefore, any individual that uses the information contained within, or elects to perform or participate in do-it-yourself repairs or modifications acknowledges that there is a risk factor involved and that the publisher or its associates cannot be held responsible for personal injury or property damage resulting from the use of the information or the outcome of such procedures.

WARNING!

One final word of advice, this publication is intended to be used as a reference guide, and when in doubt the reader should consult with a qualified technician.

FOREWORD

This Service Manual is issued as a guide to the complete servicing and repair of the MAC spring frame model Velocette and is intended primarily for the use of Agents and Repairers.

We have intentionally omitted some of the various routine maintenance jobs and adjustments already covered by the Owners' Handbook for the same model as these are usually undertaken by the rider.

References are made in places to special Service Tools which are essential for certain operations. It is earnestly hoped that Agents and Repairers will equip their workshops with them. They save so much labour and avoid the risk of damaging components that their acquisition is well justified.

It is possible that some private owners who are in the habit of doing most of their own repairs will obtain copies of this book. To any of these we suggest that in their own interest they entrust any repairs, which are likely to prove beyond their capacity, to their local Agent and not " bite off more than they can chew."

Publication No. F.469/3R/2M.   **VELOCE LIMITED.**

January, 1960

CONTENTS

A.
	Page
Air cleaner. Maintenance of	65
Ammeter. Testing	76
Automatic timing unit. Removal of	38
Automatic timing unit. (Illustration)	38
Automatic voltage regulator	74

B.
	Page
Ball valve assembly	19
Ball valve assembly. (Illustration)	17
Ballrace retaining ring tool. (Illustration)	51
Battery. Filling and charging	78
Battery. Maintenance and storage of	78
Big-end bearing. Overhauling	43
Big-end rollers. Oversizes of	44
Brake assembly. Front	10
Brake assembly. Rear	53
Brake adjustment. Rear. (Illustration)	83
Brakes. Relining	53

C.
	Page
Carburetter. (Illustration)	63
Carburetter. Sectional view	60
Carburetter. Description of	61
Carburetter. Dismantling, etc.	61
Carburetter. Setting and adjusting	64
Chain adjustment. (Primary)	82
Chain adjustment. (Primary) (Illustration)	36
Chain adjustment. (Rear)	83
Chain adjustment. (Rear) (Illustration)	83
Cleaning the machine	85
Clutch. Description of working	26
Clutch. Diagram of operating mechanism	27
Clutch. Dismantling	48
Clutch. Reassembling	48
Clutch. Adjustment of	28
Clutch adjustment. (Illustration)	28
Clutch thrust bearing	49
Commutator Cleaning	72
Commutator Connections. (Illustration)	69

	Page
Crankcase. Separating	42
Crankcase. Main bearings	42
Crankcase suction filter	20
Crankcase suction filter. (Illustration)	20
Crankshaft timing-pinion. Removal of	41
Crankshaft-pinion extractor. (Illustration)	41
Cut-out. Adjustment of	75
Cut-out. (Illustration)	75
Cylinder. Removal of	37
Cylinder. Refitting	45
Cylinder bore diameter	6
Cylinder head. Removal of	22
Cylinder head. Refitting	25

D.
	Page
Decarbonising and grinding in valves	22
Dynamo belt adjustment	74
Dynamo belt adjustment. (Illustration)	21
Dynamo belt cover. Removal of	31
Dynamo. Dismantling and reassembling	70
Dynamo. Exploded view	71
Dynamo. Removal of	31
Dynamo. Testing	73
Dynamo. Special spanner	72

E.
	Page
Engine bearings	42
Engine lubrication system	17
Engine. Overhauling	37
Engine. Removal from frame	36
Engine shaft shock absorber	22

F.
	Page
Fabric oil filter	20
Fabric oil filter. (Illustration)	17
Flywheel assembly. Lining up	44
Flywheel assembly. Overhauling	43
Flywheel assembly. Refitting	42
Fork. Description of working	12
Fork. Dismantling	15
Fork. Maintenance of	15
Fork. Reassembling	16
Fork. (Sectional illustration)	13

G.

	Page
Gearbox bearings	50
Gearbox. Dismantling	49
Gearbox end cover. (Illustration)	36
Gearbox. Reassembling	51
Gearbox. Removal from frame	36
Gearbox. Separating from engine	37
Gear operating mechanism	50

H.

Hub (Front). (Sectional illustration)	9
Hub. (Rear). (Sectional illustration)	54
Hub bearings. (Front). Dismantling	10
Hub bearings. (Rear). Dismantling	54

I.

Intermediate timing gear adjustment	47
Intermediate timing gear. (Illustration)	46
Index to Illustrations	5

K.

Kickstart mechanism. (Illustration)	35
Kickstart mechanism. Dismantling	34
Kickstart mechanism. Reassembling	35
Kickstart return spring. Replacing	35

L.

Lamps	68
Lamp bulbs	68
Lighting set	68
Lighting wiring diagram	76
Lubrication of chains	82
Lubrication of engine	17
Lubrication of fork	15
Lubrication of gearbox	8
Lubrication of magneto	79
Lubrication of wheel bearings	10, 54

M.

Main bearings. Removal	42
Main bearings. Refitting	42
Magneto. Maintenance	79
Magneto. Removal	81
Magneto. Refitting	82
Magneto. Testing	81
Magneto. Timing	47
Magneto. (Illustration)	80

O.

	Page
Oil circulation system	
Oil filter (Suction)	20
Oil filter (Suction). (Illustration)	20
Oil filter (Fabric)	20
Oil filter (Fabric). (Illustration)	17
Oil-pump. Priming	18
Oil-pump. Overhaul	40
Oil-pump. Removal	39
Oil-pump. Removal. (Illustration)	39
Oil-pump alignment tool. (Illustration)	40
Oil. Recommended grades	8
Overhead rockers. Removal	23
Overhead rockers. (Illustration)	23
Overhead rockers. Refitting	25

P.

Panniers. Fitting Instructions	87
Phases of throttle opening. (Illustration)	64
Petrol tap and strainer. (Illustration)	66
Piston. Removal	36
Piston. Refitting	45
Piston ring gaps	37
Primary chain. Removal	32
Primary chain. Refitting	33
Primary chain adjustment. (Illustration)	36
Primary chain case. Removal	31
Primary chain case. Refitting	33

R.

Rear suspension. Adjustment	55
Rear suspension adjustment. (Illustration)	55
Rear suspension. Maintenance	56
Rear suspension units	56
Retiming Ignition	47
Rocker cover. Removal	22
Rocker cover. Refitting	26
Rocker cover bolts. Location (Illustration)	23

S.

Shock absorber. Removal	22
Sleeve gear nut. Refitting	33
Sleeve gear nut adaptor. (Illustration)	34
Sleeve gear nut and spanner. (Illustration)	32
Sparking plugs. Recommended types	67

	Page.
Sparking plug. Maintenance	68
Sparking plug. (Illustration)	67
Speedometer drive	52
Steering head bearing. Adjustment	11
Steering head. (Illustration)	11
Steering head bearing tool. (Illustration)	14

T.

	Page.
Tappet adjustment. (Illustration)	23
Tappet clearances	26
Technical data	6
Theoretical wiring diagram	77
Timing gear	46
Timing gear markings. (Illustration)	46
Timing-pinion. Removal	41
Timing cover. Removal	38
Torque arms. Removal	57
Torque arms. Realignment	59
Torque arm clamp tool. (Illustration)	58

	Page.
Transfers. Instructions for fixing	84
Trunnion shaft. Removal	58
Trunnion shaft. Refitting	59
Tyres. Maintenance	85
Tyre pressures	85

V.

	Page.
Valves. Refacing and grinding in	24
Valves. Removal. (Illustration)	23
Valve guide. Renewal	24
Valve guide location. (Illustration)	25
Voltage regulator. Testing and adjusting	74

W.

	Page.
Wheel bearings (Front). Removal	10
Wheel bearing (Rear). Removal	54
Wheel bearings	10, 54

Index to Illustrations

		Page
Fig. 1	Front hub—Sectional View	9
,, 2	The steering head	11
,, 3	The Velocette telescopic fork	13
,, 4	Draw bolt for fitting head bearing cups	14
,, 5	Oil tank, ball valve, and filter	17
,, 6	Crankcase suction filter	20
,, 7	Dynamo belt adjustment, etc.	21
,, 8	Positions of rocker cover bolts	23
,, 9	Cylinder head and rocker assembly	23
,, 10	Setting of valve guides	25
,, 11	Diagram of clutch operating mechanism	27
,, 11a	,, ,, ,, ,,	27
,, 12	Adjustment of clutch	28
,, 13	Sleeve gear nut and peg spanner	32
,, 14	Sleeve gear nut adapter X2959	34
,, 15	Kickstart ratchet and springs	35
,, 16	The gearbox end cover, etc.	36
,, 17	Lucas automatic timing unit	38
,, 18	Removal of oil-pump and crankshaft pinion	39
,, 19	Pump alignment tool X2719	40
,, 20	Crankshaft pinion extractor X2721	41
,, 21	Positions of timing marks	46
,, 22	Ballrace retaining ring tool X2725	51
,, 23	Positions of selector forks	52
,, 24	Rear hub assembly. Sectional view	34
,, 25	Rear suspension adjustment	55
,, 26	Assembly tool X2992	57
,, 27	Torque tube clamp tool X2938	58
,, 28	The Amal carburetter (Section)	60
,, 29	Section of pilot passages	60
,, 30	The Carburetter	63
,, 31	Phases of throttle openings	64
,, 32	Fuel tap and strainer	66
,, 33	KLG sparking plug	67
,, 34	Miller dynamo. Commutator end	69
,, 35	Miller dynamo. Exploded view	71
,, 36	Miller bearing lock ring spanner	72
,, 37	Miller cut-out	75
,, 38	Wiring diagram (Miller lighting set)	76
,, 39	Theoretical diagram. (Miller dynamo and Regulator)	77
,, 40	Lucas type KIF magneto	80
,, 41	Rear brake and rear chain adjustment	83
,, 42	Pannier frame and bags	86

Technical Data

Identification Marks.

Engine number and Prefix letters MAC : Stamped on left-hand side of crankcase below the cylinder base flange. (Always include serial letters when quoting the identification number.) Fig. 7.

Frame Number : Prefix letters RS. Stamped on right-hand side of saddle front mounting lug.

Gearbox Number : Prefix No. 11/ or 14/. Stamped on right-hand side of housing at top.

Engine.

Capacity (Swept Volume) : 349 cubic centimetres. 21.289 cubic. in.

Bore and stroke : 68 m.m. × 96 m.m. 2.677 × 3.779-in.

Actual Bore diameter : 2.677-in.

Tappet clearance (Cold). For running. Inlet .005-in. Exhaust .005-in.

Tappet clearance (Cold). For setting timing. Inlet .030-in. to Exhaust .035-in.

Note.—Follow instructions on page 26 before checking or resetting tappet clearances.

Ignition Timing. 38° before top dead centre, fully advanced (Points open .0015-in.)

Valve Timing. (When checked with .030-in. to .035-in. Tappet clearances.)

Note.—Readjust to running clearances after checking.

	Cam marked M17/5	Cam marked M17/4	Cam marked M17/7	
Inlet opens	30°	50°	19°	Before top dead centre.
Inlet closes	60°	60°	49°	After bottom dead centre.
Exhaust opens	60°	70°	49°	Before bottom dead centre.
Exhaust closes	30°	40°	19°	After top dead centre.

Compression ratio : 6.75 to one. **Compression space :** 60—62 c.c.

Valve spring free length : Outer : $2\frac{9}{64}$ (2.1406) inches. Inner : $1\frac{15}{16}$ (1.9375) inches.

Piston Rings.

End gap—Compression rings : .0085-in. to .0115-in.
End gap. Oil control ring : .0105 to .0135-in.
Side clearance : Compression rings : .0005 to .0025-in.
Side clearance. Oil control ring : .0025 to .0045-in.

Stocked .020-in. .040-in. .060-in. oversize.

Valves. Seat angle 45°

Gudgeon-pin. .624-in. diameter (±.0001-in.) Stocked .001-in. oversize.

Small end bush. .625-in. inside diameter (+.0005-in. −.0002-in.)

Big end. Crankpin roller track diameter 1.374-in.
16 rollers—caged. $\frac{9}{16}$-in. diameter by $\frac{9}{16}$-in. long. Stocked .0002-in. and .0004-in. oversize.

Carburetter. Amal. Type 276EY/1AT. $\frac{15}{16}$-in. choke diameter.
Throttle valve. 6/4. Needle jet size 107 (No. 4/061). Main jet 130. Jet needle position 3.
Monobloc. Type 376/48. Throttle valve 3½. Needle jet 105. Main jet 200. Pilot jet 25. Needle position 3.

Magneto.	Lucas type KIF. Anti-clockwise rotation. Fixed ignition with automatic advance and retard unit type JY16A.
Dynamo.	Miller type DVR. 6-volt. Anti-clockwise rotation with automatic voltage regulation.
Lighting Bulbs.	Head lamp: 24W × 24W 6-volt S.B.C. Cap. or 30 × 24W Double Filament Bifocal Pre-focussed type.
	Parking: 6-volt, 3w. S.C.C. Cap. or 6-volt, 3W. M.E.S. Cap.
	Tail: 6-volt, 6W. S.C.C. Cap.
	Stoplight: 6-volt, 18 × 6W. Offset pin Stoplight type.
Battery.	6-volt. 13 A.H. Varley, Exide, or Lucas.
Gearbox.	4-speed. Foot controlled.
	Ratios (overall) with 21 tooth final drive sprocket: First, 14 to 1; Second, 9.6 to 1; Third, 7.3 to 1; Fourth (top) 5.5 to 1.
Sprockets.	½-in. pitch × .305-in.
	Engine 21 teeth. Clutch, 44 teeth. Final drive, 21 teeth. Rear wheel, 55 teeth.
Chains.	Primary. ½-in. pitch. .305-in. width. .335-in. roller diameter. 67 pitches.
	Rear. ½-in. pitch. .305-in. width. .335-in. roller diameter. 124 pitches.
Wheels.	Rims: Front, WM2 × 19-in. Rear, WM2 × 19-in.
	Spokes:
	Front—Brake side. 6⅝-in. × 10 SWG. 18 off.
	Front—Left side. 7¼-in. × 10 SWG. 18 off.
	Rear—Brake side. 7⅛-in. × 8/10 SWG. 20 off.
	Rear—Right side. 7⅛-in. × 8/10 SWG. 20 off.
Tyres.	Front, 19-in. × 3.25-in. Rear, 19-in. × 3.25-in.
Tyre Pressures.	Minimum solo: Front, 16 lbs. per sq. in. (1.1 atm.) Rear, 18 lbs. per sq. in. (1.2 atm.)
	For pressure chart see page 85.
Capacities.	
Petrol tank:	3 Imperial gallons. 3.6 U.S. gallons. 13.6 litres.
Oil tank:	½ Imperial gallon. .6 U.S. gallon. 2.27 litres.
Gearbox:	½ Imperial Pint. .6 U.S. Pint. .28 litres.
Front fork:	⅛ Imperial Pint. .15 U.S. pint. 71 cu. cent. per strut.
Sparking Plug.	14 m.m. diameter. 18 m.m. (extra long) reach.
	Suitable types: KLG FE70. Champion NA8. Lodge HLN.
Dimensions.	
Wheel base	(In normal loaded position) 53¾-in.—136.5-cms.
Ground clearance	(,, ,, ,, ,,) 5½-in.—14-cms.
Saddle height	(,, ,, ,, ,,) 30½-in.—77.5-cms.
Overall width	27½-in.—70-cms.
Overall length	7 feet —213-cms.
Weight unladen.	355-lbs. 161 kgs.

Recommended Lubricants

	B.P.	Duckhams.	Mobiloil.	Shell.	Wakefield.
Engine: Summer. (Ambient temperatures above 60° Fahrenheit)	Visco-Static* or Energol '40'	Q20/50* or NOL 'Forty'	Mobiloil Special* or Mobiloil B.B.	X100 10W/30* or X100 40	Castrol XXL
Engine: Winter (Ambient temperature below 60° Fahrenheit)	Visco-Static* or Energol '30'	Q20/50* or NOL 'Thirty'	Mobiloil Special* or Mobiloil A	X100 10W/30* or X100 30	Castrol XL
Gearbox	Energol '40'	NOL 'Forty'	Mobiloil B.B.	X100 40	Castrol XXL
Front Fork	Energol '20'	NOL 'Twenty'	Mobiloil Arctic	X100 20/20W	Castrolite
Wheel Hubs	Energrease C3	H.B.B. Grease	Mobil MP	Retinax A or Retinax H	Castrolease 'Heavy'
Primary Chain	Energol 40	NOL 'Forty'	Mobiloil B.B.	X100 40	Castrol XXL
Rear Chain	Energrease C3G	Laminoid	Mobil MP	Retinax A or Retinax H	Castrolease Graphited
For Grease Gun	Energrease C3	H.P.G. Grease	Mobil MP	Retinax A or Retinax H	Castrolease Medium
For Oil Can	Energol 10	NOL 'Ten'	Mobil Handy Oil	Donax A.1	'Oilit'

DO NOT use Additives in Oil or Fuel.   * These are 'Multi-grade' Oils.

THE FRONT HUB—SECTIONAL VIEW

The arrangement of the bearings etc. in the full-width type hub is identical.

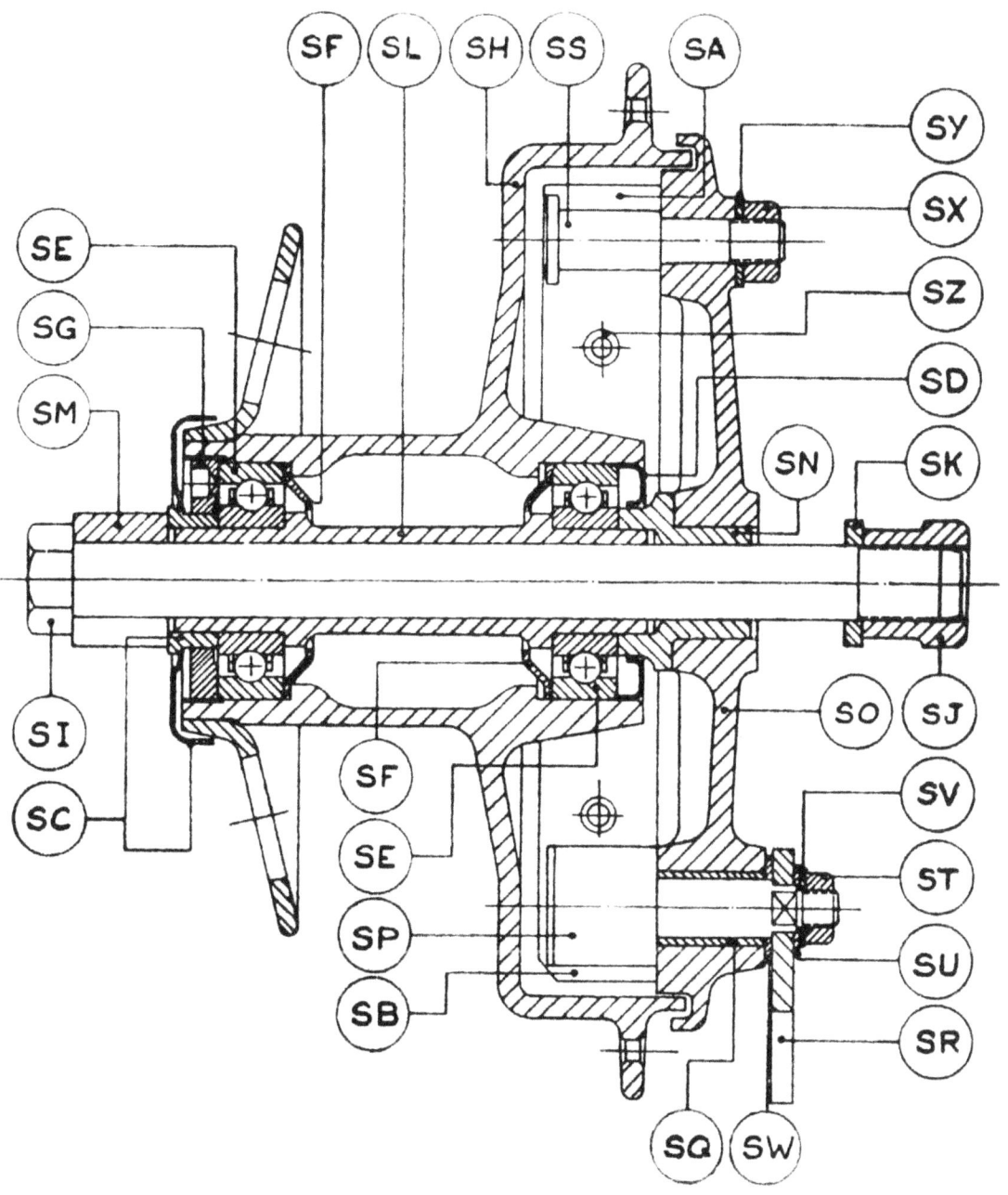

FIG. 1.

SA.	Brake Shoes	SJ.	Nut for Detachable Spindle	SR.	Lever or Brake Cam.
SB.	Brake Shoe Slipper.			SS.	Fulcrum Pin.
SC.	Outer Dust Cap and Sleeve.	SK.	Washer or Spindle Nut.	ST.	Nut for Cam.
SD.	Inner Dust Cap.	SL.	Hollow Spindle.	SU.	Square Hole Washer for Cam.
SE.	Ballraces.	SM.	Split Sleeve for Spindle.	SV.	Lock Washer
SF.	Grease Retainers.	SN.	Bearing Clamping Sleeve	SW.	Felt Washer for Cam
SG.	Ballrace Retaining Ring.	SO.	Brake Plate.	SX.	Nut for Fulcrum Pin
SH.	Front Hub Shell.	SP.	Brake Cam.	SY.	Plain Washer for Fulcrum Pin.
SI.	Detachable Spindle.	SQ.	Bush for Brake Cam.	SZ.	Brake Shoe Spring.

THE FRONT HUB, BEARINGS AND BRAKE. (Fig. 1.)

The front hub is supported on a hollow spindle (SL) by two non-adjustable Journal ball bearings (SE) which are a parallel-press fit in the hub (SH) and on the spindle. They are packed during initial assembly with high melting point grease which is sufficient for at least 20,000 miles running without attention, in normal circumstances.

Dismantling.

Dismantling the bearings for renewal or for repacking with grease is carried out as follows: Remove the front wheel assembly from the fork. On removal of the wheel the fork sliders will tend to spring over to the right. They are set in this way intentionally to keep the springs secured in their mountings when the wheel is in place.

Pull out the brake plate and brake shoe assembly from the drum. The bearing clamping sleeve (SN) will probably come away with the brake plate.

Enter a brass or aluminium punch in the opposite end (left-hand side) of the hollow spindle and drive the spindle and the brake side ball bearing out towards the brake drum. A punch about 9-in. long by just under $\frac{7}{8}$-in. diameter reduced to just under $\frac{5}{8}$-in. diameter for about $\frac{1}{2}$-in. at one end will be needed. (The same punch also suits the rear hub.) The dust caps (SC and SD) from both sides, will be removable now, together with the grease retainer (SF) from the brake side. The left hand ballrace and retaining ring (SG) will remain.

Unscrew the ballrace retaining ring and drive out the bearing (SE) towards the left, using a punch about 9-in. long $\times 1\frac{3}{16}$-in. diameter, reduced at one end to just under $\frac{7}{8}$-in. for about $\frac{1}{2}$-in. The other grease retainer (SF) will now be free.

Reassembling Front Hub Bearings.

Place one grease retainer (SF) convex side inwards into the ballrace housing in the left side of the hub and enter the ballrace into position. Press or drive the ballrace home in the housing and pack firmly with high melting point grease. Refit and tighten the ballrace retaining ring. Replace the other grease retainer in the brake side ballrace housing, convex side inwards, and pack the housing with grease. Take the hollow spindle with ballrace fitted to it and enter the spindle through the grease retainer and hub, locating the end in the left-hand ballrace, and the brake side ballrace in its housing. Press the spindle and ballrace home. Note that if the brake side ball bearing was removed from the spindle that it is fitted to the shorter ground end of the spindle. Incorrect mounting (on the longer end of the hollow spindle) will make it impossible to assemble the hub correctly.

Pack the bearing with grease and press the inner dust cap (SD) into the hub. On the opposite side, press the outer dust cap and sleeve assembly (SC) on to the protruding end of the hollow spindle.

Refitting the Brake Plate and Shoe Assembly.

Verify the condition of the brake liners and renew them, or fit a pair of "service" relined brake shoes, if the liners are worn flush with the rivet heads. See that the cam works freely and ease off if tight. See that the bearing clamping sleeve (SN) is in place in the brake-plate and fit the brake plate and shoe assembly in the drum, locating the sleeve over the protruding end of the hollow spindle. Refit the front wheel, and check fork for freedom of working. See page 16.

THE STEERING HEAD AND BEARINGS. (Fig. 2.)

Adjustment.

Final adjustment must leave the column quite free without trace of play. To take up play, slack back the top cross member clamp bolt nut (3) and tighten down the column lock-nut (2) until the column begins to bind when checked with the front of the machine supported so that the front tyre clears the ground. Gradually slacken the lock nut until the column is just free, with no trace of play or roughness in working. When correctly adjusted tighten clamp bolt nut (3).

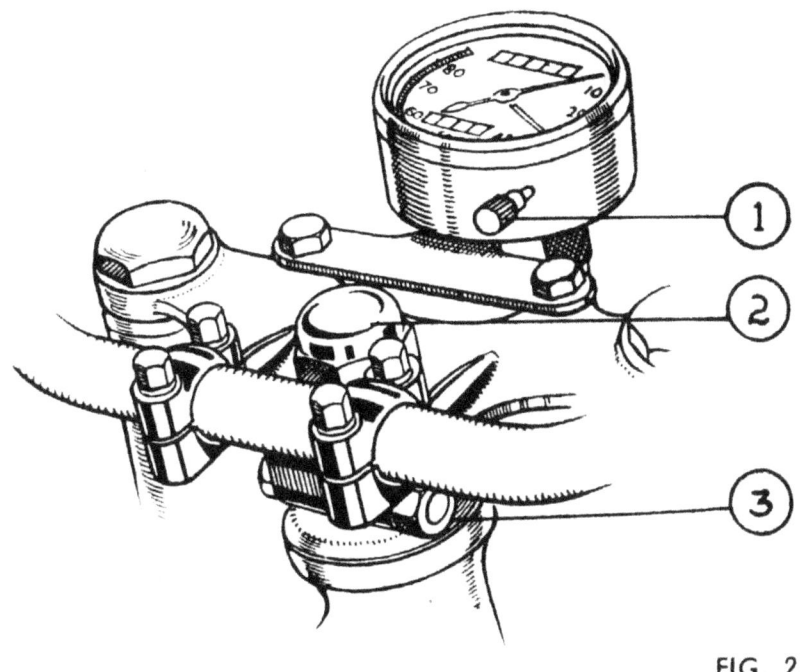

FIG. 2

THE STEERING HEAD

(1) **Trip Mileage Resetting Knob.**
(2) **Steering Column Nut.**
(3) **Clamping Bolt Nut.**

Should the column turn jerkily or roughly suspect that the head race cups and cones are pitted, and dismantle the column from the steering head for inspection and if necessary renew the bearings.

Removal of Steering Column. (Fig. 3.)

This will involve removal of the front fork assembly from the steering head, and is easier if the front wheel is removed first, together with the front mudguard and stays.

Disconnect the leads from the battery + terminal. Disconnect the speedometer driving flex from the instrument. Remove the handlebar clip bolts and caps and lay the handlebar across the tank top after putting a covering of rag or corrugated paper to protect the tank enamel. Replace the handlebar caps and bolts in the positions from which they were taken. The headlamp may be taken right off after removing the front and reflector and disconnecting all wiring from the switch and lamp, or it may be left connected to the wiring and laid back on the tank, after the front fork crossmember (4) Fig. 3, page 13, has been removed.

Unscrew and lift up both fork damper piston rod adaptors (3) and attach to each rod a length of wire, say 22 S.W.G., and about 18-in. long. These wires are essential to pull up the damper piston rods (24) on reassembling, and unless secured in this way they will drop down into the fork tubes on removal of the adaptors and will be difficult to retrieve.

Loosen the adaptor lock nuts (39) and screw the adaptors right off the rods. Loosen the clamp bolt nut (5) and remove the column lock nut (32). Support the fork underneath and tap the top cross member (4) up and off the column and fork tubes (12). If the headlamp has not been detached from the wiring, remove it from the brackets (37 and 40) and lay it on the tank. See that it is protected from damage.

Take off the dust cover from the top steering head bearing, and lower the fork gently through the steering head of the frame, meanwhile catching any bearing balls which fall out of the races. The upper bearing cone will be left in the top bearing. Store the fork upright to prevent loss of oil.

Renewal of Steering Head Bearings.

Remove the top cone and all the bearing balls and wipe the parts clean. Inspect them carefully for wear or pitting of the ball tracks. To remove the bearing cups from the steering head lug they must be driven out using a suitable steel punch passed through the head and engaged with the edges of the cups. Work from below to remove the top one and from above for the bottom one.

New cups have to be drawn into place quite square with the housings and a convenient way of doing this is to use a $\frac{3}{4}$-in. bolt $8\frac{1}{2}$-in. long, threaded B.S.F. for about $2\frac{1}{2}$-in., and two stout washers to locate in the cups.

The washers should be not less than $\frac{3}{16}$-in. (.1875-in.) thick and must be $1\frac{31}{32}$-in. (1.968-in.) diameter recessed on one edge to 1.860-in. diameter to a depth of about $\frac{1}{16}$-in. (.0625-in.) to locate in the cups. (Fig. 4.)

Enter the cups lightly into the housings and with one washer over the bolt, spigot upwards, thread the bolt up through the steering head, fit the other washer, spigot downwards, and thread the nut on to the bolt to hold all parts in place. See that the washers are located in the cups, and the latter quite square, and tighten down the nut until the cups are fully home.

Reassembling the Steering Column.

The bottom steering head cone may be tapped off the column if in need of renewal, and a new one pressed on. Note that the top and bottom cones differ. The top cone is deeper than the bottom one and its inside diameter is smaller.

Stick the bearing balls into the cups with grease, nineteen $\frac{1}{4}$-in. diameter balls in each cup. Push the steering column up into place through the steering head and hold it up firmly into the bearing. Push the top cone down over the column followed by the dust cap. See that the top locating cups (10), the buffers (8), and their housings (9) are all in place on the lamp bracket assemblies. Bring the headlamp forward, leading the wiring down between the lamp bracket tubes and the frame head lug and place the top cross member in position, threading the wires from the damper piston rods through the holes. Fit the column lock nut and screw the adaptors on to the damper piston rods, and tighten the locknuts. Remove the wires and tighten down the adaptors.

Readjust the head bearing as previously described and refit the handlebar, tightening the clip bolts evenly.

THE FRONT FORK. (Fig. 3.)

Description of Working.

Suspension is by coil springs (19), oil damped. The oil for damping and lubrication is carried in the fork struts.

The working is as follows: On extension of the fork, that is on recoil after a shock, the damper tubes (45) attached to the unsprung sliders

FIG. 3. THE VELOCETTE TELESCOPIC FORK WITH STEERING DAMPER

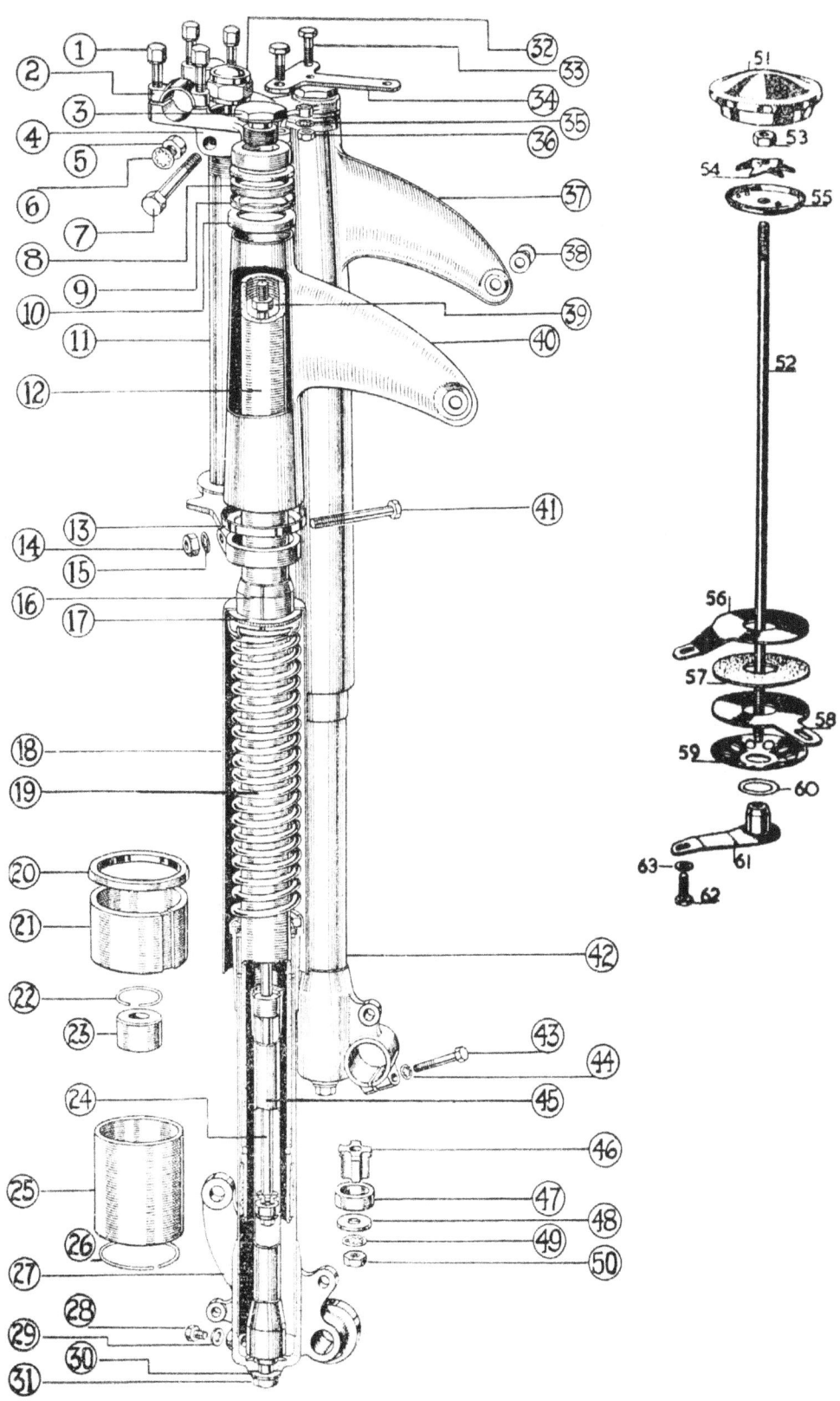

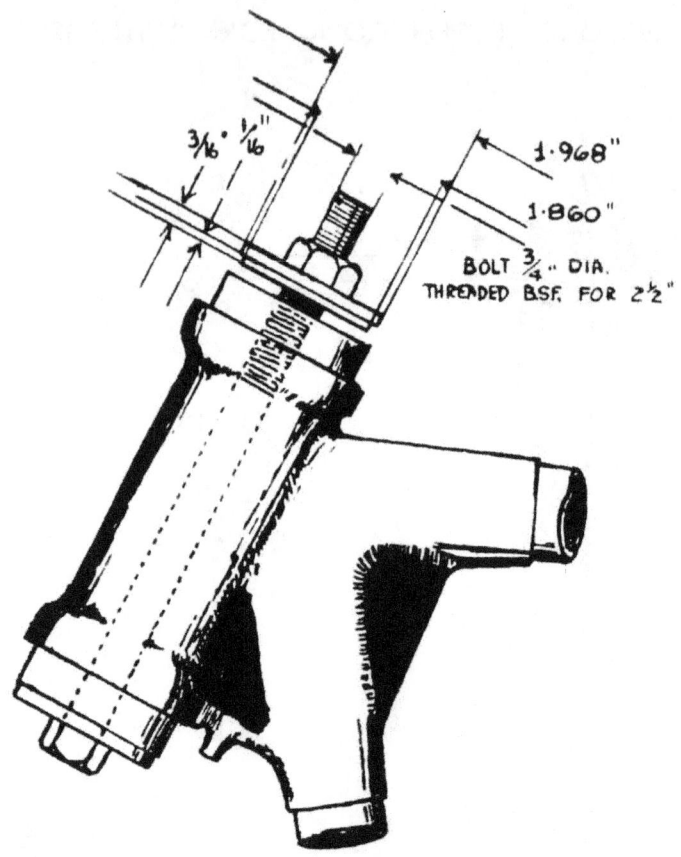

FIG. 4.
STEERING HEAD BEARING CUP TOOL.

move downwards away from the damper piston rods (24) which are fixed at the top to the adaptors (3) on the sprung part of the fork. The damper pistons (47) move into contact with the damper piston rod washers (48) closing the valves. The upward movement of the pistons relative to the damper tubes causes oil from the sliders (27 and 42) to be drawn through radial holes in the damper tubes to fill the spaces below the pistons.

On compression of the fork the movement is reversed and the damper tubes move upwards relative to the piston rods, and the pistons lift off the piston rod washers, allowing oil to pass freely from below the pistons through the damper valves (46) into the upper parts of the damper tubes.

Again on recoil the damper tubes below the pistons are replenished, but the oil above the pistons is trapped and can get out only through restricted openings at the top ends of the damper tubes, providing the resistance necessary to give the desired degree of damping.

Oil from the upper ends of the damper tubes drains down into the sliders and is available for use again.

The outer lower ends of the damper tubes are shaped to form cones, and any impact sufficient to force the sliders up almost to their limit brings the open ends of the fork tubes (12) over the cones, and a hydraulic lock is formed which prevents metallic contact and "bottoming" in severe conditions.

During the whole time the machine is running over rough surfaces the above cycle of operations is going on, and the more irregular the surface the greater is the degree of damping. It has been found that over almost smooth surfaces the fork works almost undamped and moves freely over slight inequalities in the road, thus overcoming the objection usually found with most damping systems that they prevent movement of the fork altogether under slight impact.

Maintenance.

Apart from external cleaning, the fork needs no attention. The oil supply lasts almost indefinitely and topping up is unnecessary. Should an owner wish to do so the oil may be drained out and fresh oil put in after 10,000 miles running.

Drain plugs (28) are fitted into the bottom of the sliders at the rear. After refitting the drain plugs, unscrew the two adaptors (3) from the top of the fork tubes. They can then be lifted far enough to get oil in quite easily. ⅛ pint (71 c.c.) will be needed in each side.

The Fork Spring Dust Covers. (Fig. 3.)

Occasionally a slight rattle may develop due to a loose dust cover. This must be rectified at once otherwise the rubber washers (17) between the inside of the dust covers and the split sleeves (16) will be damaged and will have to be replaced.

To eliminate rattle the split sleeve on the side needing attention has to be moved up the fork tube to " nip " the buffer. To do this first drain out all oil from *both* fork sliders. Slightly loosen the clamp bolt (41) on the side required. Do not slack it right off.

Bounce the front wheel sharply several times on the ground until the cover is prevented from rattling and retighten the clamp bolt. The dust covers will never be held so firmly that they cannot be turned by hand, but they must be secure and unable to rattle.

Complete draining of the fork is essential to avoid forming a hydraulic lock which otherwise will prevent the full closure of the fork springs, and the split sleeve will not move. Only partial slackening of the clamp bolt is required as if it is loosened too much the sleeve will move down again when the spring extends.

Dismantling the Fork. (Fig. 3.)

After removal from the machine—described previously—hold the steering column in a vice so that the fork is horizontal. Cover the jaws to prevent damaging the column. The procedure deals with only one strut, but it applies equally to both. Only the sliders (27 and 42) and the lamp bracket assemblies (37 and 40) are " handed " and their positions must be noted for correct reassembly.

Pull off the two buffer housings (9) and the locating cup from the top of the lamp bracket assembly. Remove the lamp bracket assembly and the cup (13) in which it is located at the bottom. Slacken off the clamp bolt (41) fully and pull the split sleeve (16) with the main tube, spring, dust cover, and slider, etc., through the bottom cross member of the column assembly away from the column. Twist the assembly when pulling which will make it come away easier.

Remove the column and the other assembly from the vice. Pull off the spring dust cover (18) and the rubber buffer (17) from the split sleeve. Hold the top end of the main tube (12) horizontally in the vice, hold the spring, and tap the split sleeve round until it comes free of the spring. Take the tube out of the vice and remove the split sleeve from it. Hold the slider in the vice and by grasping the spring firmly, twist it out of the mounting on the slider.

Take the slider in one hand and the main tube in the other and after pushing the slider up the tube as far as it will go, draw them apart as sharply as possible to dislodge the oil seal (20) and the slider bush (21) from the top of the slider. The main tube with the fork tube bush (25) will then come away. To remove the fork tube bush first prise the the circlip (26) from its groove in the end of the tube and tap the bush carefully off the tube.

The Fork Damper Assembly is removable from the slider after removing the nut (31) and washer (30) from the end of the slider, and will tap out of place. To dismantle remove the damper bush circlip (22) from the damper tube and remove the bush by a similar process to that adopted to remove the slider bush and oil seal from the slider. The damper piston rod (24) with the piston and valve, etc., will then pull out. If the piston (47) or damper valve (46) are removed note the correct order of replacement and see that the shiny face of the piston is set facing the bottom (next to the washer (48). Also when replacing the damper bush (23) note that the end with the chamfer fits uppermost, otherwise the circlip will not go into place.

Reconditioning—a Warning. The slider assemblies will be seriously damaged if stoved at temperatures exceeding 212° Fahrenheit after re-enamelling.

Reassembling the Fork. (Fig. 3.)

Fit the assembled damper to the slider being careful to locate the damper tube spigot properly in the hole in the slider. Fit the washer and nut and tighten. See that the fork tube bush and circlip are properly fitted to the main tube, slide the upper bush (21) over the tube and towards the bottom, noting that the groove across the end face must be facing the bottom bush.

Hold the tube horizontally in the vice and after lubricating the bushes fit the slider over it, entering the damper piston rod through the tube and the bottom bush (on the tube) in the slider. Twist the slider bush (21) to bring the groove, which is cut down the outside, to the top. Hold the slider so that the wheel spindle mounting lug points downwards. Enter the slider bush into the slider and drive it firmly into place using Service Tool LET 796, which consists of a specially shaped split collar which can be fitted over the tube. Remove the tube from the vice and fit the oil seal (20) over it and slide it down to the top of the slider into which it must be fitted by using Service Tool LET 796 once more. Slide the spring down into position and by holding the slider in the vice twist the spring firmly into its mounting. Extend the slider along the tube as far as it will go.

Push the split sleeve (16) down the tube until the upper edge of its taper section is set exactly 7.187-in. (7 $\frac{3}{16}$-in.) from the top of the tube. Hold it firmly in this position and push the slider and spring towards it, engaging the spring in its mounting on the split sleeve and twisting it firmly into place. Invert the assembly until the damper piston rod protrudes from the tube and attach a piece of wire to it as described on page 12. Fit the rubber buffer (17) and dust cover (18) over the sleeve, thread the wire, and the tube through the bottom cross member, and partly tighten the clamp bolt. Note that the assembled tube, spring and slider are fitted on the correct side. The slider which carries the wheel spindle clamp is always on the left (remote from the brake drum).

When assembling the fork—prior to refitting it to the machine—always set the struts so that the fork ends of the sliders point over to the right at about 20° off the centre line. This ensures that when the wheel is fitted after the clamp bolts (41) are tightened the sliders tend to hold the springs firmly into their mountings.

Reassembly of the lamp brackets only calls for care in fitting them to their respective sides and seeing that they are located properly in their top and bottom collars and that the top buffers are fitted between the hollow (concave) sides of the buffer housings.

The wires attached to the damper piston rods enable these to be drawn up for the attachment of the adaptors (3).

Before refilling with oil verify that the dust covers do not rattle, and after fitting the wheel make certain that the fork works freely before finally tightening the spindle clamp bolt. If the dust covers are loose see page 15.

Setting the Front Mudguard Stays.

As a fork is seldom removed and dismantled unless the machine is accidentally damaged, care should be taken when fitting the front mudguard stays, whether new or repaired ones, that they go into place without having to be forced. Before fitting them therefore they must be set to the correct widths between the ends as follow : Front stay 6⅝-in. (6.625-in.); Central stay, 6¾-in. (6.75-in.); Bottom (rear) stay fitted outside the centre stay, 6½-in. (6.5-in.).

In any instance where the fork does not work freely, and this is not due to the wheel mounting, remove the stays and reset them if needed.

ENGINE LUBRICATION SYSTEM.

Description of Working.

From the oil tank oil is taken to the feed side of a double gear pump in the crankcase, through a non-return ball valve fitted between the oil tank and the oil feed pipe (Fig. 5). The oil feed pipe is primed with oil during original assembly—in this connection refer to page 18.

The oil pump body carries two pairs of gears, one pair forming the feed pump and the other pair which are much wider, form the return pump and return oil to the oil tank after it has circulated through the engine. Due to the greater width of the return gears the feed cannot overtake the supply and cause the crankcase sump to become flooded. The pump is driven from a worm on the timing side mainshaft.

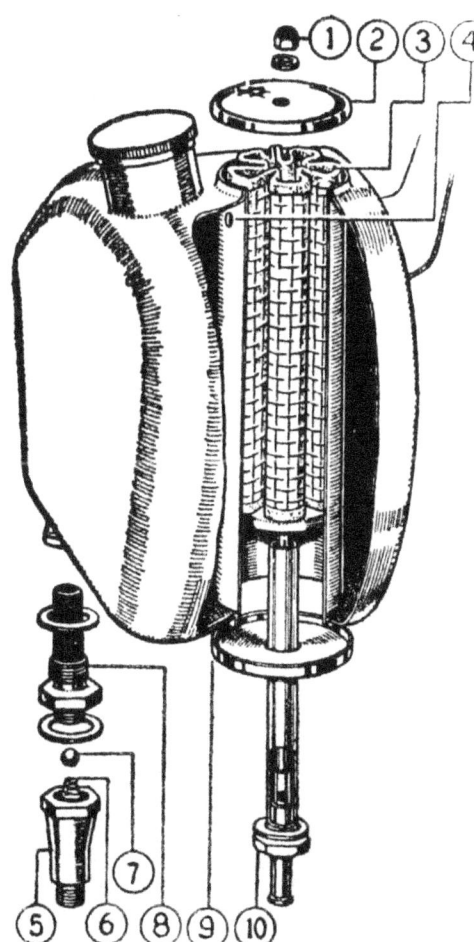

FIG. 5

OIL TANK, BALL VALVE AND FILTER.

(1) Oil Tank Filter Stud Nut.
(2) Oil Tank Filter Cap—Top.
(3) Oil Filter Element.
(4) Outlet to Tank.
(5) Ball Valve Body.
(6) Ball Valve Spring.
(7) Ball Valve Ball.
(8) Oil Strainer Assembly.
(9) Oil Tank Filter Cap—Bottom.
(10) Oil Tank Filter Tube Assembly.

From the feed pump gears the oil is forced through a drilling in the crankcase to the timing cover in the face of which is a hole which matches with the outlet of the drilling in the crankcase. The timing cover acts as

ENGINE LUBRICATION SYSTEM (continued).

a distributor for the oil supply and carries feeds to the big end bearing through the crankshaft oil jet, to the cams, bottom rockers, and to the overhead rocker gear.

The feed to the cams and bottom rockers is through the cam oil jet, one end of which locates in a hole in the cover. The rocker oil feed pipe leading to the rocker cover is attached to a union at the top of the timing cover. By the removal of the oil pipe from this union it is possible to check whether the pump is working and it is essential that this check is made should the oil feed pipe or oil tank have been removed, or the oil-pipe emptied of oil. A fourth outlet from the cover feeds the cam wheel bush.

From drillings in the rocker cover oil is directed into the rocker bearings in the overhead rocker bearing bracket assembly, and from here lubricates the valve stems, guides, and the ball cups at the top ends of the push rods. The surplus drains down to the timing case through the push rod cover tubes, lubricating the push rod ball cups formed in the bottom rockers, and falls on to the timing gears.

The surplus oil from the cam wheel bush and the cam oil jet drains into the timing case, from which it goes back into the crankcase through a hole in the wall between the crankcase and timing case.

The piston, cylinder, and small end are lubricated by oil dissipated by the rapidly revolving big-end, and oil draining down the crankcase wall on the timing side is caught in a drilling leading to the intermediate gear bush. Both main bearings are kept constantly supplied.

From the bottom of the crankcase the oil is taken up to the return half of the pump, but before reaching the pump has to pass the Suction Filter (Fig. 6). The filter is formed by a plug screwed into the oil return passage at the bottom right hand rear corner of the crankcase. The diametric clearance between the filter plug and the passage is so small that it is quite impossible for anything which might damage the pump to pass.

The oil from the crankcase is piped to a connection under the oil tank, and passes up a tube inside the oil filter chamber in the tank, and after passing through a fabric filter element enters the main oil tank through a hole at the upper end of the filter chamber below the filler cap opening. (Fig. 5.)

The fabric filter is easily removed for replacement and should be discarded and replaced by a new one every 10,000 miles.

Oil in circulation may be observed issuing from the opening in the filter chamber when the engine is running.

Checking the Oil Circulation.

Owing to the use of a spring loaded non-return ball valve between the oil tank and the pump, the pump will not feed oil to the engine unless the feed-pipe is full of oil. After a normal spell of running this pipe will always be left full and priming is only needed during initial assembly, after a full engine overhaul, or if for any reason the oil feed pipe has been disturbed and emptied of oil.

After priming the oil pump, and before starting the engine it is essential to disconnect, temporarily, the union at the lower end of the overhead rocker oil feed pipe. A moment after starting the engine oil should be seen to be forced out of the union on the cover. Allow the engine to run for about two minutes at slow speed to make certain that the flow is continuous before stopping the engine and refitting the union nut.

ENGINE LUBRICATION SYSTEM (*continued*).

In normal circumstances the flow may be checked occasionally by noting the oil returned to the tank through the hole in the filter chamber.

Bear in mind that this flow will usually be somewhat intermittent and irregular. It may be constant and greater than normal after starting an engine which has been stationary for some time, because an accumulation of oil which has had time to drain to the bottom of the crankcase off all the internal parts will be cleared. After this, and if the throttle is opened and the engine speed increased the flow may be observed to cease temporarily, only to resume again at a greater rate on the engine slowing down. This is due to the time taken for the suddenly increased amount from the pump, to get round the system and to find its way back to the oil sump.

These symptoms are quite normal, but it should be noted that if the oil filter chamber in the tank is not refilled with oil after cleaning the tank, or replacing the filter element, no return into the tank will be seen until the chamber has filled up to the outlet hole with oil pumped back from the engine. Also the level of oil in the main tank will be reduced by the amount trapped in the filter chamber. It is, therefore, advisable to refill the filter chamber as well as the tank during an oil change.

The Ball Valve Assembly (Fig. 5.)

This is composed of a threaded union screwed into the oil tank carrying a gauze strainer (8) and formed to act as a seating for the ball (7), which is kept into contact with it when the engine is stationary by the spring (6) carried below the ball in the lower part of the assembly, the Ball-valve Body (5).

The purpose of the ball valve is to prevent oil from the tank draining into the engine by gravity through the pump when the engine is standing, as this would eventually flood the crankcase and make starting very difficult.

In the ordinary way the ball valve will seldom need attention, but if there are indications that the valve is leaking, such as excessive and prolonged smoking at the exhaust after starting up, or if the crankshaft is felt to be very sluggish to rotate on starting (provided that this is not due to excessive cold or the use of summer viscosity oil in cold weather) the ball valve assembly can be dismantled for attention. Excess oil can be drained from the crankcase before attempting to start if the ball valve has been leaking.

After detaching the oil feed-pipe union nut from the Ball-Valve Body (5) the Ball-Valve Assembly may be unscrewed from the tank using a spanner on the upper hexagon formed on the Oil-strainer assembly (8). Unless the tank has previously been drained a tin must be provided to catch the oil as the Oil-strainer assembly is removed.

By holding the Ball-valve Body upright in the vice the strainer assembly may be unscrewed out of it leaving the ball and spring exposed.

Note that a gasket is used between the strainer assembly and the body and do not remove the spring needlessly. The body may be cleaned out with the spring in place.

The seating for the ball in the strainer assembly may be inspected, but if leaking, the strainer assembly should be replaced. The expedient sometimes adopted of tapping the ball sharply against the seating to bed it in is deprecated because this widens the seating, and consequently reduces the unit pressure of the ball upon it, making subsequent leakage more likely, and should only be used as a temporary measure.

When reassembling the strainer to the body see that the gasket is in place, and the ball resting on top of the spring. The ball *must be above the spring as illustrated*, otherwise the flow of oil will be cut off effectively with disastrous results to the engine. See Fig. 5 for order of fitting. If the spring has been taken out make certain that when refitted it is seated right home

ENGINE LUBRICATION SYSTEM (*continued*).

in the ball valve body otherwise the spring pressure upon the ball will be too high and prevent the ball opening when the engine starts.

Refit the Ball-valve assembly to the tank not omitting the gasket, and if the oil pipe is full of oil re-attach it to the Ball-valve body and tighten the union nut. If the oil pipe has been disturbed, or is empty, prime it by filling with oil. See that the drain plug is in place and tighten. Refill the tank.

Before starting the engine undo the union nut of the Rocker oil pipe and free the nipple. Start up and check the oil flow (see page 18). If there is no flow stop the engine at once, reprime the oil-feed-pipe and test again.

The oil pipe may be filled more easily if the banjo union hollow bolt is loosened to relieve air locks. Tighten up as soon as the pipe is full.

When all is in order refit and tighten the rocker-oil pipe union nut.

The Suction Filter. (Fig. 6.)

The Filter Plug (Fig. 6) should be unscrewed and removed for cleaning at intervals of 2,000 miles, or if at any time continuous and excessive smoking at the exhaust indicates that the crankcase is not being cleared satisfactorily of oil. Wash the plug in clean petrol, dry off and replace. Note that a gasket is fitted between the head of the plug and the crankcase. Make certain that this is in good condition and replace if faulty. Tighten the plug fully to eliminate air leakage.

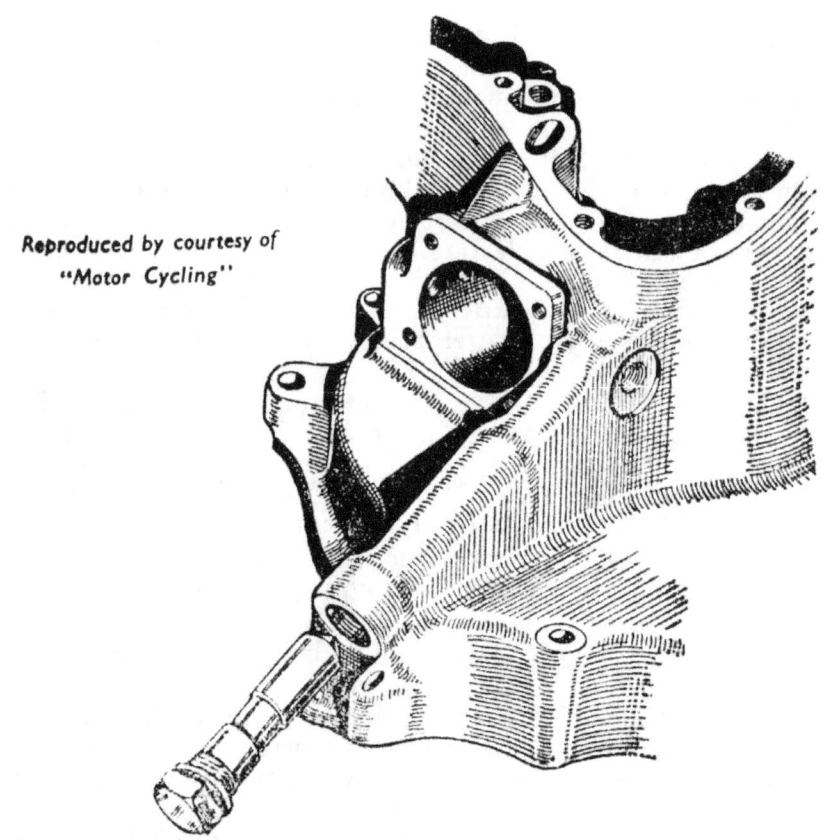

Reproduced by courtesy of "Motor Cycling"

FIG. 6. THE CRANKCASE SUCTION FILTER

Fabric Oil Filter (Fig. 5).

The filter element should be renewed every 10,000 miles or less and the old one discarded. To replace the element it is not necessary to remove the oil tank, although if it is desired to wash out the tank this is easier if it is taken off.

ENGINE LUBRICATION SYSTEM (*continued*).

Drain out all oil, by removing the oil tank drain plug. Drain the filter chamber by loosening the filter stud nut (1) sufficiently to permit the bottom cap (9) to pull away a little from the bottom of the tank, and catch the oil from the filter chamber in a tin.

When all oil has drained away, remove the nut and top cap and pull down the stud and bottom cap clear of the tank and take them away. Pull the old filter element out from the top.

Wash the filter chamber, filter tube assembly (10) and both caps in clean petrol and dry off. Fit the replacement filter element and put back the bottom cap with its gasket and thread the filter tube assembly up through the filter chamber. Have the top cap, with its gasket, nut, and washer handy for refitting. Hold the filter tube assembly firmly up to the cap and the cap against the bottom of the tank and fill the filter chamber with clean oil up to the level of the outlet hole (4). Refit the top cap with its gasket and the washer and nut, and tighten up the nut. The gaskets must be properly centralized to prevent leakage.

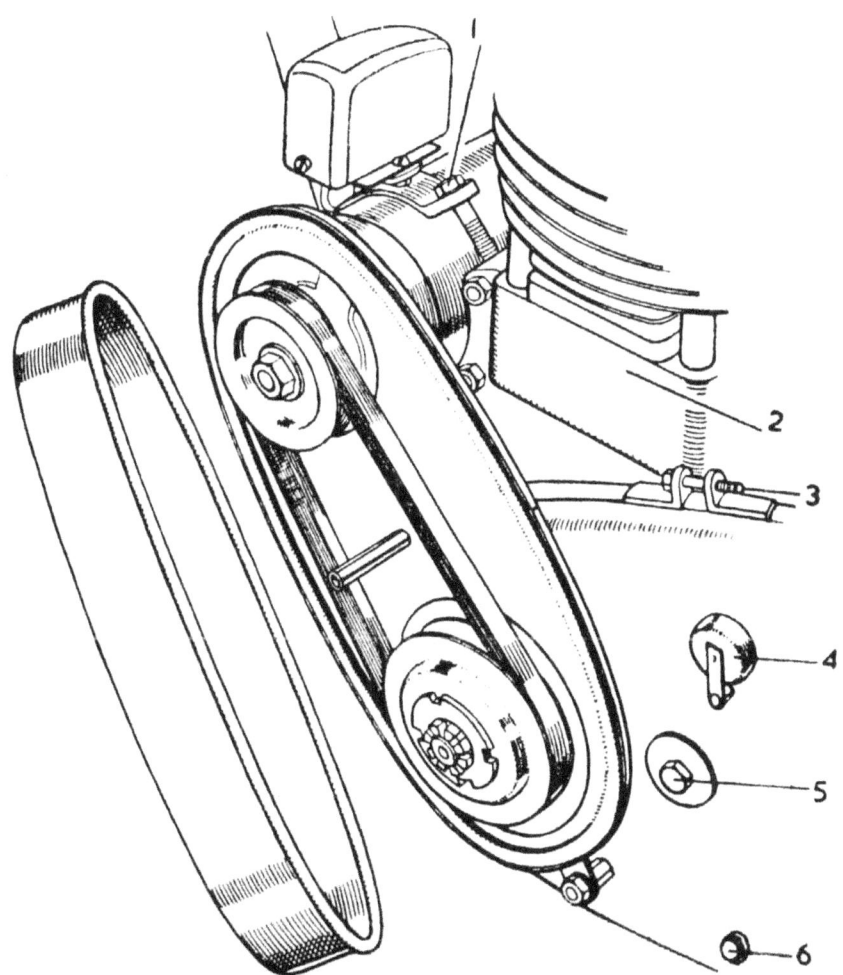

FIG. 7. DYNAMO BELT ADJUSTMENT
(1) Dynamo Clamp Bolt.
(2) Location of Engine Serial Number and Prefix.
(3) Chain Case Strap Fixing Pin.
(4) Chain Case Inspection Cap.
(5) Chain Case Bolt.
(6) Chain Case Drain Plug.

Replace the tank drain-plug and refill the tank with oil.
Additives are unnecessary and should not be used.

If the oil feed pipe has been disturbed fill it with oil and check the circulation. See page 18.

ENGINE SHAFT SHOCK ABSORBER.

The shock absorber spring, and the splined shock absorber clutch can be removed for inspection or replacement without removing the front half of the primary chaincase and are accessible after removal of the front of the dynamo belt cover, the belt, and the mainshaft nut or shock absorber spring collar (Fig. 7).

Dismantle the cover as shown, take off the belt and withdraw the split cotter from the mainshaft. Engage top gear and hold the rear brake on whilst the nut is loosened and removed. The spanner A229 is required. A hammer will be needed on the spanner to start the nut.

As the collar unscrews the dynamo pulley flange and pulley, which locate on the collar, will come off with it. The spring and shock absorber clutch will then pull off.

When refitting, grease the splines and shock absorber cam-faces liberally and note that the projection on the pulley must engage the slot in the pulley flange, and the projection on the pulley flange must be engaged with one of the slots in the edge of the collar.

Replace the plain washer on the end of the shaft, and fit the collar. Tighten fully, and fit a new split cotter, afterwards spreading out the ends of the cotter.

DECARBONISING THE ENGINE AND GRINDING IN VALVES.

The mileage that an engine will run efficiently without being decarbonised depends to a great extent upon driving conditions. A new engine is the better for receiving this attention after the first 2,000 to 3,000 miles have been covered. Afterwards it will probably be found to run perfectly satisfactorily for very much greater distances without similar attention. Whilst it is impossible to lay down any hard and fast rule it may be said that generally the average private owner does the work too often rather than too seldom.

If the engine is running well, and there is no noticeable loss of power, or other evidence such as a tendency to " pink " excessively it is best not to disturb it.

During the operation do not remove the cylinder barrel, unless there is good reason to do so. Removal means disturbing the piston rings, which can never be replaced in exactly the positions in which they have settled and bedded in to the cylinder and piston, and their frequent removal and reassembly may cause an increase in oil consumption.

Dismantling Cylinder Head.

Disconnect the petrol pipe from the tank. Take off the tank strap from beneath the front end of the tank. Pull off the sleeve connecting the carburetter to the air filter. Remove the fuel tank and take off the carburetter. Note that a special heat insulating gasket is used between the carburetter flange and the cylinder head.

Remove the silencer and the exhaust pipe together. Unscrew the banjo hollow bolt and the bottom union nut from the rocker oil pipe, and remove the pipe.

Remove the rocker cover. It is held by eight bolts of five different lengths—the positions they occupy should be noted for subsequent replacement (Fig. 8).

Should the cover not come clear easily, rotate the crankshaft until the inlet valve is full open. The front of the cover will then slide over towards the left of the machine and the rear edge can be tipped over the inlet rocker quite easily.

LOCATION OF ROCKER COVER BOLTS

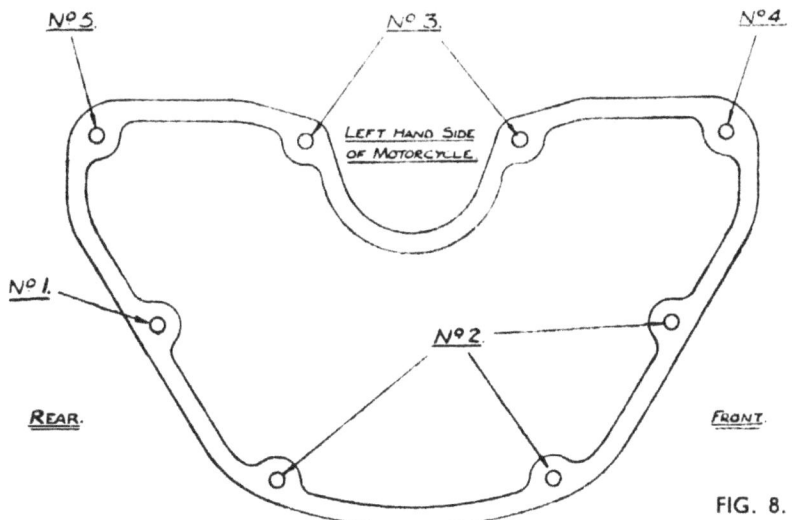

FIG. 8.

No. 1 is the longest Bolt. The others are indicated numerically in decreasing length.

Take out the sparking plug. If this is found to be tight in the threads do not force it, but drip a little penetrating oil or paraffin round the body of the plug and allow time for this to percolate between the plug and the head.

Rotate the crankshaft until both valves are seen to be closed. Take out the two bolts at the ends of the rocker bearing bracket and the one in the centre. Do not undo the other two—these hold the bearing caps. (Fig. 9).

Lift off the rocker bearing bracket assembly and rockers, and remove the gasket from the platform on the head. Lift out both push rods and mark them for replacement in the same positions. Do not interchange them.

THE CYLINDER HEAD AND ROCKER ASSEMBLY

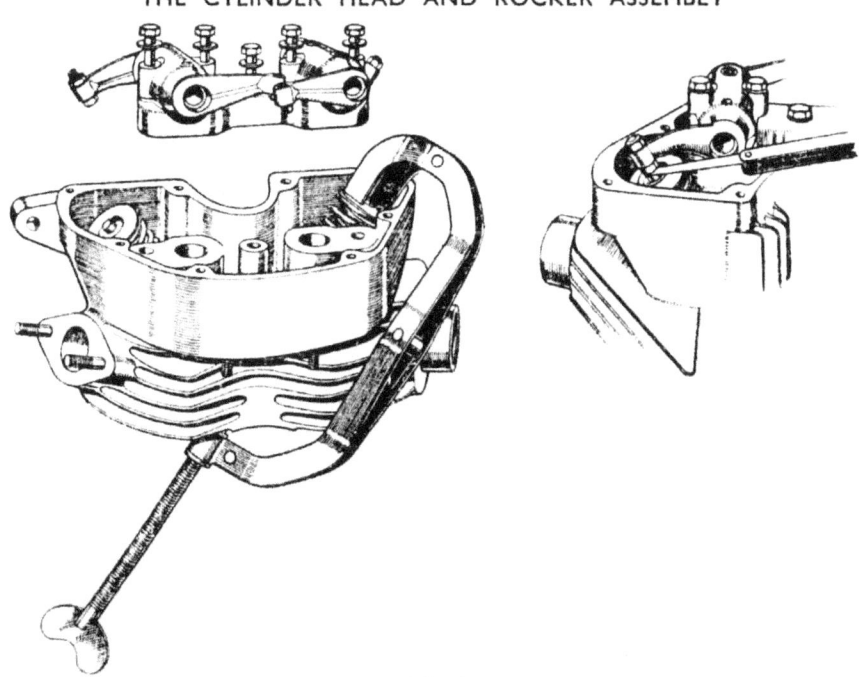

FIG. 9.

LEFT. Rocker bearing bracket assembly removed. All five bolts are shown withdrawn, but only the two end ones and the centre one need be removed, and the other two which hold the bearing caps should be left tight. The Compressor KA163 2 is shown in use.

RIGHT. Checking tappet clearance on exhaust valve.

Unscrew and remove the four cylinder head nuts and washers. Two nuts are outside the rocker box on the left, the other two down inside the cavities in the rocker bearing bracket platform.

Take off the nuts and washers from the flange studs of the upper push rod cover, and telescope the tube into the lower one. Keep the two gaskets and the guide plate for reassembly later. Unscrew and lift out the four long cylinder studs from the cylinder base studs.

Remove the cylinder head—preserving the copper gasket for refitting.

Removing Valves.

Compress the valve springs with the compressor tool KA163/2 (Fig. 9), and pick out the cotter. Keep the halves of each cotter together and do not interchange them or the valves and springs.

Refacing Valves.

The valves should be refaced on a valve refacing machine—the seat angle is 45°. This reduces the amount of grinding-in needed and saves unnecessary wear on the seatings in the head. Also clean up and polish the valve head but be careful not to reduce the diameter of the stem. The scale which may be found on the exhaust valve due to additives in the fuel, is often very hard, but can usually be cleaned off by holding a piece of carborundum against the scaled surface whilst the valve is rotated rapidly in a lathe or drilling machine.

Grind in each valve to its own seating using " fine " grade compound. Grind in only enough to give an uninterrupted matt grey surface all round the seatings on the valve and in the head.

Reconditioning the Cylinder Head Valve Seats.

As the valve seating material is very hard and durable, the seatings seldom need any other truing up than can be given by grinding in the valves, and they cannot be recut with the normal type of seating cutter.

After prolonged use and when refacing is needed they must be trued-up by grinding with a 45° valve seat refacing stone. Special equipment for this purpose is obtainable from various machine tool manufacturers.

Cleaning off Carbon Deposit.

Use only brass or copper scrapers on the piston crown and combustion chamber to avoid scratching the surfaces. The ports in the head may be cleaned by using emery cloth. Do not remove the ring of carbon which will have formed round the top of the cylinder bore.

After cleaning the piston crown rotate the crankshaft to bring the piston down the bore and clean off all carbon dust from the bore. After cleaning thoroughly bring the piston back to the top.

Replacement of Valve Guides. (Fig. 10.)

The valve guides are bored to allow diametrical clearances from the valve stems of .00125-in. to .0025-in. and are fitted during manufacture to the head when the head is heated.

Removal of worn guides for replacement purposes must not be attempted unless the metal of the head around the guides is heated up before pressing them out. The temperature should not exceed 100° Centigrade (boiling point of water). Immersion of the head in boiling water is a suitable means of heating, or the metal round the guide may be heated with a blow lamp provided the flame is moved about and not concentrated on one spot.

The head must also be heated before fitting new guides, which are pressed in leaving ⅝-in. protruding beyond the machined surface around the valve guide hole (Fig. 10).

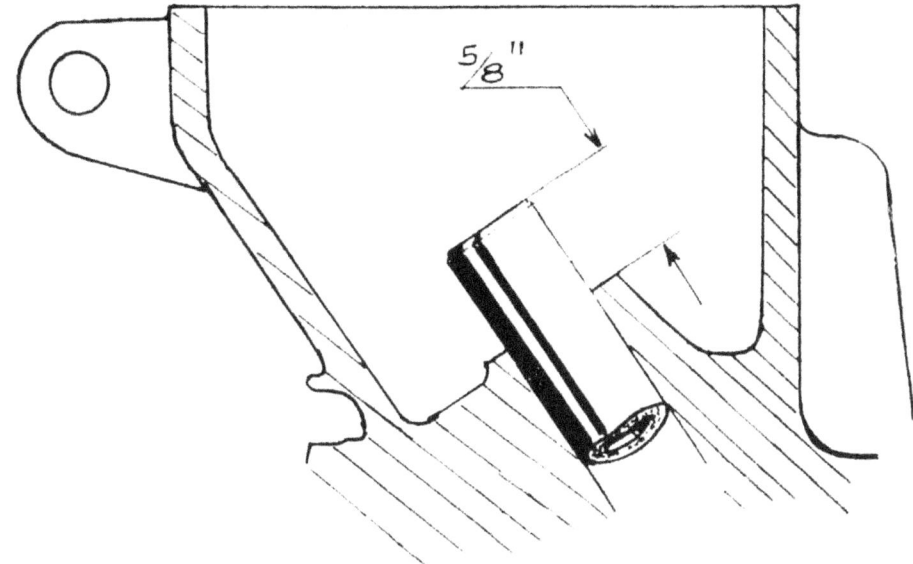

FIG. 10.
SETTING OF VALVE GUIDE IN CYLINDER HEAD.

After fitting new guides the valve seatings must be lightly trued up concentric with the guide bores, and the valves ground in.

Refitting Valves and Springs.

Place the valve spring bottom washers over the valve guides, concave side up, fit the springs with top collars. Lubricate the valve stems and push the valves into place and through the top collars. Compress the springs with the compresser KA163/2 and fit the cotters.

These may be stuck to the stem with grease to hold them whilst the compressor is released. After removing the compressor depress each valve smartly once or twice to seat it properly. The head is ready for refitting.

Refitting the Cylinder Head.

Inspect and if necessary renew the cylinder head gasket. Place the cylinder head in position and thread in the four long cylinder holding studs, screwing these into the cylinder base studs. Fit the cylinder head nut washers and nuts. Tighten down each nut a little at a time working from the first nut to the one diagonally opposite, and then doing the same with the other two, working round the head until they are all tight. *Caution*: The tension on the studs increases when the cylinder and head heat up and overtightening in the first place will cause damage.

Replacing the Overhead Rockers.

Refit the two gaskets with the push-rod guide plate between them on the flange of the push-rod cover, and fit and tighten the two nuts. It is most important not to omit the guide plate. Thread the push rods into position observing that they go back as marked during dismantling. If the piston is not already at top dead centre of the compression stroke, turn the crankshaft forward with a finger resting on each push rod. Observe the inlet one (nearer the cylinder) lift and fall, and as it reaches its lowest point the piston will be rising on the compression stroke. Bring it to the top.

Stick the rocker bearing assembly gasket, or a new one, in place on the platform and fit the bracket assembly and rockers, engaging the rocker tips with the cups on the push rods. Also check that the lower extremities of the push rods are seated correctly in the ball cups in the bottom rockers. Tighten the bearing assembly bolts evenly.

Readjusting the Tappets.

The clearances must be checked and set when the engine is cold. The running clearances, as distinct from the clearances used when checking the valve timing, are .005-in. on both valves.

Before checking or setting, the crankshaft must be turned so that the heel of the bottom rocker of the valve being dealt with is resting as nearly as possible midway on the neutral of the cam. Thus, when checking or setting the inlet tappet the exhaust valve must be just opening and when dealing with the exhaust clearance the inlet valve must be just on the point of closing.

Clearance is varied by turning the adjustable tappet in the rocker end after slackening the lock nut. One turn of the tappet will alter the clearance about .038-in. After adjustment retighten the locknut and check again.

Refitting Rocker Cover.

Clean both joint faces, stick a new gasket to the face of the head and fit the cover into place. Screw in the eight bolts having previously placed the lock washers over them. Note the positions occupied by the different length bolts (Fig. 8, page 23). Tighten carefully. Refit the rocker oil feed pipe, being careful not to overtighten and shear off the banjo bolt.

The remainder of the work calls for no special mention, except that before fitting, the threads of the sparking plug should be smeared with a little " Oil Dag," or graphite grease. For sparking plug recommendations, and instructions for cleaning and adjusting see page 66.

THE CLUTCH.

Description of Working. (Fig. 11.)

The clutch is operated by a thrust cup carrying a thrust bearing instead of by the more usual single thrust rod operating through a hollow gear shaft as on the LE model, and most other makes. The adjustment which becomes necessary periodically to allow for settling and wear on the friction linings is made by means of the screwed clutch spring holder threaded into the front plate of the clutch, and not by alteration to the cable adjustment. A cable adjuster is fitted, but this is used for controlling the cable adjustment only and must not be used as a " first aid " remedy for a slipping clutch.

Before attempting any adjustment to the clutch it is important that the operation of the clutch is properly understood and the following explanation should be studied by anyone unfamiliar with the design.

The operating mechanism is shown diagrammatically on page 27 (Fig. 11).

The movement of the handlebar lever (A) raises the operating lever (F) in the gearbox and the raised tip of the lever forces the large thrust pin (G) against the projecting lip of the thrust cup (J), causing the thrust cup to hinge outwards with the opposite side acting as the fulcrum.

If the outer clutch plate is observed whilst the handlebar lever is operated, with the clutch stationary, the plate will be seen to tilt outwards, as only that part of the plate nearest the thrust pin side of the clutch is freed from contact with the friction linings.

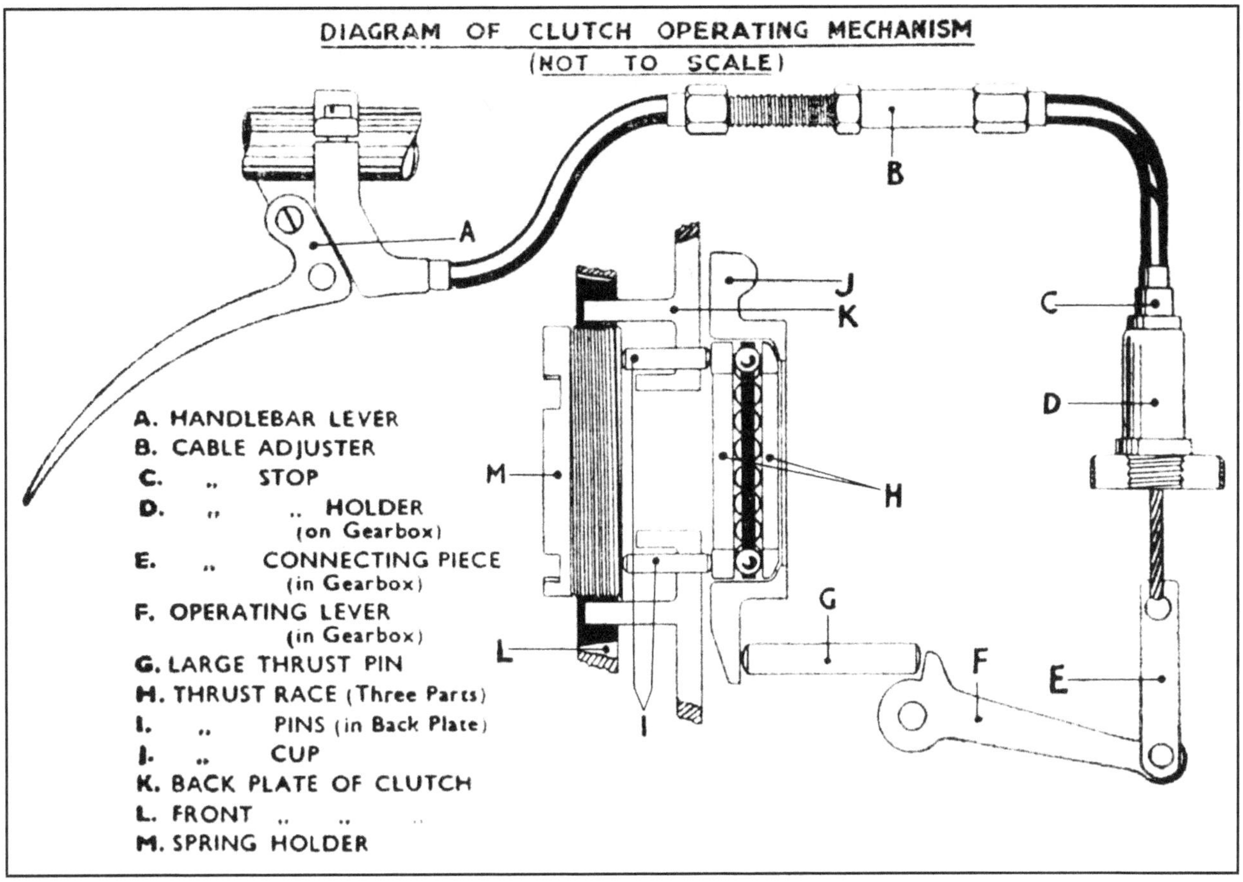

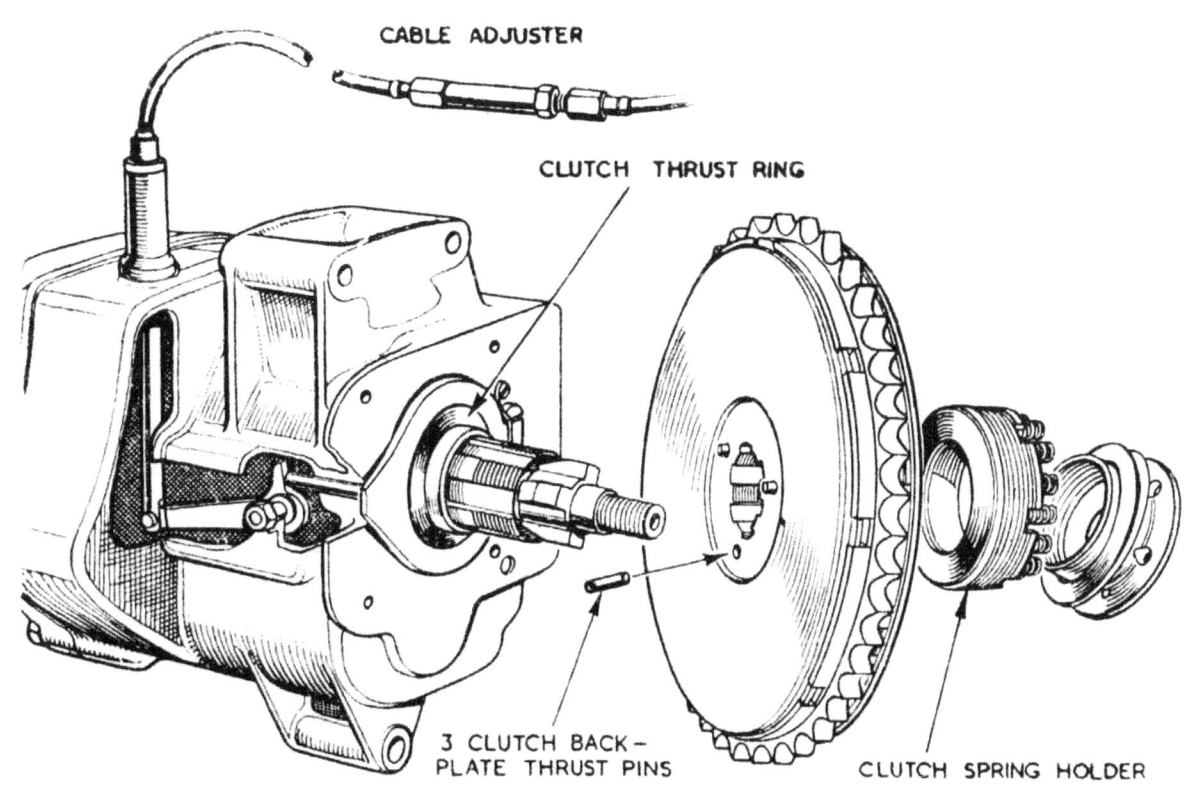

FIG. 11

A. HANDLEBAR LEVER
B. CABLE ADJUSTER
C. ,,   STOP
D. ,,   ,, HOLDER (on Gearbox)
E. ,,   CONNECTING PIECE (in Gearbox)
F. OPERATING LEVER (in Gearbox)
G. LARGE THRUST PIN
H. THRUST RACE (Three Parts)
I. ,,   PINS (in Back Plate)
J. ,,   CUP
K. BACK PLATE OF CLUTCH
L. FRONT ,,   ,,
M. SPRING HOLDER

By courtesy of "The Motor Cycle." FIG. 11a

THE CLUTCH OPERATING MECHANISM: SHOWING INTERNAL LEVER AND THRUST PIN

For the clutch to become fully disengaged the plates have to complete one revolution, after which the spherically seated, self-aligning ball thrust bearing (H) seated in the thrust cup levels the plates and frees them from the friction linings.

The disengagement of the front plate is arranged by the transmission of the outward movement of the thrust through the bearing (H) and three thrust pins (I) against the adjustable clutch spring holder (M) screwed into the front plate (L).

The thrust pins (I) are fitted freely in holes in the back plate (K).

Because of the tilting of the front plate the plates are " peeled off " from contact with each other so that when correctly adjusted and maintained this type of clutch does not cause the unpleasant grating of the gears on starting away which is often noticeable with other makes.

It will be understood that in normal use and a condition of correct adjustment the thrust pins and thrust bearing are free of all thrust loading. It will also be noted that settling or wear of the friction linings will allow the outer plate (L) to close in slightly towards the backplate (K) due to the reduction in friction lining thickness. As the thrust cup (J), when not in operation, is held against its seating and the face of the gearbox by a spring clip (not shown), it follows that the initial freedom in the thrust bearing and thrust pins will gradually be reduced, until a stage is reached in which, if adjustment is not carried when needed the thrust pins and bearing will be carrying part of the pressure of the clutch springs. The result will be clutch slip and premature wearing of the thrust bearing.

In such circumstances adjustment has to be made to the clutch spring holder (M) which must be turned forward (anti-clockwise) in relation to the front plate (L) to restore free movement in the thrust mechanism.

ADJUSTMENT OF CLUTCH.

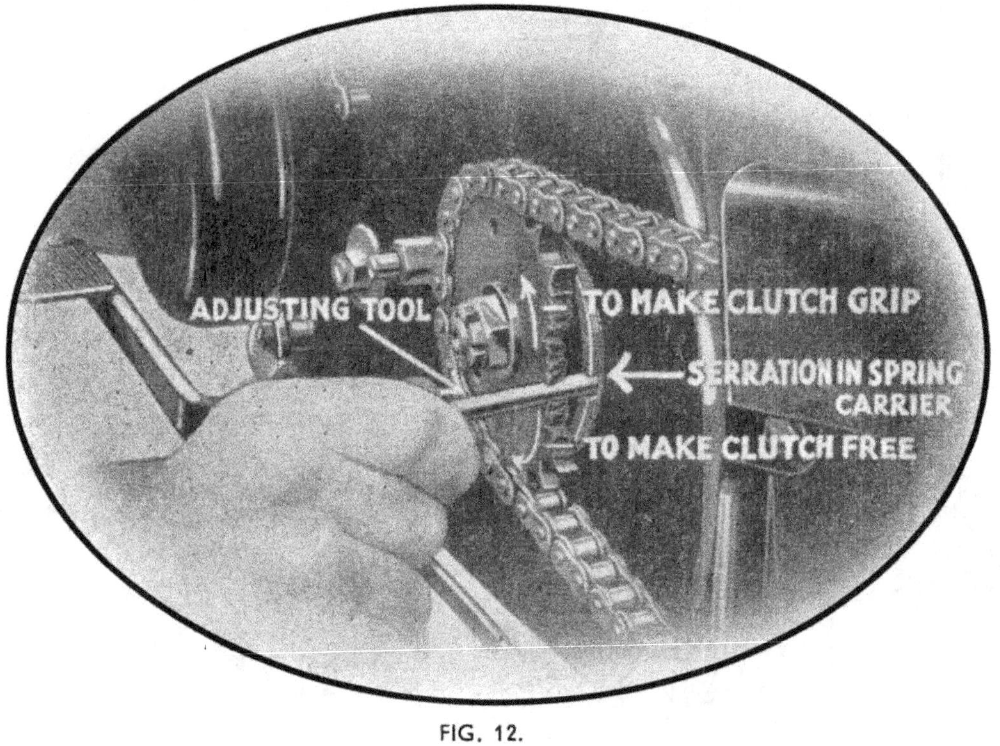

FIG. 12.

For clarity the sprocket is shown " broken away " to show the adjusting tool engaged in the clutch spring holder. Note that the movement is reversed if a gear is engaged whilst adjusting.—See page 30.

Adjustment of Clutch. (Fig. 12.)

Only in special circumstances, as described later, is adjustment of the clutch cable midway adjuster required.

In the ordinary way the adjustment is made by turning the clutch spring holder in the clutch front plate by engaging the flat end of the adjusting tool KA62/2 with one of the notches in the edge of the clutch spring holder through the ¼-in. hole in the final drive sprocket and moving the rear wheel in the direction required (Fig. 12).

To use the adjusting peg in the sprocket the front section of the rear chain guard has to be detached from the primary chain case. The chain guard is marked to indicate the need for its removal.

The adjustment is made normally with the gears in neutral, and only in an exceptional case is it made when an indirect gear is engaged. Such contingencies will be dealt with later.

To prevent clutch slip, i.e., to increase free movement in the operation, pull the rear wheel forward so that the final drive sprocket and adjusting tool will move the clutch spring holder forward in relation to the clutch front plate.

Should the clutch fail to free properly after this adjustment, the clutch cable adjustment may need a little correction : see next section.

Adjustment of Clutch on New Machines or after fitting New Cable Assembly.

The adjustment of the clutch is correct when a new machine is despatched from the factory, but the friction linings (clutch inserts) may settle during the first few hundred miles running, and readjustment may be needed fairly soon.

The clutch cable adjustment seldom needs attention after the initial compression and settling of the outer casings and ferrules of a new cable assembly has taken place. The control cable itself does not stretch, but very slight shortening of the total length of the casings may occur with new parts and has the same effect as a lengthened inner wire.

A careful watch should be kept on the clutch lever during the running in period of a new machine, if the clutch has been relined, or a new cable assembly has been fitted.

The settling down of the clutch inserts allows the clutch front plate to close in gradually towards the back plate and reduces the freedom allowed in the thrust bearing during assembly.

This in turn causes the control cable to lose some free movement. On the other hand any shortening of the control cable casings due to compression will tend to hide the fact that the inserts have settled and clutch slip is possible even whilst there is still some lost motion in the cable.

It is recommended, therefore, that during the service check normally carried out after the first 500 miles running, the clutch adjustment should be dealt with by carrying out a series of operations, each very simple, exactly as described later and in the order given.

With the clutch in correct adjustment it must be possible to pull back the clutch lever quite freely, and without operating the clutch at all, far enough to move the inner wire (or clutch cable) $\frac{1}{8}$-in. to $\frac{3}{16}$-in. Should this free movement be seen to have decreased, re-adjustment must be made at once.

The sequence of operations for adjusting as mentioned previously as follows :

Operation 1.—Slacken off the midway cable adjuster fully to allow the nipple to be detached from the handlebar lever and slip it out of the hole in the lever.

Operation 2.—Open both throttle and air controls fully. Select neutral position of the gears, and depress the kickstart against compression and test for clutch slip. If the clutch is felt to slip omit Operation 3 and carry on with Operation 4.

If no slip can be felt carry on with Operation 3.

Operation 3.—Using the clutch adjusting peg as already described, pull the rear wheel backwards a quarter of a turn at a time checking for clutch slip after each movement. This will involve taking out the adjusting peg from engagement with the clutch spring holder before each test. As soon as the clutch can be felt to slip (and only just slip), proceed with Operation 4.

Operation 4.—Refit the cable nipple to the handlebar lever. Readjust the midway adjuster until all lost motion is taken out of the cable and the lever is just drawn up against the lever bracket on the handlebar. Do not force the adjuster but *only just* remove all play. When correct tighten the cable adjuster locknut.

Finally, refit the adjusting peg to the sprocket, engage it with the clutch spring holder, and pull the rear wheel forward a little at a time until free movement begins to appear on the cable when the handlebar lever is checked.

Adjust until there is free travel on the cable of $\frac{1}{8}$-in. to $\frac{3}{16}$-in.

The adjustment is now completed.

Although the foregoing may seem complicated at first sight the whole " drill " is both easily and quickly carried out, and after the initial settling of a new cable assembly has taken place is only likely to be needed in special circumstances, as for instance if it is not known whether adjustment is needed to the cable or the spring holder. The effect of the two adjustments is inter-related.

If in doubt as to whether the cable or spring holder should be adjusted the following should be referred to :—

Symptom : Clutch slipping. No lost motion on control cable.
Remedy : Readjust clutch spring holder forward.
Symptom : Clutch slipping. Lost motion present on control cable.*
Remedy : Carry out Operation 4 of Adjustment " drill."
Symptom : Clutch not freeing. Normal or excess lost motion on cable.
Remedy : Carry out full Adjustment " drill."
Symptom : Clutch slipping and also not freeing.*
Remedy : Carry out Operation 4 of Adjustment " drill."

It can be accepted that if clutch trouble is not eliminated by carrying out the " drill " exactly as described the clutch will have to be dismantled to attend to a mechanical fault, to rectify incorrect assembly, or to replace worn parts.

* See next section.

Adjusting a Tight Clutch Spring Holder.

If excessive slip through neglect of the adjustment, or a spring holder which is tight in the clutch front plate, causes the clutch front plate to move round with it when adjustment is attempted, the adjustment should be made in the following manner.

Engage either second or third gear, and after passing the adjusting peg through the sprocket, move the clutch by means of the kickstart until one of the notches in the spring holder is opposite the peg and engage the peg in the notch.

To make the clutch grip *move the rear wheel backwards*. This is the opposite direction to that used when adjusting with the gears in neutral.

By adjusting with an indirect gear engaged advantage is taken of the difference in the rates of movement of the clutch sleeve gear (to which the clutch driven plates are attached) and the final drive sprocket.

Oil in the Clutch.

The primary chain case is intended to carry enough oil to lubricate the chain, and the clutch will grip satisfactorily even if there is an excess of oil in the cover provided that from the outset the cover has had oil in it.

It has been found however, that a clutch which has been run completely free of oil over a period will be subject to slip if oil is subsequently introduced on to the friction surfaces. In such circumstances the clutch must be relined, and assembled with oil in the cover.

REMOVAL OF DYNAMO AND BELT COVER. (Fig. 7.)

Remove the outer half of the cover by unbolting it from the back half and taking off the nut holding it to the primary chain case.

Disconnect the positive (+) leads from the rear (red) terminal of the battery. This is most important.

Remove the dynamo clamp bolt (1) and turn the dynamo carcase in its mounting to loosen the belt. Take off the belt.

Pull out the single pin plug from the socket which protrudes through the commutator cover. The cover is marked +B at this point. (Fig 34, page 69.)

Take out the two screws holding the voltage regulator base to the dynamo strap.

Pull the dynamo and the back half of the belt cover out to the left side of the machine from under the strap, at the same time leading the two cables connecting the regulator to the dynamo out between the crankcase and strap.

To take the back half of the cover off the dynamo, remove the armature nut and draw the belt pulley off the taper. If a claw extractor is used be careful not to break the flange of the pulley.

It is usually possible to remove the pulley, after taking off the nut, by supporting it from the back and delivering a light sharp blow on the end of the armature. Always use a soft punch to avoid harming the thread if this method is used.

PRIMARY CHAIN COVER.
Removal of Front Half.

Proceed as described in the preceding section to remove the dynamo belt, but do not take out the dynamo clamp bolt. Remove the front part of the rear chain cover to expose the rear chain driving sprocket. Remove the split cotters from this sprocket and from the shock absorber collar nut. Drain the primary cover.

With the rear brake held on; loosen and remove the sprocket nut and the shock absorber collar nut, using spanner A61/2AS for the former and A229 for the latter. Preserve the plain washers which are fitted behind

PRIMARY CHAIN COVER (continued).

these nuts. The driving pulley, and pulley flange will come off with the collar nut. Remove the shock absorber spring and shock absorber clutch from the engine shaft.

The rear half of the belt cover can be raised over the engine shaft and the cover swung round out of the way of the primary cover.

Unscrew the primary chain cover strap fixing pin (3), Fig. 7, page 21, from the lug on the strap. Free the strap from the cover all round and push it off and over the back half of the cover. Remove the chain case fixing bolt (5) with washer and inner distance piece and pull out the joint moulding.

Remove the cover. Preserve the distance tube fitted between the halves of the cover, and the felt oil seal around the opening for the clutch spring holder.

Removal of Primary Chain.

Fix the sprockets to prevent them turning by mounting a sprag from the bottom of the engine sprocket to the top of the clutch chain wheel. Take off the sleeve gear nut locking plate, held to the sleeve gear nut by a $\frac{1}{8}$-in. Whit. screw, and unscrew the sleeve gear nut, using the pegged end of the spanner A61/2AS. It will have to be started by driving it round, using a mallet on the spanner (Fig. 13).

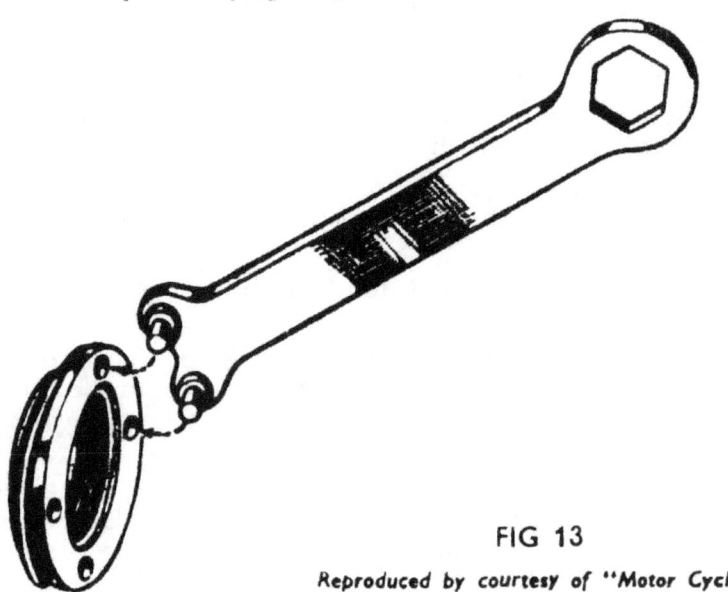

FIG 13

Reproduced by courtesy of "Motor Cycling".

SPANNER A61/2AS AND SLEEVE GEAR NUT.

As the chain is endless the engine sprocket and clutch assembly have to be drawn off their respective shafts together. The clutch may have to be levered off to start it by using levers carefully between the clutch back plate and the chain case. If care is taken to hold the clutch front plate and back-plate firmly together the clutch can then be refitted afterwards without it having been separated, unless of course it needs attention. Preserve the three thrust pins from the clutch back plate.

Removal of Rear Half of the Primary Chain Cover.

Having removed the clutch, the clutch thrust bearing is accessible, and the four screws securing the half cover to the gearbox can be taken out after cutting and drawing out the locking wires from the screw heads.

A gasket is fitted between the cover and the gearbox, and an oil seal ring between the cover and crankcase.

Refitting the Rear Half.

Verify that the chain case oil seal is in good order and in place on the crankcase main bearing boss. Stick the gasket—or a new one if needed—to the face of the gearbox with grease, and mount the chain case back half in place. Insert the four fixing screws and tighten fully. Fit new locking wires and twist the ends round securely to lock them. Use two lengths of wire passed through the screws horizontally. Do not wire upper to lower screws as this will interfere with the working of the thrust cup.

Refitting Primary Chain.

Engage top gear to prevent the sleeve gear slipping through its ballrace as the clutch is fitted. Verify the condition of the clutch thrust bearing, grease well, and replace, and see that the sleeve gear distance piece is in place on the sleeve gear and fitted through the thrust bearing.

Take up the clutch assembly, holding the back and front plates firmly together and stick the three thrust pins with grease into the holes in the clutch back plate. These pins are each $\frac{3}{16}$-in. dia. $\times$ .453-in., and must not be confused with the thrust pins used in the kickstart ratchet—so that if this also has been dismantled the point should be checked.

Hang the chain over the clutch chain wheel, and rest the engine sprocket in the loop. The clutch assembly and engine sprocket with the chain in place have now to be placed on their respective shafts. Care is necessary not to allow the clutch plates to separate, and assistance is desirable for this part of the work.

Refitting the Sleeve Gear Nut.

In order easily to refit the sleeve gear nut, which sometimes makes it necessary to compress the clutch spring slightly, the use of Service Tool X2959 sleeve gear nut adaptor (Fig. 14) is advisable. This is fitted over the gearshaft with the pegs engaged in the holes in the sleeve gear nut and the gear shaft nut used to compress the springs enough to start the sleeve gear nut on the thread. The four holes in the adaptor are to enable the peg spanner A61/2AS to be used to turn it.

After starting the sleeve gear nut on the threads, and having fitted the shock absorber clutch, spring, pulley, washer, and shock absorber collar nut sprag the chain and tighten both the sleeve gear nut and the shock absorber collar nut fully, finally driving the spanners round with a mallet. Fit the split-pin to the engine shaft. Readjust the clutch. See page 30.

Refitting Front Half of Primary Chain Cover. (Fig. 7.)

Put the chain case sealing strap in place over the back of the rear half of the primary chain cover. Fit the oil seal felt into its housing inside the cover around the opening for the clutch spring holder.* Fit the front half into place setting it in line with the back half, locating the chain case bolt distance piece over the plunged in edges of the bolt holes in the covers, fit the bolt and washer (5) and tighten up.

Press the joint moulding into place round the edges of the two halves of the cover with the ends at the top, and see that the centre rib fits between the cover faces. Bring the sealing strap over from the back into place over the moulding and tighten the bolt (3).

The reassembly of the dynamo belt cover calls for no special mention.

Refill the chain case with oil.

* A new felt must be soaked in oil or molten tallow before fitting.

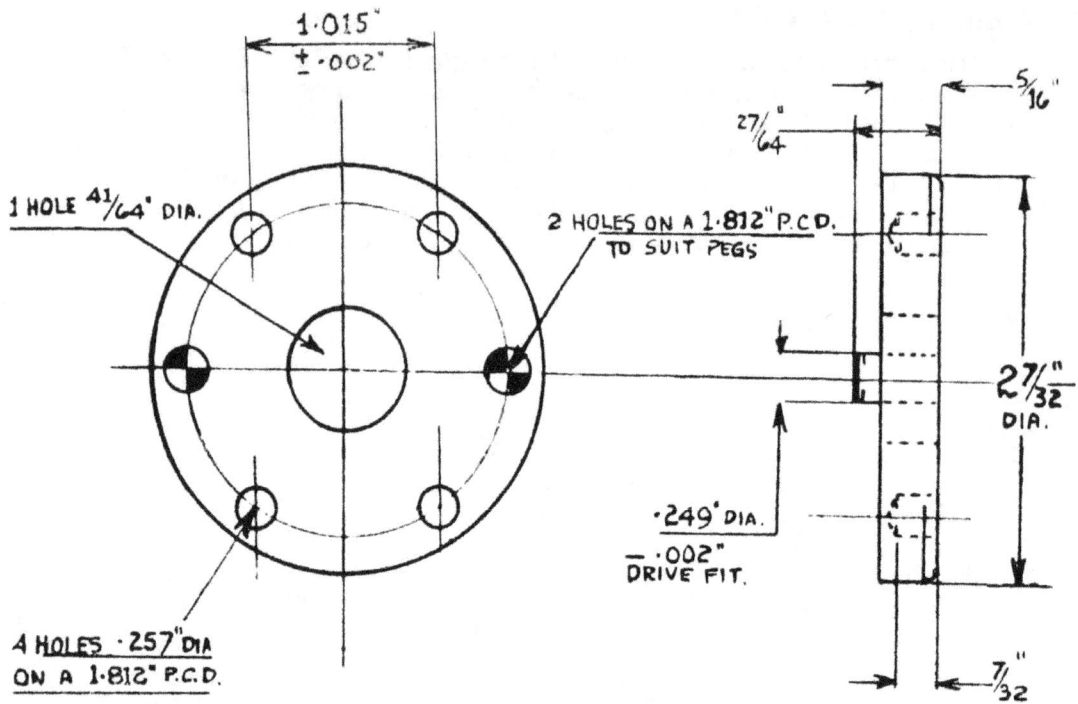

FIG. 14.
X2959. SLEEVE GEAR NUT ADAPTOR.

THE KICKSTART.

Dismantling Kickstart Ratchet and Spring. (Fig. 15.)

Drain the oil from the gearbox by removing the plug from the end cover (Fig. 16). Take out the three ¼-in. bolts holding the kickstart bearing to the end cover and draw it out of position with the ratchet, and kickstart crank, etc. Preserve the layshaft thrust washer from inside the ratchet.

Should the spring be broken the kickstart crank cotter may be removed at once, but if not the bearing and ratchet have to be held against the tension of the spring whilst driving out the cotter.

Remove the cotter nut and washer. Obtain two 2-in. nails of small enough diameter to enter the breather holes in the ratchet. Knock these into the bench 1$\frac{19}{32}$-in. (1.593-in.) apart, or into a piece of wood held in the vice. Cut off the heads leaving about ½-in. protruding from the surface of the wood.

Place the kick-start assembly, with the ratchet teeth downwards over the nails, entering the nails into the breather holes. Turn the kickstart bearing in a clockwise direction against the spring sufficiently to allow the head of the cotter to clear the disengaging ramp on the bearing. Drive out the cotter and gradually release the bearing.

If the spring is broken the ratchet will pull out of the bearing when the crank is tapped off. If unbroken tap the ratchet through far enough to expose the loop of the spring where this is fitted to the ratchet. Unhook the spring from its mounting and pull the ratchet out.

Note that the ratchet carries three thrust pins, $\frac{3}{16}$-in. dia. × $\frac{9}{16}$-in. long (.187-in. × .5625-in.) which must be preserved for refitting. These must not be confused with the three clutch thrust pins which are much shorter.

Take out the engaging spring which will be loose inside the kickstart bearing. Unscrew the kickstart spring anchor peg and remove the return spring—or the part of it if broken.

Replacement of Kick-start Spring. (Fig. 15.)

Push the end of the spring with the smaller loop (X) into the mouth of the kickstart bearing and by twisting the spring clockwise whilst holding the bearing firmly it will be found possible to work round the spring coil by coil and get it into place. In its free state the outside diameter of the spring is greater than the internal diameter of the kickstart bearing, but by twisting it round as described the coils will be compressed and will enter easily.

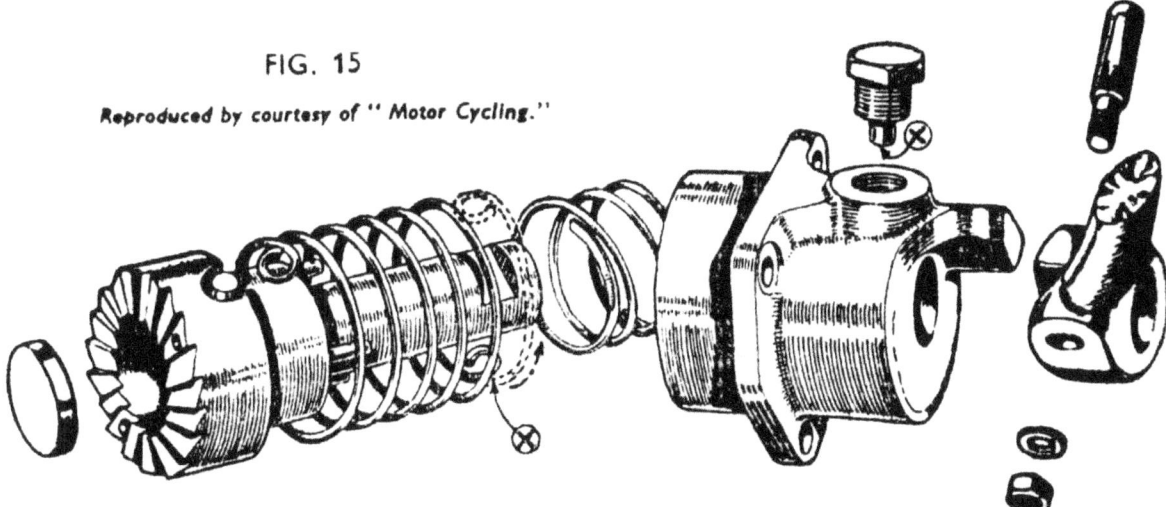

FIG. 15

Reproduced by courtesy of " Motor Cycling."

KICKSTART RATCHET AND SPRINGS.

Leave the end of the spring with the larger loop, and one coil protruding, and manoeuvre the smaller loop in the kickstart bearing under the hole which carries the anchor peg and screw the peg home with its tip (X) through the spring loop.

Fit the three thrust pins into the ratchet. There are six holes, but the three which act as breather holes are slightly smaller than the others. **Note specially** that the correct thrust pins must be used. These are $\frac{3}{16}$-in. $\times \frac{9}{16}$-in. and are the same part as the big-end rollers. Discarded big-end rollers may be used as replacements. Do not, however, confuse them with the clutch thrust pins which are only .453-in. long. Stick them in place with a little grease.

Fit the engaging spring over the ratchet and push the ratchet into the kickstart bearing, engaging the loop of the spring (that was left protruding) over the anchor lug, that is formed on the ratchet. Twist the ratchet round clockwise and push it further into the bearing at the same time entering the spring.

Place the ratchet over the two nails that were used in dismantling and fit the kickstart crank over the end of the ratchet.

Turn the housing round clockwise just far enough to allow the cotter to go through the crank across the flat on the ratchet. It fits from front to back. Do not in any circumstances turn the housing further than is needed to fit the cotter. Any extra tensioning of the spring will permanently distort and damage it.

Refitting Kickstart Assembly. (Fig. 15.)

Before fitting the assembly to the gearbox see that the layshaft washer is in place against the ratchet gear, the kickstarter bearing bush on the end of the layshaft, and the kickstart layshaft thrust washer in the ratchet.

Do not use a gasket between the face of the kickstart bearing and the gearbox end cover. Tighten the three bolts fully. Refill the gearbox.

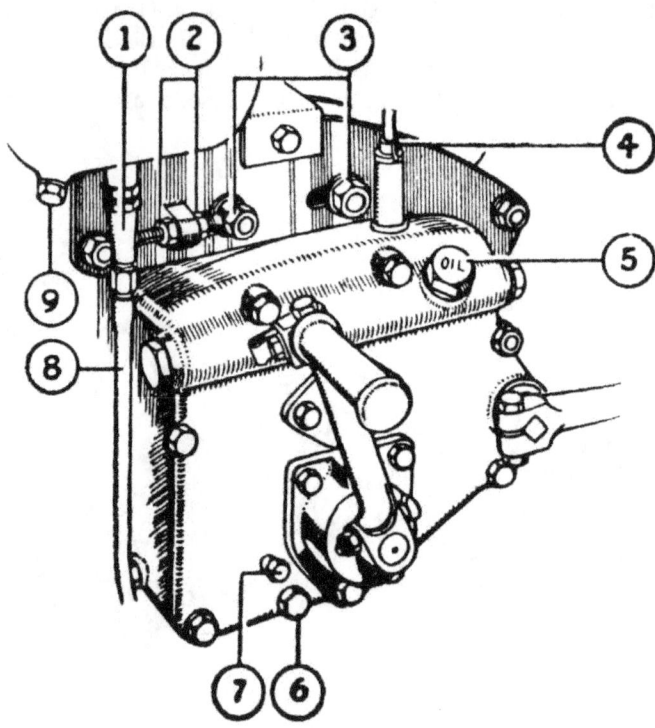

FIG. 16.

GEARBOX END COVER, KICKSTART AND PRIMARY CHAIN ADJUSTMENT.

(1) Ball Valve Assembly.
(2) Chain Adjuster Nuts.
(3) Gearbox Mounting Bolt Nuts.
(4) Clutch Cable Stop.
(5) Gearbox Oil Filler Plug.
(6) Gearbox Oil Drain Plug.
(7) Gearbox Oil Level Plug.
(8) Engine Oil Feed Pipe.
(9) Oil Tank Drain Plug.

REMOVAL OF ENGINE AND GEARBOX FROM FRAME.

The engine and gearbox are held together as a unit by the rear engine plates and any extensive overhaul of the engine that involves separating the crankcase will necessitate removing the engine and gearbox units together. The primary chain cover, etc., should also be left in place.

It is possible, however, to renew any of the gears or shafts in the gearbox without removing the housing from the frame, and only the replacement of the sleeve gear ball bearing, or lay-shaft ball-bearing that are both fitted to the housing would require its removal. The engine would then have to come out as well. The cylinder head steady, carburetter, and exhaust pipe must, of course, be removed.

The air cleaner assembly and oil tank have to be removed as a preliminary to reach the rear engine plates. These are attached to the frame at the top and to the rear engine plates at the bottom.

The oil tank need not necessarily be drained before removal.

Remove the dynamo; see page 31. Take off the front section of the rear chain guard, it is attached to the primary chain cover by two ¼-in. B.S.F. nuts.

Disconnect the clutch and exhaust lift cable assemblies at the handlebar levers and pull the cables clear from any clips on the frame.

Pull out the split cotters from the gear box mainshaft nut and shock absorber collar. If the gearbox is to be dismantled it is a help if at this stage the gearbox end cover plate is removed from the gearbox end cover, and the gearbox mainshaft nut inside the opening loosened. The shaft can then be held from turning by applying the rear brake.

Also loosen the shock absorber collar. Next remove the gearbox sprocket nut and pull the final drive sprocket off the shaft with the chain. The chain need not be removed unless it is to be cleaned or replaced.

Take the weight of the unit on a block below the crankcase, and remove all bolts from the front engine plates and three from the rear plates. One at the top rear corner, one from the bottom rear corner, and one bolt passing through the frame lug and bottom front ends of the engine plates. On this last is a distance piece, between the frame lug and the engine plate on the right hand side.

The whole unit may now be levered forwards and lifted out of the frame.

Separation of Gearbox from Engine.

Remove the primary chain cover front half, the clutch, engine sprocket, and primary chain, and the rear half of the chain cover from the gearbox (see page 32). The bolt holding the engine plates to the crankcase is now accessible for removal after which the gearbox assembly and rear engine plates will pull away from the crankcase.

OVERHAULING THE ENGINE.

Removal of Cylinder and Piston.

The removal of the cylinder head is dealt with on page 22.

Remove the cylinder barrel. This will be made easier if the crankcase bolts and studs are freed off first. Note that if compression plates are fitted between the cylinder and crankcase they must be kept aside for refitting when rebuilding the engine.

The piston is removable after taking out one circlip and driving out the gudgeon pin. A slot will be found running into the circlip groove at one side of the piston for the purpose of allowing a sharp bradawl or scriber to be inserted under the circlip to prise it out. Use a soft metal punch against the opposite end of the gudgeon pin, have an assistant support the piston against the force of the blows and drive out the gudgeon pin. Help is essential here otherwise there is a risk of bending the connecting rod and setting it out of line. The pin is a light driving fit when the piston is cold.

Inspection of Cylinder, Piston and Rings.

Examine the bore for wear or scoring. The original bore diameter is 2.677-in. Reboring is generally considered necessary if wear in excess of .008-in. has taken place or the bore is damaged or scored. Cylinders do not wear uniformly, but the maximum wear will be found to have occurred towards the top of the bore at the back. To measure the wear therefore, take an accurate reading of the diameter from front to back, just below the ridge left at the top end of the ring travel. This reading may then easily be compared with a measurement taken below the part traversed by the rings which will usually be found almost unworn.

Piston rings should be examined for uneven bearing on the cylinder, excessive gap, or side play in the grooves. Any patches of discolouration on the bearing surfaces of the rings indicate that blow-by has been taking place and renewal may be necessary. The ring gaps of course increase with wear and may increase up to .025 to .030-in. before replacement.

New piston rings are supplied by us correctly gapped and in an unworn bore the gaps are : Compression rings .0085-in. to .0115-in.
Oil control ring .0105-in. to .0135-in.

Side clearances are : Compression rings : .0005-in. to .0025-in.
Oil control ring : .0025-in. to .0045-in.

Pistons and rings are obtainable in three oversizes +.020-in. and +.040-in., and +.060-in. on diameter. Oversize piston rings cannot be fitted to a worn bore unless the bore is reground to the correct diameter of the replacement rings, in which case an oversize piston would be essential also.

Dismantling the Timing Cover and Timing Gears.

The timing cover is held to the crankcase by ten screws. Remove these and tap the cover gently at the edges with a mallet or soft hammer to free it from the joint face and pull it off. Do not insert wedges between the faces.

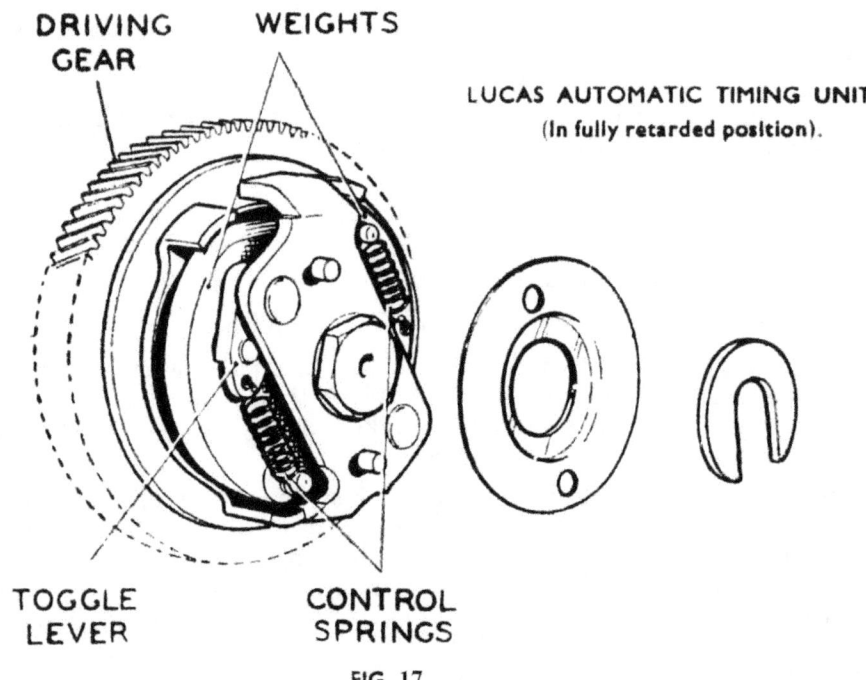

FIG. 17

Remove four bolts (2; $\frac{5}{16}$-in., and 2; $\frac{1}{4}$-in.) holding the timing gear steady plate to the crankcase and the bottom rocker and intermediate gear spindles, also take off the nut from the end of the camwheel spindle. The second nut on the steady plate holds the cam oil jet and should be left in place. Remove the steady plate.

Undo the magneto armature nut in the centre of the timing unit. After loosening, the nut will tighten and begins to withdraw the timing unit from the armature.

Pull the cam followers off the spindle, being careful to preserve the " Belleville " thrust washer which is fitted between the inlet cam follower and the crankcase. Draw from their respective spindles the camwheel assembly and intermediate gear assembly. The crankshaft pinion and oil-pump worm cannot be drawn off the shaft until the oil pump is out of the way, but the mainshaft nut (left-hand thread) may be removed at this stage. Preserve the timing shaft (tongued) washer which is behind this nut.

Removal of Oil Pump. (Fig. 18.)

It is important not to attempt to take out the oil pump assembly before heating the crankcase around the pump to expand the pump housing. If forced out cold the housing will be scored which may scrap the crankcase.

Take out the four oil pump fixing screws which hold the pump base plate to the crankcase. Three of the holes in the base plate and two of those in the crankcase are visible in the illustration. Note that the screw fitted to the inner front corner is longer than the other three.

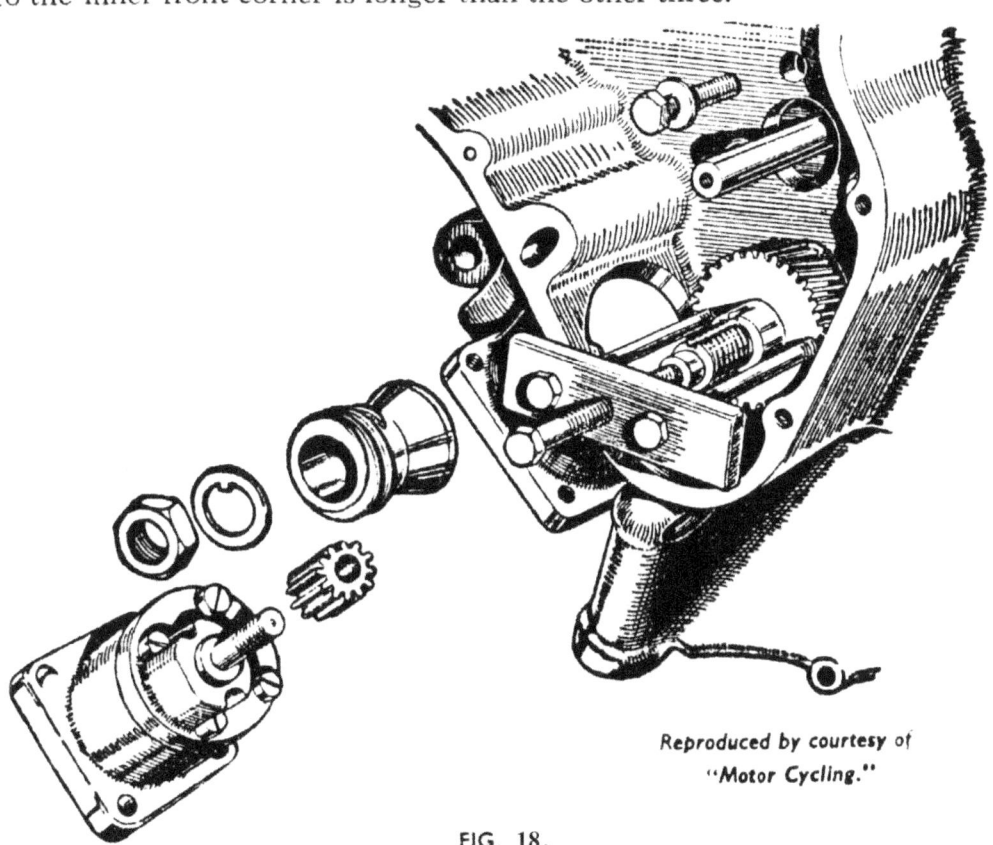

Reproduced by courtesy of "Motor Cycling."

FIG. 18.
REMOVAL OF OIL PUMP AND CRANKSHAFT PINION.

The Oil-pump is illustrated after removal, and with small driven pinion taken off. The Crankshaft Timing-pinion is about to be pulled off the shaft with the extractor X2721.

Heat the crankcase around the oil pump housing. A blow lamp may be used if care is taken not to play the flame continuously on one point and overheat the metal. As the metal is warmed up tap the pump carefully on the top from inside the timing case until it comes clear. Do not tap on the end of the pump spindle. Do not take the oil pump apart unnecessarily. It is seldom that it needs any attention, and if working freely, and if there has been no lubrication trouble it is best left alone, as a special tool is needed to rebuild it.

Dismantling the Oil Pump.

Take out the four screws securing the pump body and its cover to the base plate. Removal of the plate exposes the two return gears and the cover will pull off the pump body bringing with it the pump spindle and the feed gear cut integral with it. The two return gears and the loose feed gear are then removable from the housing, but as they are taken out mark them with indelible pencil for replacement in the same positions, as it is possible for the two loose gears to be fitted inverted. This is not recommended once the gears have been working and have bedded in to the respective matching gears on the driving spindle.

Overhauling the Oil Pump.

When inspecting the pump make sure that the fixed spindle is firm in the body, and scrutinize the recesses in the pump body, in which the gears run, for any signs of scoring on the walls.

To work efficiently the pump gears must have the minimum clearance possible between the tops of the teeth and the body. They must also revolve freely when the pump body and cover are bolted to the base plate with as little end float as possible.

End float is removable by lapping down the appropriate end face of the pump body so that when in place the gear end faces are practically flush. Any lapping needed must be most carefully done using medium grade grinding compound and rubbing the pump face whilst held quite flat on a surface plate or sheet of plate glass.

Should new gears be fitted, carefully inspect them for any roughness or fraize around the edges and remove this very carefully indeed by polishing with a strip of superfine emery cloth (Grade OO) held on a small file. To take out the spindle from the oil pump cover remove the driving gear which meshes with the worm on the mainshaft. Hold the spindle firmly and unscrew the gear anti-clockwise. A convenient method of holding the spindle to avoid damage is to get a scrap splined return oil pump gear, file flats opposite to each other, and hold it in a vice. The splines of the spindle can then be held in the splines in the gear whilst unscrewing the driven gear.

Reassembling the Oil Pump.

After reassembling the gears and spindle to the pump the pump cover has to be accurately lined up to the body before tightening the four oil pump screws holding the pump to the base plate. For this work Service Tool X2719 oil-pump alignment tool is required (Fig. 19).

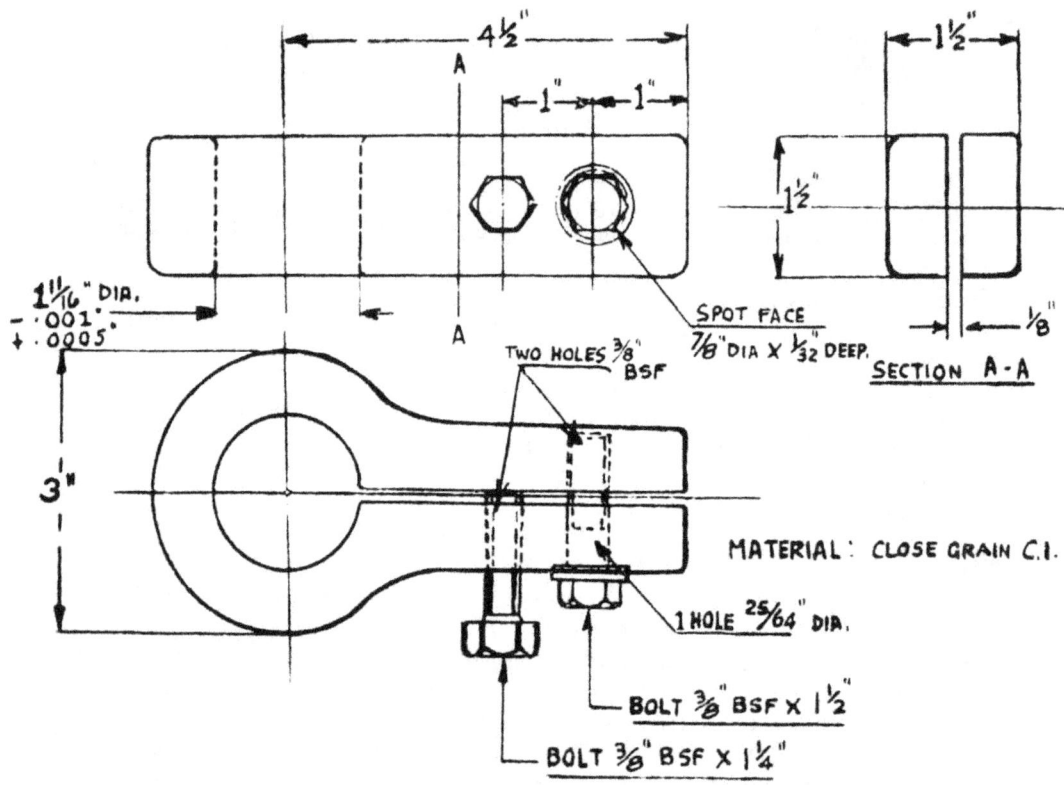

FIG. 19. X2719 OIL PUMP ALIGNMENT TOOL.

The pump body and cover, loosely mounted to the base plate, are clamped in the tool and the four screws tightened up. Test the pump for freedom of working by turning the spindle. If tight, try slackening off the four screws. If this frees the pump gears the trouble is lack of end play and the pump must be dismantled, the offending gear or gears located, and eased off by lapping down their end faces perfectly square to the bore.

Slight roughness or "lumpiness" can be cured by running a mixture of oil and Turkey stone powder through the pump whilst the pump spindle is rotated in a lathe or drilling machine. After this treatment complete dismantling and scrupulous cleaning in petrol are essential before putting the pump together again in the alignment tool, tightening the body to the base plate and refitting to the engine.

Refitting the Oil Pump to Crankcase.

Heat up the crankcase around the oil pump housing using a blow lamp, but taking care to keep the flame moving about and not concentrated on one spot. Make certain that the crankshaft timing pinion and oil pump drive worm are fitted as they cannot be got into place after fitting the pump. Fit a new base plate gasket over the pump.

Push the pump into the housing lining up the holes in the pump base plate with the screw holes in the crankcase and meshing the driven gear with the worm. The illustration on page 39 (Fig. 18) shows how the pump is located. Tap the pump home and fit the four fixing screws. Note that the short screw fits into the inner front screw hole. This hole is just visible in the illustration in the right-hand bottom corner of the base plate.

Removal of Crankshaft Timing Pinion. (Fig. 20).

After removal of the oil pump and the left-hand thread mainshaft nut (unscrewed by turning clockwise) pull off the tongue washer behind the nut, and draw the pinion off the shaft, using Service Tool X2721 (Fig. 20).

This is attached to the pinion as shown in Fig 18 and the tightening of the centre bolt draws the pinion from the mainshaft.

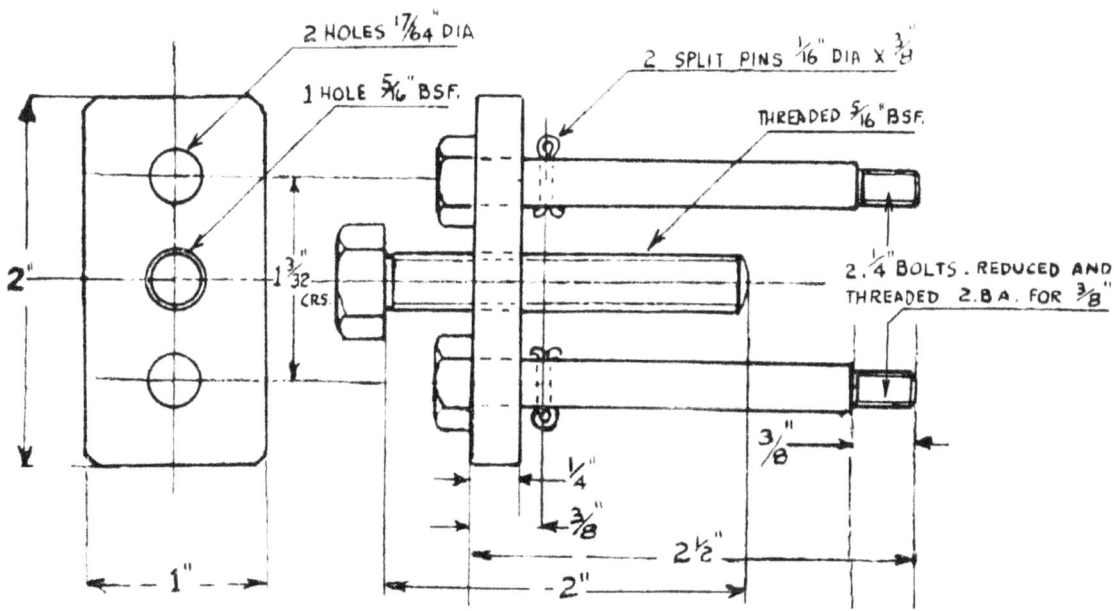

FIG. 20 X2721 CRANKSHAFT TIMING PINION EXTRACTOR.

Separating the Crankcase Halves.

Removal of all crankcase bolts and studs enables the case to the opened up. The roller race centre will easily come out of the bearing outer ring in the driving side crankcase, but it may be necessary to tap the timing side shaft out of the timing side ball bearing which should be left in the case.

The ballrace can be tested for play or roughness whilst in place, and it is possible to inspect the roller track in the driving side bearing outer ring. If it is suspected that the roller track on the inner ring is worn or pitted, one of the rollers may be pulled out of the cage to enable an examination to be made.

Removal of Main Bearings.

The crankcase must be heated around the bearing housings to free the ballrace and the roller race outer ring. A blow lamp may be used or the case may be heated over a gas ring, provided that care is taken not to concentrate the flame on one point. It is safer to immerse the case in boiling water and allow it to reach the temperature of the water.

When hot take up the case, protecting the hands with rag, and bring-down the open side smartly and quite square on the bench top or on a large block of wood to jarr the bearing or roller race outer ring out of place.

The end float on the flywheel assembly is controlled by the distance between the bearings and during initial assembly it is usual to fit packing shims of various thicknesses between the outer rings of the bearings and their housings in the crankcase, to take up excess end float. These shims are produced in three thicknesses, .003-in., .005-in., and .012-in. Any shims found in the housings on removal of the bearings must be retained and a note made of the side from which they were taken.

The centre ring, rollers, and cage of the driving side bearing can be removed from the mainshaft by levering off the centre ring.

Refitting or Renewing Main Bearings.

The mainshafts taper gradually from the flywheels outwards, and the bearings are internally tapered to suit. The taper cannot be detected by eye, but the " large " ends of the bearing inner rings are noticeably radiussed from the end face into the bore—the " small " ends being sharp cornered. If in doubt offer the bearing up to the shaft and, with the fingers only, try to push it on to the shaft. If it is the wrong way round it will hardly go on at all with the finger pressure. All Hoffmann bearings have the maker's name and identification number on the " small " ends, so that these will be outwards and remote from the flywheels when fitted.

Fit the roller race centre to the shaft, tapping it into position up to the shoulder of the flywheel.

Heat the crankcase around the bearing housings (see above), and fit into the bearing housings any packing shims that were removed on dismantling, or new ones of the same total thickness. Fit the ball bearing to the timing side case placing it quite square into the housing and tapping it home quickly, being careful that it is the right way round. Fit any shims needed to the driving side case and place the outer ring squarely in position, noting that the internal lip on this must be towards the bottom of the housing, otherwise the rollers will not enter.

Refitting the Flywheel Assembly.

The work on the big end, described on page 43, is assumed to have been carried out, or to have been unnecessary and the flywheel assembly ready for replacing in the crankcase. See that the intermediate gear spindle is fitted. It cannot be put in after the crankcase is assembled.

With the timing side crankcase resting on the bench upon its timing case face, place the flywheel assembly in position entering the timing side mainshaft into the timing side ballrace, and push the shaft home. See that both joint faces are scrupulously clean and place the driving side case into position entering the rollers into the ring in the crankcase.

Fit all the bolts and studs, and tighten these slowly and evenly so as to bring the faces together quite square. As the tightening proceeds keep testing the freedom of the flywheel assembly and as soon as there is any sign of stiffness due to the bearings being " nipped " by the closing of the crankcase stop tightening the bolts and nuts.

With clearance (feeler) gauges find the extent of the gap left between the crankcase face joint, checking the gap all round so as to be quite certain that the bolts and nuts have been tightened evenly.

It is possible that the halves of the crankcase will pull right up together and still leave the flywheel assembly quite free to turn in the bearings. If this is so tap the assembly first to one side, and then to the other to find the extent of the end float present. If there is end float this must be checked and a note made of the amount to be taken out, and the extent of shimming required.

The flywheel assembly must be assembled into the crankcase finally so that with all studs and bolts tightened fully, there is perfect freedom of rotation with no noticeable side play, or at least as little as possible, so as to give about .001-in. freedom when the crankcase gets hot. It is, however essential to avoid any trace of stiffness, and consequent artificial side load on the bearings.

Should alteration to the shimming be required the crankcase must be separated, the ball bearing, and roller bearing outer ring removed, and shims taken out or fitted according to whether additional freedom is needed, or whether play is be removed.

To give freedom remove a packing shim or shims whose total thickness is equal to, but in no circumstances less than the gap which was measured between the crankcase halves at the point where tightening began to " nip" the bearings, being careful to arrange as far as is possible for an approximately equal thickness to be left at each side. For instance should .012-in. shimming be needed, it would be undesirable to fit one .012-in. shim, and two each of .005-in. should be fitted at each side. Should .008-in. shimming be needed there would be no objection to .003-in. one side and .005-in. the other, as the difference is not so great.

If there is too much play fit shims equivalent in thickness to the amount of play to be taken up (or slightly less). In this case also if two or more shims have to be used try to make up about the same thickness at each side.

If no alteration is needed just separate the faces far enough for them to be coated lightly with jointing compound (Gasket Goo—made by The Wilcott Parent Co., Fishponds, Bristol, is recommended) after which the bolts and nuts may be finally tightened.

Overhauling the Flywheel Assembly and Big-end.

The shanks of the crankpin taper outwards towards the threaded ends and it is secured by nuts to the flywheels. To separate the flywheels for the purpose of inspecting the big-end bearing one nut must be removed and the crankpin pressed out of one of the flywheels. A special box spanner—Service Tool No. X2720, is required for the removal and refitting of the crankpin nuts which are $\frac{3}{4}$-in. Whitworth (1.3-in. across the flats). The outside diameter of the spanner around the hexagon must not exceed $1\frac{3}{4}$-in.

The nuts are invariably very tight, good leverage is essential to move them, and the flywheel has to be held really firmly whilst loosening or tightening up. After taking off the nut, support the flywheel to be removed and drive out the pin using a brass or aluminium drift to protect the threaded end.

The connecting rod is then removable, leaving the cage and rollers on the pin. Mark the connecting rod so that it may be replaced the same way round. Inspect the bearing outer ring in the connecting rod for signs of pitting or uneven wear, and if necessary to renew, press out the worn ring and press in a new one, locating it centrally in the eye of the rod.

Whilst dealing with the big end check the fit of the gudgeon pin in the small end bush so that this bush may be replaced at the same time should it be worn. See also page 45.

Pull the cage and rollers off the crankpin and inspect the roller track for wear and possible pitting, or breaking up of the hardened surface.

Some wear will almost certainly be noticed at the sides of the roller track where the roller cage bears on the crankpin sleeve. Provided that this is not excessive so as to leave the roller track unsupported it may be disregarded.

Oversize rollers may be employed to take up slight play, but must only be fitted if the tracks are even and free from pitting. These rollers are obtainable .0002-in. and .0004-in. oversize on diameter. The standard diameter is .1875-in. ($\frac{3}{16}$-in.). The standard sleeve diameter is 1.374-in.

The final assembly of the big end should leave the connecting rod quite free and a hardly perceptible amount of vertical play is permissible without oil in the bearing. There will be about .008-in. side play. Slight stiffness may be overcome by carefully lapping the ring in position in the connecting rod, or lightly polishing the crankpin sleeve.

To fit a new crankpin the nut at the other end must be taken off and the pin driven out of the flywheel.

Before fitting a new pin make certain that the oil-passage through the timing side mainshaft and flywheel is quite clear, and also that there is no restriction in the oil hole in the crankpin sleeve.

Place the pin in position lightly in the timing side flywheel setting the oil outlet hole in the roller track to point towards the centre of the flywheel, i.e., vertically downwards at top dead centre. Tighten the nut enough to draw the shoulder of the crankpin assembly (the side of the sleeve) just up to the flywheel, but no more. With a force feed oil can squirt oil into the hollow timing side shaft and verify that it comes through and out of the oil hole in the sleeve.

Fit the roller cage with the rollers which if desired may be stuck into place with a little clean soft grease. Fit the connecting rod over the rollers the same way round as originally fitted. Place the driving side flywheel in position roughly lining up the rim with the timing side and pull down the nut to bring the flywheel up to the side of the crankpin sleeve.

Lining up the Flywheel Assembly.

A pair of V blocks of suitable size, a surface plate, and Dial indicator are required to carry out this work. The assembly has to be supported in its bearings—temporarily fitted to the mainshafts—in V-blocks on a surface plate. The V-blocks must be large enough to support the main shafts (at least 5-in. centre height from the surface plate).

Line up the flywheel rims using a straight-edge across them, testing at several different points round the circumference. A heavy copper headed hammer or a lead lump is needed to jar the flywheels on the pin to alter the alignment.

Mount the assembly in the V-blocks, rotate, and check the shafts for accuracy with the Dial indicator. Any malalignment is corrected by taking up the assembly and striking whichever wheel needs correction at the point indicated by the spinning test. The setting must bring the shafts running to within .001-in. of exact truth.

Tighten the nuts and check again. Finally, line up if needed by using the lead lump.

Replacement of Small End Bush.

Any vertical play on the gudgeon pin in the small end bush calls for replacement of the gudgeon pin or bush, or both. If the pin is worn it is worth trying a new pin in the original bush before deciding to renew the bush. Gudgeon pins are listed .001-in. oversize so that even if the bush is worn it might be satisfactory with an oversize pin.

Whilst it is possible to draw out a small end bush and draw a new one into the rod with a suitable bolt and collars, etc., we do not recommend attempting to renew it unless the engine is dismantled and the connecting rod removed.

All connecting rods are checked and trued in production after the bushes are fitted and finished to size, ensuring perfect alignment between the small end and big end bearings, and this cannot be guaranteed when other methods of fitting are employed. Further, as the replacement bush has to be filed in position to match up with the oil hole in the connecting rod there is a serious risk of filings getting into the crankcase. Connecting rods sent to us for rebushing will be lined up, before return, on a special fixture.

Refitting the Piston and Cylinder.

If the magneto has been removed refit it before fitting the cylinder. It is essential after reassembling the flywheels and crankcase, particularly if a new small end bush has been fitted, to check that the bore of the small end is in line with and parallel to the big end. To test; obtain an accurately ground mandrel of $\frac{3}{8}$-in. diameter to fit closely and without play in the small end bush. Set the flywheels so that the lower edges of the small end bush are nearly flush with the cylinder face on the crankcase. Push the mandrel through the bush and check that it lies flat on the face at both sides of the small end. Should it touch at one side, but not on the other, the connecting rod must be reset.

The small end eye must also lie centrally in the mouth of the crankcase to avoid side thrust on the piston and this point should be checked, making due allowance for side play on the big end.

Fit the piston in place and push the gudgeon pin through the bush, finally driving it home up to the circlip, which will have been fitted to the piston. It is a help when fitting if the pin is first pushed into one boss so that it just protrudes inside the piston. The protruding end is then easily entered into the small end bush. Get help to support the piston from the opposite side when tapping the pin home. Note that the split in the piston skirt must be at the front. Finally fit the second circlip verifying that it fits properly down in its groove, and see that the ends do not touch.

New circlips are occasionally found to need a small amount removing from one end to prevent the ends touching, which would prevent proper seating in the circlip groove.

Smear the cylinder bore with clean oil, fit a new gasket over the cylinder base, sticking it in place with a little grease, and if any compression plates were fitted originally fit these in place on the crankcase. Set the ring gaps 120° apart.

Support the piston and lower the cylinder over it compressing the rings one at a time to enter them in the bore. Lower the cylinder into place and push it firmly into the crankcase.

The reassembly of the cylinder head and overhead valve gear is dealt with from page 25.

The Timing Gears.

The timing gear bushes in the camwheel and intermediate gear wheel assemblies seldom need replacement, but if renewed must be bored to suit the spindles and not reamed. Boring is essential to ensure the bearing being concentric with the gear teeth. The camwheel bush must be bored to .001-in. above the spindle diameter, and the intermediate gear bush to .0015-in. larger than its spindle. End float on the gears must not exceed .0015-in.

End float must be checked after fitting the steady plate with this bolted firmly in place.

POSITIONS OF TIMING MARKS.

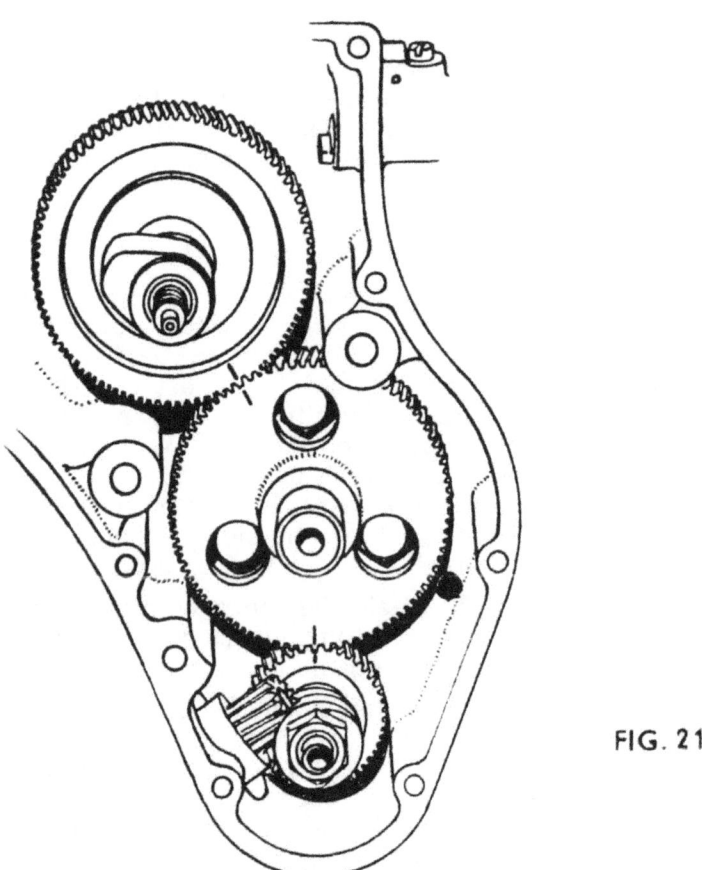

FIG. 21

The Intermediate Gear Spindle Bolt Heads are also visible through the holes in the gear.

The gears are marked for refitting (Fig. 21). To fit, turn the crankshaft to bring the mark on the crankshaft pinion to the top. Fit the camwheel to its spindle setting the timing mark as illustrated and the cams pointing rearwards. Slide the intermediate gear into place and mesh its teeth with the camwheel and crankshaft pinion so that the marks register. There are two marks on the intermediate gear, but as they are not diametrically opposite the gear can only be fitted in one way to register the marks properly, i.e., with the longer section between the marks facing the front.

Note specially that owing to the intermediate gear having one more tooth than the camwheel it changes its position in relation to the other gears and lags behind the camwheel one tooth in every two turns of the crankshaft.

The result is that after resetting the timing gears with all marks coinciding, and then turning the crankshaft two complete turns, the marks on the intermediate gear will be out of register with the crankshaft, and cam gears which will be back in their original positions.

This sometimes leads to the assumption that an engine is incorrectly timed as obviously the chance of the engine stopping so that the marks are in register or even nearly so is exceedingly remote. The marks will all coincide only once every 93 turns of the crankshaft. This feature of the design avoids loading the same teeth at each revolution of the camshaft and evens out any wear which takes place.

The Adjustable Intermediate Gear Spindle.

Mainly for purposes of original assembly the spindle carrying the intermediate gear is arranged to be adjustable, so that the backlash between the teeth of the gears may be varied. The adjustment normally does not need any alteration, and the spindle is set when new to give freedom in the gears at all positions with minimum clearances between the teeth.

The flange of the spindle is secured to the inner wall of the crankcase by three ¼-in. B.S.F. bolts which pass through clearance holes in the crankcase thus permitting a certain degree of movement. The flange which is machined with a flat is located by this flat portion fitting against a corresponding flat machined on the crankcase, thus allowing the spindle lateral movement only.

The heads of the spindle holding bolts are accessible through the three holes in the intermediate gear and are shown in Fig. 21, page 46.

Should excess backlash develop between the gears the adjustment may be made by removing the steady plate, slightly slacking off the three bolts and pushing the intermediate closer into mesh towards the rear (towards the left of the illustration).

It is important not to set the gear too close as this will cause gear whine.

Retiming the Ignition.

Refit the automatic timing unit loosely to the magneto armature. Attach a timing disc to the driving side mainshaft and fix a pointer made of stiff wire to some convenient fixed point, i.e., one of the engine or crankcase bolts. Bring the piston to top dead centre with both valves closed and bend the pointer to indicate zero on the timing disc. Turn the crankshaft backwards 38° as indicated by the pointer. With finger and thumb turn the front plate of the timing unit backwards to its limit, to advance it fully. The plate referred to carries the toggle levers and is shown in Fig. 17, page 38. The illustration shows the unit fully retarded. Holding the timing unit fully advanced set the contact breaker points just opening (apart by .0015-in.) The contact breaker gap must of course have been adjusted previously to the setting recommended by the magneto makers. Tighten the centre bolt to fix the timing unit to the taper on the armature. Check the timing before fitting the timing cover as follows :

Turn the crankshaft backwards and see that the contact points close. Open the points with the fingers and place between them a piece of cigarette paper, allowing the points to close on it. Obtain assistance to hold the timing unit fully advanced or insert a small block between the projections of the front plate and the back plate on the gear to wedge them apart. Very slowly move the crankshaft forward maintaining a light pull on the cigarette paper meanwhile. As soon as the paper will withdraw from between the points stop moving the crankshaft and check the position of the timing disc. The reading must be 38°.

Remove the wedge from the timing unit, if one was used, and check the tightness of the timing unit bolt.

Refitting the Timing Gear Cover.

It is advisable always to use a new gasket which may be stuck to the cover with Gasket Goo before fitting. Check that the crankshaft oil feed jet is clear and entered in the bore in the timing side mainshaft. Also engage the holes in the cover over the projecting tip of the cam-wheel spindle and cam oil jet. Tighten the cover screws firmly and evenly. The rocker oil pipe should be left disconnected at the bottom end for the time being so that the oil feed may be checked before finally connecting it and tightening the union (see page 18).

THE CLUTCH.
Dismantling.

If the gearbox has not been removed from the frame the preliminary work of removing the dynamo belt cover, and primary chain (see page 30 onwards) will be required, but the back half of the primary chain cover may be left attached to the gearbox.

Having drawn the clutch off the sleeve gear and taken out and preserved the three thrust pins from the back plate, the component parts of the clutch can be lifted off one by one. The condition of the inserts and chain wheel ballrace can be verified. The inserts will wear until flush with the metal surface around them, but should be reasonably secure in their places. The chain wheel ballrace must be free without excessive play and should be a sliding fit on the back plate, but secure in the chain wheel.

Relining the Clutch.

Worn inserts can be pushed out of place and renewed if necessary. Press in new inserts leaving them projecting an equal distance each side and make certain that the working surfaces are all level. Pressing them up against a truly flat surface will ensure this.

Reassembling the Clutch.

The back plate must be held firmly from rotating during re-assembly otherwise the spacing plates cannot be engaged with the front plate. The best thing to hold the plate is a disused sleeve gear from any single cylinder model Velocette. This is gripped in the vice by the gear teeth or driving dogs, and the clutch back plate fitted loosely over the splines.

Fit the first clutch plate in position followed by a spacing plate, second* clutch plate, and the second spacing plate. Note that the external tongues on the clutch plates and internal tongues on the spacing plates must all point away from the chainwheel, i.e., downwards.

Centralise the four plates with the back plate, bring the tongues on each pair of plates into line and engage the internal tongues of the spacing plates in the slots machined in the back plate just inside the ground friction surface.

Hold the chainwheel with the deeper slotted rim underneath and fit it into position with the ballrace over the boss of the back plate. Enter the tongues of the clutch plates in the chainwheel and see that all friction surfaces come into contact. With the chainwheel fitted, put on the third spacing plate and clutch plate in that order and with their tongues pointing upwards, those of the clutch plate being engaged in the slots in the rim of the chainwheel. Centre the spacing plate carefully as its internal tongues must engage in slots on the clutch front plate.

* Earlier models have only one 'insert' plate and one spacing plate at each side of the chain wheel. The method of assembly is similar.

Fit the front plate over the tongues of the back plate and move the chain-wheel backwards and forwards maintaining light pressure on the front plate until it is felt to go into place and lie flat on the friction linings as the tongues on the spacing plate enter the slots.

See that the spring holder is screwed into place in the front plate, and fit the three thrust pins into the holes in the back plate sticking them in with a little grease.

The clutch assembly is now ready for refitting.

The Clutch Thrust Bearing.

This is a ball thrust bearing seated spherically in the clutch thrust cup and located centrally upon the sleeve gear by a distance-piece pushed over the sleeve gear behind the clutch back plate. There are three parts to the bearing; a hardened steel thrust ring flat on both sides, a cage carrying the bearing balls, and a spherical thrust washer. This has a spherical face to fit the thrust cup and a flat face providing a bearing for the balls during the operation of the clutch. (Fig. 11, page 27.)

The thrust bearing should be inspected for wear. If pitted the parts affected should be replaced. The plain thrust ring if pitted on one side only may often be reversed to give it a new lease of life. Inspect the distance piece for grooving due to wear and replace if worn. If a new caged ballrace is fitted see that there are no rough edges on it which would prevent it sliding freely on the distance-piece. Coat all parts with grease before refitting.

The clutch thrust bearing is not intended to carry a constant thrust load, and when the clutch is correctly adjusted is only called upon to take the load when the clutch lever is operated, and the clutch is disengaged. It is therefore important at all times to keep the adjustment correct and when driving to avoid keeping the machine standing in gear with the engine running for longer than is necessary. In circumstances where the engine cannot be stopped, i.e., in traffic blocks, always select neutral.

THE GEARBOX.*
Dismantling.*

It is possible to remove all the shafts and gears from the gearbox without dismounting the housing from the frame, but if the layshaft ballrace and sleeve gear ballrace need renewal the housing must be taken out. The gearbox and engine are removed, together as a unit. See page 36.

Drain out all oil by removing the drain plug from the end cover (Fig. 16, page 36). Take out the two ¼-in. B.S.F. bolts from the gearbox cover (above the kickstart bearing) and remove the cover. Hold the gearshaft from turning and unscrew the gearshaft nut which is exposed by the removal of the small cover.

Unless the kickstart spring or ratchet need attention the kickstart bearing should be left in place attached to the gearbox end cover. (For attention to kickstart see page 34.) Tap the gearshaft into the gearbox a little way to free the ballrace, remove the seven ¼-in. B.S.F. cover bolts and pull the cover off the housing. Note the two dowels which may be left in the face of the housing or come away with the cover, and preserve these for refitting. The gear control pedal may be left attached to its spindle.

The layshaft is supported in the kickstart ratchet by a floating bush and this may be left on the end of the layshaft or come away in the ratchet. There is also a hardened steel disc in the ratchet (Fig. 15), this must be carefully retained for refitting. Also remove from the layshaft the layshaft washer fitted up against the ratchet gear.

* 'Light' type boxes Series 11/, are dealt with in exactly the same way as the 'Heavy' types Series 12/ or 14/.

Pull the gearshaft first gear wheel off the gearshaft.

Draw out the two selector fork rods—these are grooved near the ends to provide a means of gripping them. Pull the gearshaft right out towards the clutch side of the machine and pull out the double sliding gear and upper fork, also the layshaft assembly and lower fork.

Special Note.—In all gearboxes that have sleeve gears with more than sixteen gear teeth, that is those that have ' Close ' or ' TT Close ' ratios (fitted to special order) the top gear pick-up dogs overlap the spaces between the gear teeth in all but one position. If the layshaft will not come out of mesh with the sleeve gear with light pressure, turn the sleeve gear round to bring the ' clear ' space to the bottom. This applies to all gearboxes with serial number prefixed by the figures 12/.

If the clutch has been removed the sleeve gear will tap through its ballrace into the gearbox and can then be removed. Only the layshaft ballrace and the sleeve gear ballrace, together with the camplate and its attendant mechanism remain in position.

The Operating Mechanism.

Experience has shown that attention is practically never required to this part of the gearbox mechanism and it should not be disturbed needlessly.

Should the camplate be taken off its spindle note that it is mounted on a loose centre-piece—the camplate ratchet plate—and it must be set correctly in relation to this part. Accordingly the two parts are marked and if removed from the ratchet plate the camplate must be fitted with the V mark on it facing the corresponding mark on the ratchet.

After very long use indeed some wear may be found on the steel pegs in the selector forks which engage the operating slots in the camplate. These are renewable separately by driving them out of position and pressing in new ones. No attention whatever is likely to be required to the gear change lever shaft and bearing in the end cover, the rocker shaft bushes, or connecting linkage.

The Gearbox Bearings.

The gearshaft bearing in the end cover will jar out of place after removal of its locating circlip if the cover is heated, and the gearbox housing should be heated in order to free the layshaft ballrace which also will jar out of its housing. To refit or replace heat the housing and cover and tap the bearings into place.

The sleeve gear ballrace which is fitted between two thin steel oil retaining shims is held by a retaining ring threaded into the housing. To reach this ring the back half of the primary chain cover must be removed, and the thrust cup taken away. The thrust cup is held into its seating by a small wire clip retained by two $\frac{1}{8}$-in. screws.

The metal at the edge of the hole for the ballrace retaining ring is punched into the notches in the ring for locking purposes. The overlapping metal must be chiselled off carefully to clear the ring.

To unscrew the retaining ring use Service Tool No. X2725 (Fig. 22), which will avoid damaging the ring. The oil retaining shim outside the ballrace will lift out and the ballrace can be tapped out after heating the housing around the bearing. The second shim will now come away.

Examine the shims carefully and if in the slightest degree worn or showing any signs of splitting they must be replaced. When refitting the shims and the ballrace—or renewing them—great care must be taken to centralise the shims accurately, otherwise the sleeve gear oil thrower and the distance piece will rub against them and cause wear, eventual failure, and oil leakages.

The ring when finally tightened should be in such a position that one of the grooves at the back of the ring, is at, or near the bottom so that any oil passing the shims and collecting in the recess behind the retaining ring may drain away back into the gearbox through the drilling in the housing. Preferably the ring should tighten up fully with one of the outer slots at or near the top which will ensure that one groove at the back will be near the bottom.

Refit the sleeve gear noting that the oil thrower is in place with its concave side next to the gear teeth.

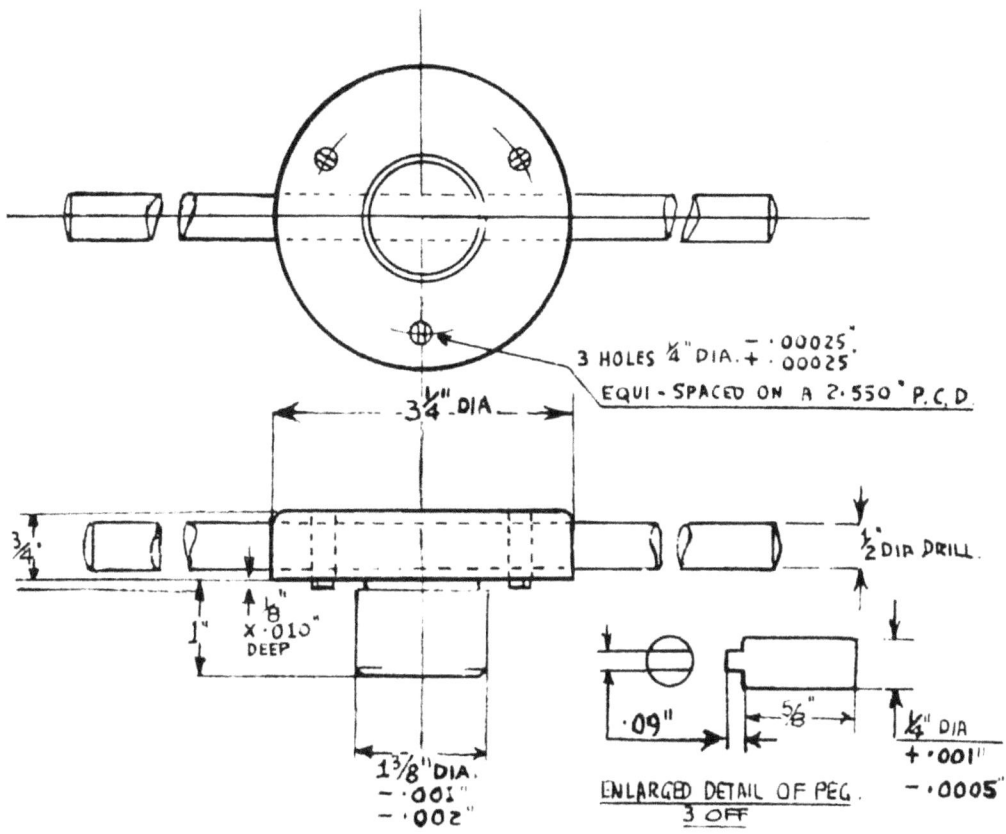

FIG. 22.
X2725 BALLRACE RETAINING RING TOOL.

The bushes in the second and third speed layshaft gears and the low gear bush are easily replaced, but to renew the former the layshaft assembly must be dismantled as described in the next section.

The sleeve gear bush is pegged in position and before attempting to press it out the peg, which passes through the plain ground part of the sleeve gear, must be drilled out. A new sleeve gear bush must be located before pressing in so that the oil holes in the bush will come directly below the oil holes drilled through the gear between the teeth, and after fitting, the bush must be drilled and pegged, and bored out to .001-in. above the gear-shaft diameter. The bush must be bored to ensure concentricity with the ground part of the sleeve gear. Reaming is unsatisfactory.

It is unlikely that the bushes in the low gear, and in the second and third speed layshaft gears will need renewal, but if so they can be pressed out of the gears and new ones pressed in.

After fitting, the low gear bush must be finished bored to .625-in., and the layshaft gear bushes to .8125-in. The limits are plus .0007, minus .0005-in. in both cases.

Note that current models have two bushes in the low gear. These are pressed in from opposite sides so as to provide bearing flanges at both sides of the gear.

The Layshaft Assembly.

Whilst the layshaft assembly is removed the teeth of the sliding dog, and the corresponding pick up teeth on the second and third gears should be inspected for wear on the edges. The edges must be clean and sharp and if broken away, chipped, or rounded the part must be replaced.

A worn sliding dog can be replaced after removal of either of the end gears—these are splined to the shaft. They may be pressed or levered off the layshaft and will then allow the second and third speed layshaft gears to come off.

When reassembling note that the third speed gear—the larger one—fits next to the ratchet gear, and when pressing them back into place, press them on far enough to locate them without excess end float, but perfectly free to rotate. End float must not exceed .015-in. and is best left at about .005-in.

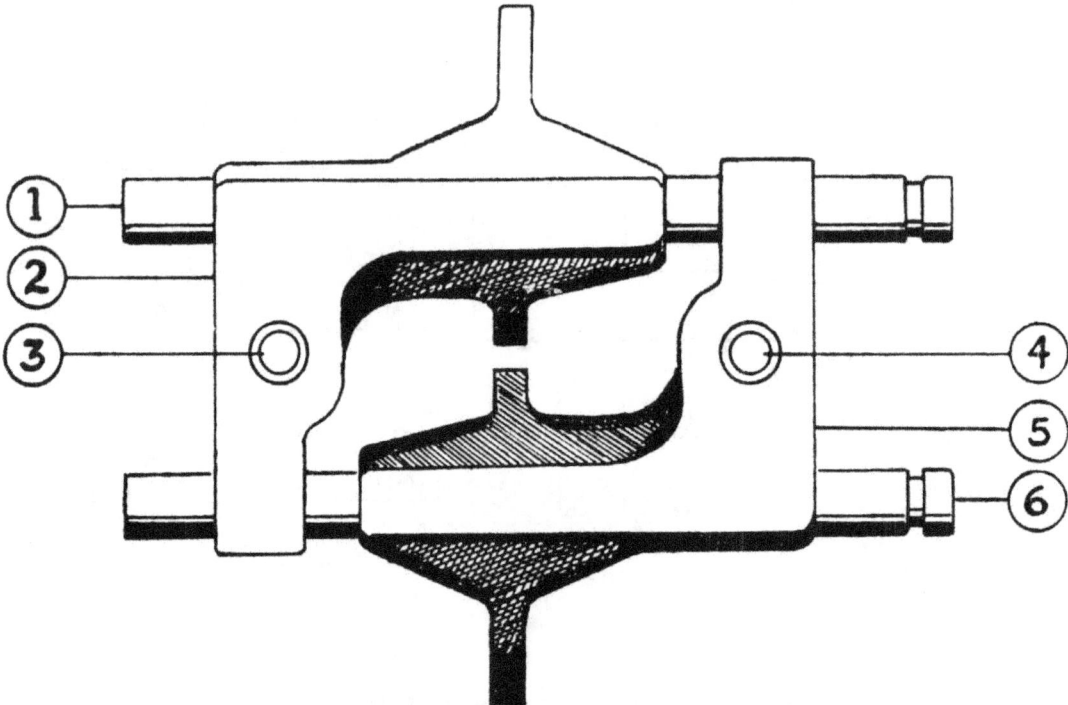

FIG. 23. POSITION OF SELECTOR FORKS FOR REFITTING. (Viewed from rear.)

(1) Selector Fork Rod (1st and Top Gears).
(2) Selector Fork. (1st and Top Gears).
(3) }Selector Fork Pegs.
(4)
(5) Selector Fork. (2nd and 3rd Gears).
(6) Selector Fork Rod. (2nd and 3rd Gears).

Refitting the Gears to the Housing.

The layshaft assembly should be held in one hand and the double sliding gear rested in position on the second and third speed sliding gears, noting that the larger gear of the double gear (the one with the internal pick up teeth) faces towards the largest gear on the layshaft (i.e., remote from the ratchet gear).

Engage the selector forks in the grooves of the double gear and sliding dog with the forks set so that in the case of the top one the lug carrying the selector fork peg is downwards and the peg between the actual fork and the clutch side of the gearbox (Fig. 23) and the bottom one the other way round.

Place the layshaft assembly, double gear, and forks into the housing, manoeuvring the end of the layshaft into the layshaft ballrace and meshing the layshaft gear with the sleeve gear. Engage the selector fork pegs in the cam tracks in the camplate, and push the fork rods through the selector forks entering their plain ends in the holes in the gearbox housing. **Note.—** The lower selector fork rod on all gearboxes 12/ or 14/ is now $\frac{1}{16}$-in. longer overall than originally, so that if the rods are seen to be of different lengths always fit the longer one through the lower fork. The grooved ends fit into the end cover.

Push the gearshaft through the sleeve gear from the clutch side and enter the splines through the splines in the double gear. Refit the gearshaft first gear wheel over the end of the gearshaft, meshing it with the ratchet low gear.

Refitting the End Cover.

Should the kickstart bearing, and kickstart be attached to the cover, make sure before fitting that the kickstart layshaft thrust washer is in place in the kickstart ratchet. If the kickstart bearing is not attached to the cover it may be left for the time being and fitted after the end cover is in place.

Place the layshaft washer over the splines protruding beyond the ratchet low gear, place the kickstart bearing (floating) bush on the layshaft, and, after checking that the end cover ball bearing is in place, with the circlip fitted, put the cover in position using a new gasket on the face joint, and the dowels in position. It will be necessary, as the cover is pushed home to enter the ends of the selector fork rods in their holes in the cover, and the gearshaft through the end cover ballrace. Also the gear control lever must be held up so that the peg at the rear end of the gear change rocker shaft is engaged in the slot in the striking plate assembly. Tighten the holding bolts. Fit and tighten the gearshaft nut against the ballrace and refit the end cover-plate, using a new gasket. See that the drain plug is fitted.

Refit the kickstart assembly as described on page 35. Note when doing so that the kickstart bearing bush, the layshaft washer, and the layshaft thrust washer are all in their places, and do not use a gasket or paper joint washer between the kickstart bearing and the gearbox end cover.

Refill gearbox with oil and refit the level and filler plugs.

THE REAR WHEEL AND BRAKE.

Removal of Rear Wheel and Brake.

If attention is needed to the brake it is easier to take out the wheel with the brake assembly attached as follows :

Remove the rear detachable section of the mudguard, and the rear chain guard from the left-hand torque tube assembly. Detach the rear brake torque arm, the rear end of the speedometer drive flex from the reduction gearbox, and remove the rear brake adjusting nut. Take out the rear chain connecting link and take off the chain.

Loosen the rear wheel spindle, and the nut on the brake-plate locking bolt on the left-hand side (Fig. 41, page 83). Pull the rear wheel, with brake assembly out rearwards from the fork ends. Complete removal of the nut from the brake plate locking bolt permits the withdrawal of the brake-plate assembly from the drum, and by taking out the wheel spindle and removing the three wheel nuts the drum is freed from the wheel hub.

Relining the Brake.

Replacement brake liners and rivets are available, but it is preferable to fit a pair of replacement relined brake shoe assemblies in exchange for the worn ones. When fitting replacement shoes be careful to fit the steel slippers which protect the ends of the shoes from wear by the cam, and see that the cam works freely in its bearing in the brake plate.

A limited amount of wear may be taken up by inserting thin steel packings between the brake shoe ends and the slippers, but the brake lining rivets must be below the surface of the liner and unable to rub the drum.

Dismantling the Rear Hub Bearings. (Fig. 24.)

This may be necessary to repack the bearings with grease or to renew them. The barrel of the hub does not carry any grease and the amount needed for adequate lubrication is kept in the bearings by grease retainers fitted between the bearings and the hub.

To dismantle drive out the hollow spindle JD, after pulling off the speedometer reduction gearbox (JA), and the ballrace clamping sleeve (JK). The spindle is driven out from the right-hand side of the machine towards the left and will take with it the left-hand side ballrace (JF) and dust cap (JE). A punch, 9-in. long, slightly less than $\frac{7}{8}$-in. diameter, and reduced at one end to just under $\frac{5}{8}$-in. for a distance of $\frac{1}{2}$-in., will be needed. The same punch is used for dealing with the front hub.

REAR HUB ASSEMBLY (Sectional View).

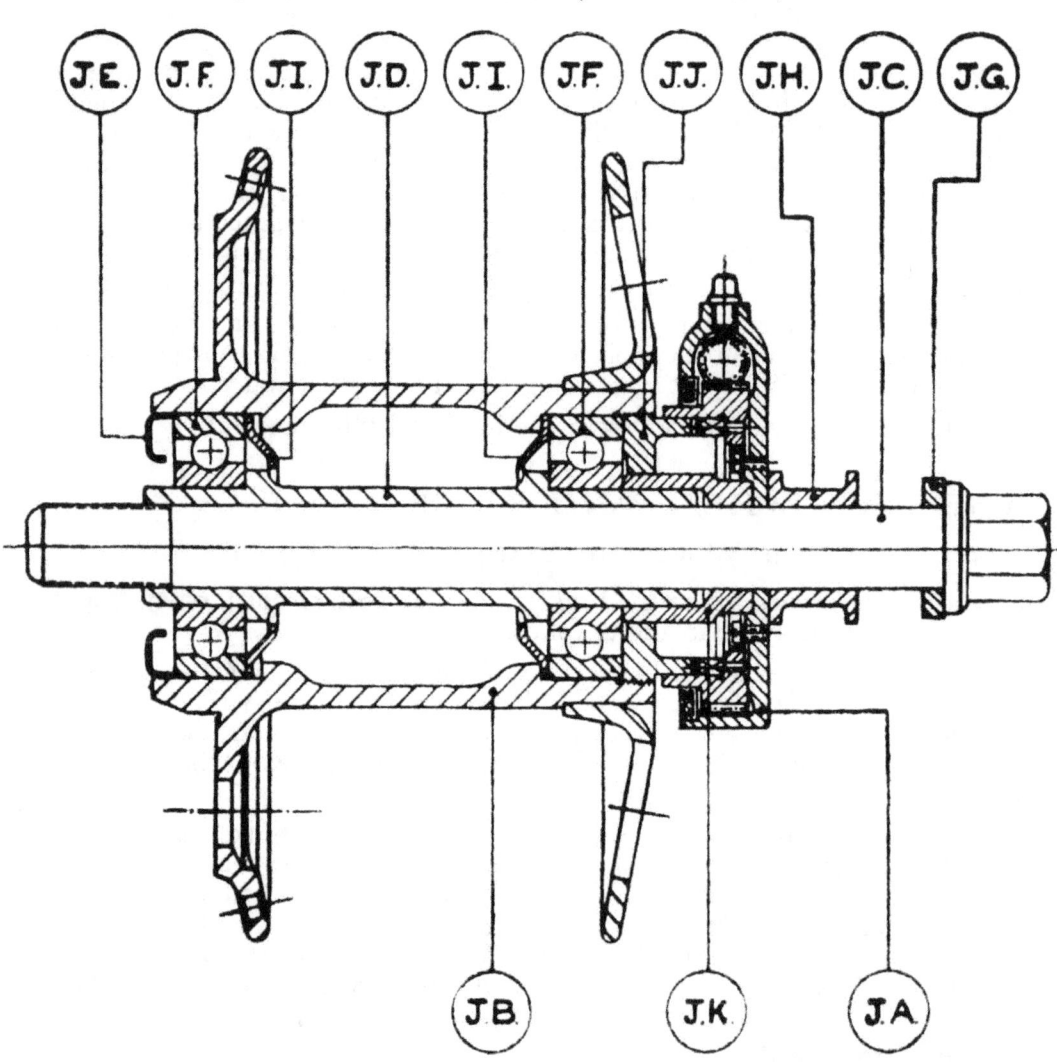

FIG. 24.

JA Reduction Gearbox for Speedometer Drive.	JD Hollow Spindle.	JH. Distance Piece.
JB. Hub Shell.	JE. Dust Cap (Brake Side).	JI. Grease Retainers.
JC. Detachable Spindle.	JF. Ballraces.	JJ. Ballrace Retaining Ring.
	JG. Spindle Washer.	JK. Ballrace Clamping Sleeve.

Unscrew and remove the **left-hand thread** ballrace retaining ring (JJ). The edge of this is slotted in four places. The wider slots will take a bar for undoing the ring. If the ballrace is in good condition and only needs repacking with grease, this can be done without removing it. If renewal is needed drive the bearing out towards the right-hand side using a suitable punch inserted through the hub or insert one end of the hollow spindle into the bearing after removing the left-hand side ballrace, inserting the punch (previously described) into the other end of the hollow spindle.

Reassembling the Rear Hub. (Fig. 24.)

Place the right-hand side grease retainer (JI) in position, hollow (concave) side outwards as illustrated and press the ballrace into its housing. Pack it well with high melting point grease. Fit and tighten the retaining ring (JJ) using a bar across the two wide slots. Press the other ballrace on to the hollow spindle taking care to fit it to the shorter parallel ground end —refer to illustration. Place the left-hand side grease retainer in the housing hollow (concave) side outwards—pack the housing with grease and fit the hollow spindle through the hub entering the longer parallel ground end in the right-hand side ballrace, and the outer ring of the left-hand side ballrace in the hub. Press the ballrace home. Pack a little more grease into the ballrace and press in the dust cap (JE) hollow side towards the ballrace.

Push the ballrace clamping sleeve (JK) on to the hollow spindle, and fit the reduction gearbox—engaging its driving dogs with the two narrow slots in the ballrace retaining ring. The hub is then ready for refitting.

Reassembling the Brake Plate Assembly.

Push the brake plate support bolt through the brake-drum grease shield. Fit the brake plate washer in place over the support bolt and fit the brake

REAR SUSPENSION-ADJUSTMENT FOR LOAD

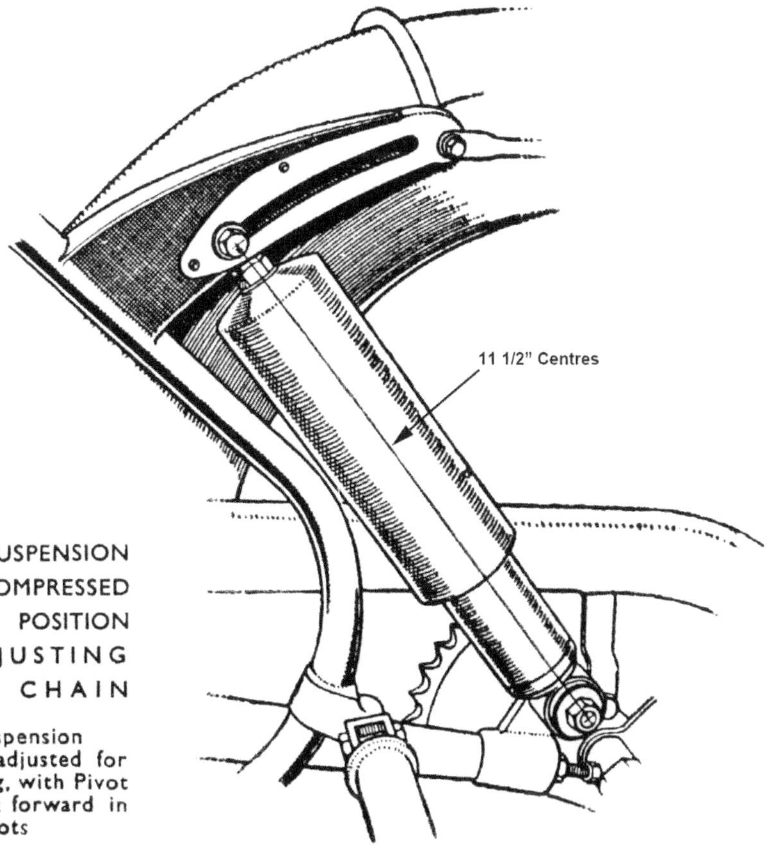

11 1/2" Centres

REAR SUSPENSION UNIT COMPRESSED TO MID POSITION FOR ADJUSTING REAR CHAIN

The Suspension is shown adjusted for Solo Riding, with Pivot Bolts right forward in slots

FIG. 25.

plate assembly, at the same time entering the brake shoes in the drum and the end of the support bolt through the hole in the brake cam steady. If desired the hub may now be attached to the brake drum and the wheel with brake assembly fitted to the machine.

THE REAR SUSPENSION. (Fig. 25.)
Description.

The rear suspension is by two self-contained suspension units containing the springs, the damper mechanism, and the oil necessary for damping and lubrication.

The objection to most rear springing systems is that they are unable to cope equally well with both solo and pillion riding conditions. Thus, if the springing is arranged for the heavier load it hardly works at all with a solo rider; and if arranged for solo use tends to bottom when a passenger is carried.

The MAC rear suspension is easily and quickly adjustable for load in a manner which makes it unique in motor-cycle practice by means of the patented adjustment incorporated and proper working and consequently reasonable comfort are obtainable by a light rider solo, or by two heavy persons.

By altering the positions of the top mountings of the spring suspension units along the slots in the support lugs on the frame, the springing may be adjusted from " light "—furthest forward as illustrated—to " heavy "—right back. Any intermediate setting may be used, provided that the suspension units are in line, with the upper mounting bolts the same distance along the slots at each side.

Maintenance—Suspension Units.

Apart from external cleaning no attention is necessary. Should it be required to replace the dust covers, or springs these are removable after taking the units off the machine. Removal of the covers discloses the buffers and springs.

To remove a cover for access to the spring or felt washer first remove the suspension unit from the machine by detaching it at the upper and lower pivots.

Hold the unit vertically in a vice gripping the bottom fixing lug between protected vice jaws.

With both hands press down the dust cover against the spring far enough to allow the removal of the two halves of the split dust cover retainer. Help will be needed to pull them out whilst the spring is held compressed (a valve cotter is removed in the same way).

The dust cover, washer and spring will then come away over the top lug.

On earlier types the removal of the dust covers is carried out differently as follows :—

Hold the locknut below the top fixing lug and unscrew the lug by turning it, with a bar passed through the distance piece in the eye of the lug. Hold the threaded end of the damper spindle with a screwdriver in the slot and screw the locknut right off. The cover and spring will then lift off.

The remainder of the unit consisting of the lower part containing the damper mechanism cannot be taken apart, and will be found to function indefinitely.

Occasionally the eye bushes may need renewing. Those at the bottom are easily fitted by pushing them into place in the lower eyes, but the top ones call for the use of a special pressing tool—Service Tool No. X2992 (Fig. 26).

This tool is used by first pressing the rubber sleeve into the eye, by resting the fixing lug on the tool and with the shoulder bush (I) entered in the sleeve. Before attempting to fit the sleeves lubricate them with soapy water.

Remove the shouldered bush (1). Rest the eye, with rubber sleeve fitted, on top of the tool. Fit the distance piece over the Opening Bush (3) and shouldered bush (1) and fit the Opening Bush over the locating rod. Press down the shoulder bush until the distance piece is fully home in the rubber sleeve.

Maintenance—Rear Swinging Fork.

Periodical lubrication of the trunnion shaft bearings through the grease nipples at each side of the trunnion lug on the frame is all that is needed. The greasers are on the underside of the lug.

Do not in any circumstances dismantle the swinging fork assembly needlessly.

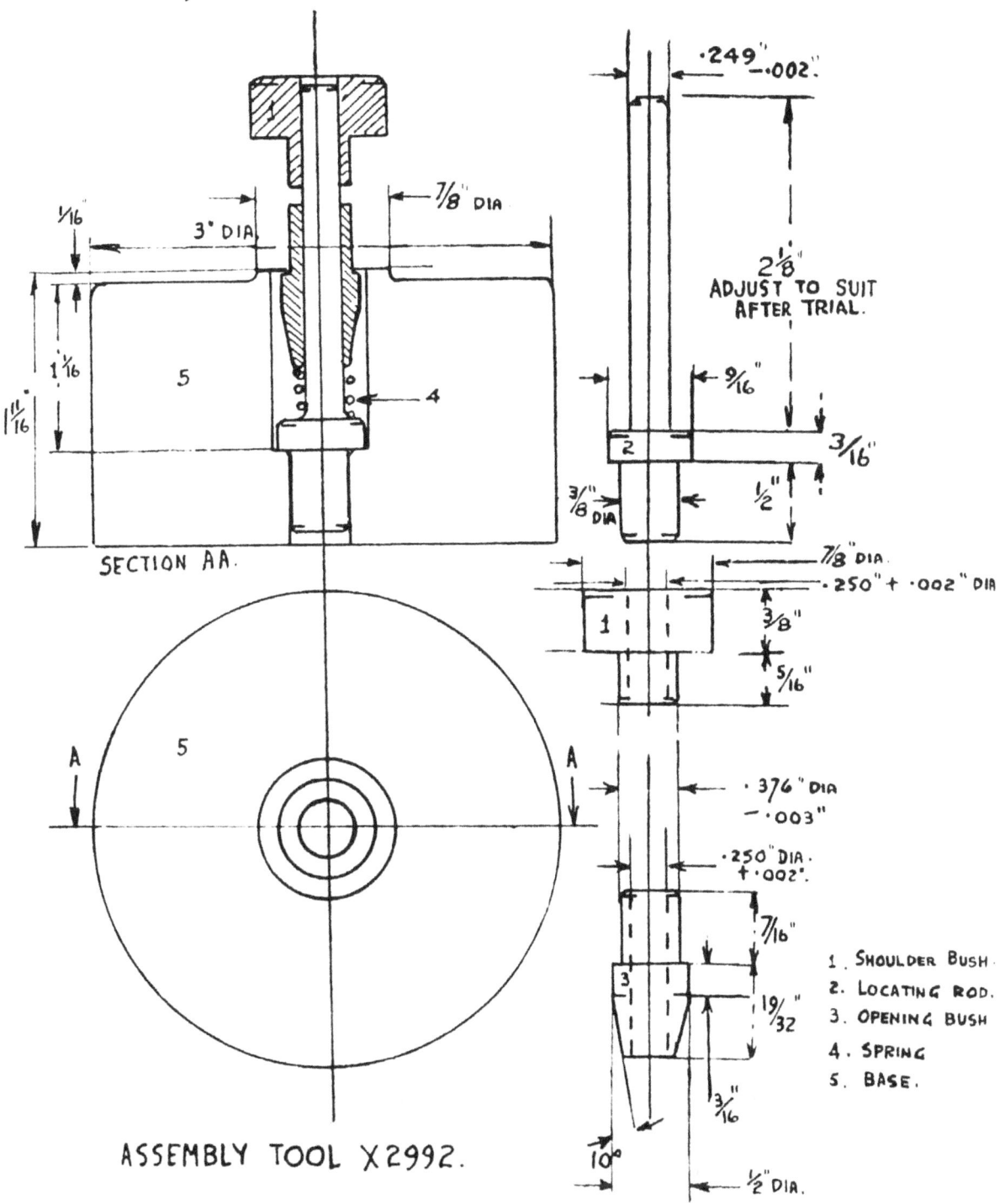

FIG. 26.

The torque arm assemblies are very carefully and accurately lined up with each other during assembly at the factory, and are held in alignment with special equipment, while the clamping bolts are tightened up and the torque tube ends clamped to the trunnion shaft.

In the event of accidental damage or if it is essential for the assembly to be taken apart for any other reason the frame with the rear swinging fork assembly should be returned to the factory.

As this may be impractical in the case of Overseas Agents the method of dismantling, and reassembling the trunnion shaft and torque tube assemblies is detailed in the next section.

Dismantling the Trunnion Shaft.

As stated previously the torque arm assemblies should not be loosened or moved on the trunnion shaft, except in cases of absolute necessity, such as to enable repairs to be carried out after accidental damage, or to renew the trunnion shaft bushes in the frame.

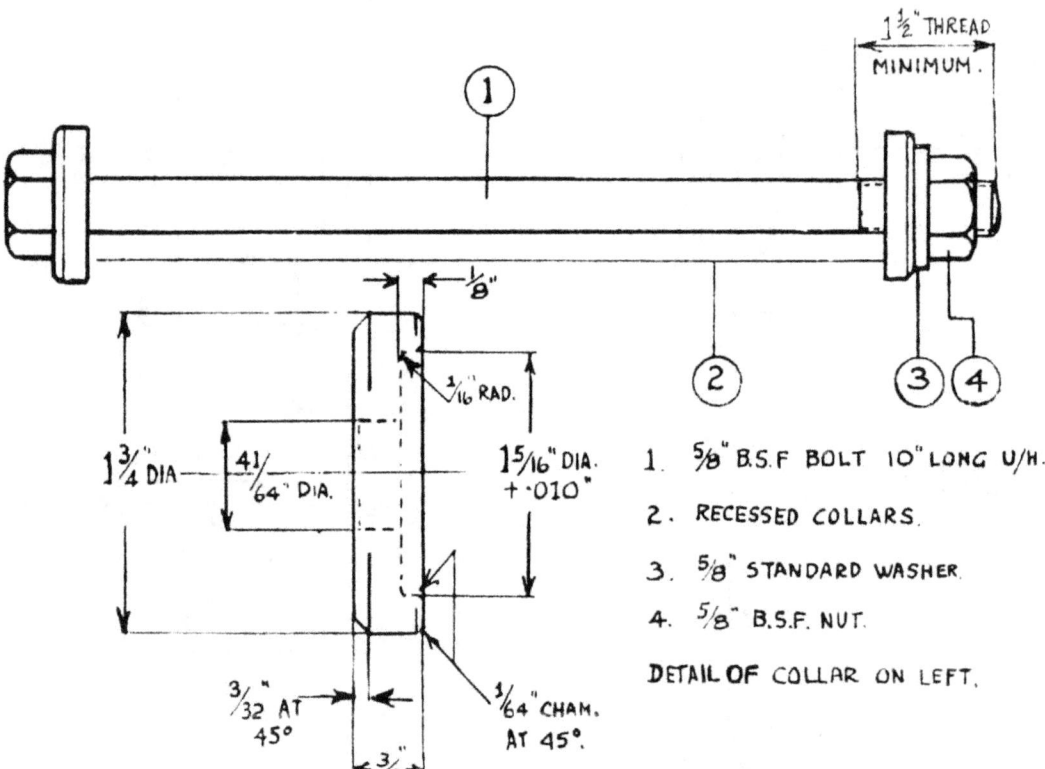

FIG. 27. X2938 TORQUE TUBE CLAMP TOOL.

During initial assembly the two torque arm assemblies are lined up using a special torque tube-assembly Alignment Tool No. X2939, which ensures that when the rear wheel is in position the rear wheel spindle is parallel to the trunnion shaft. In addition, a clamp is needed to hold the torque arm assemblies compressed against the trunnion lug felt washers to take up all excess end float. This tool is the Torque Tube Clamp Tool X2938. (Fig. 27).

The trunnion shaft is finished in three diameters, the offside (right-hand) end to take the offside torque arm assembly being .002-in. larger than the centre parallel portion which bears in the trunnion shaft bushes. The nearside (left-hand) end which carries the nearside torque arm assembly is .002-in. smaller than the centre section.

To dismantle the shaft, therefore, it must be driven out towards the right or offside, after slacking off both trunnion lug clamp bolts and expanding the lugs from the shaft with suitable wedges driven into the slots in the lugs. The lugs must be expanded to avoid scratching the shaft. Care must be taken not to over-expand them and they must be opened only enough to free the shaft.

Before attempting to drive out the trunnion shaft (for which a soft metal spigoted punch is essential) remove the two rubber trunnion shaft end plugs.

After removal of the shaft the felts and felt housings will pull off the shoulders on the frame trunnion lug.

The Trunnion Shaft Bearing.

In the event of worn bushes these must be driven out of the trunnion lug, and new ones pressed in, after which they must be accurately bored or reamed out to 1.250-in. +0.00075-in.
$\qquad$ − 0.00025-in.

Reassembling the Trunnion Shaft and Torque Arms.

Fit the trunnion shaft felt washers and felt housings to the machined shoulders on the trunnion shaft lug on the frame—The housings fit on first, with their flat faces against the lug, and the felts in place in their recessed faces.

See that the felts are well soaked in oil before fitting, particularly if they are new. Alternatively, soak them for a moment or two in molten tallow.

Set out the torque arm assemblies in the correct positions for replacement, noting that the offside (right-hand) one has an annular groove turned in the bore for identification purposes, and that there is a lug for carrying the rear chain guard on the upper part of the nearside (left-hand) torque tube.

Hold the right-hand torque arm assembly against the right-hand side of the trunnion lug, and having oiled the trunnion shaft push the smaller end through the torque arm assembly and into the bearings.

As the end comes out at the left-hand side, put the left-hand torque arm assembly (with the lug wedged open slightly) into position and push the trunnion shaft into it. Wedge open the right-hand lug slightly and press the shaft through. When the shaft has been pushed through until the chamfered end just protrudes beyond the face of the lug on the right, the wedges may be removed and the clamp bolts and nuts fitted. Tighten the bolt on the right-hand side fully, but for the time being leave that on the left loose.

The torque arms must now be drawn together towards the frame to compress the felts and to take up the side play. For this the torque tube clamp tool X2938 is required (Fig. 27). Clamp the torque arms to remove all side play, but leave the shaft free to turn in the bushes.

With the torque arms held with the clamping tool fix the Alignment Tool X2939 in position and locate it on the frame lugs with the two pegs. Bring the torque arms up into line with the holes in the rear ends of the alignment tool and pass the mandrel through the tool and the fork ends. With the torque arms thus held in alignment tighten the left-hand side clamp bolt.

As an alternative, but less satisfactory method of lining up the assembly before tightening the left-hand side clamp bolt, push two well-fitting ⅜-in. bars through the two bolt holes for the rear engine plates. One hole is in the trunnion lug, and the other in the lug at the bottom of the seat tube. A third ½-in. diameter mandrel is then placed through the fork ends and the assembly is then raised and a sight taken across this mandrel and the upper one at the front. When the torque arms have been adjusted on the trunnion shaft until the mandrels are seen to be parallel and the clamp bolt lightly tightened, the fork should be lowered and a similar test made by sighting across the bottom mandrel. If there is any variation set the fork by moving one of the torque arms on the trunnion shaft so that a mean between the two " sights " is obtained.

When correctly aligned tighten the clamp bolt fully and recheck.

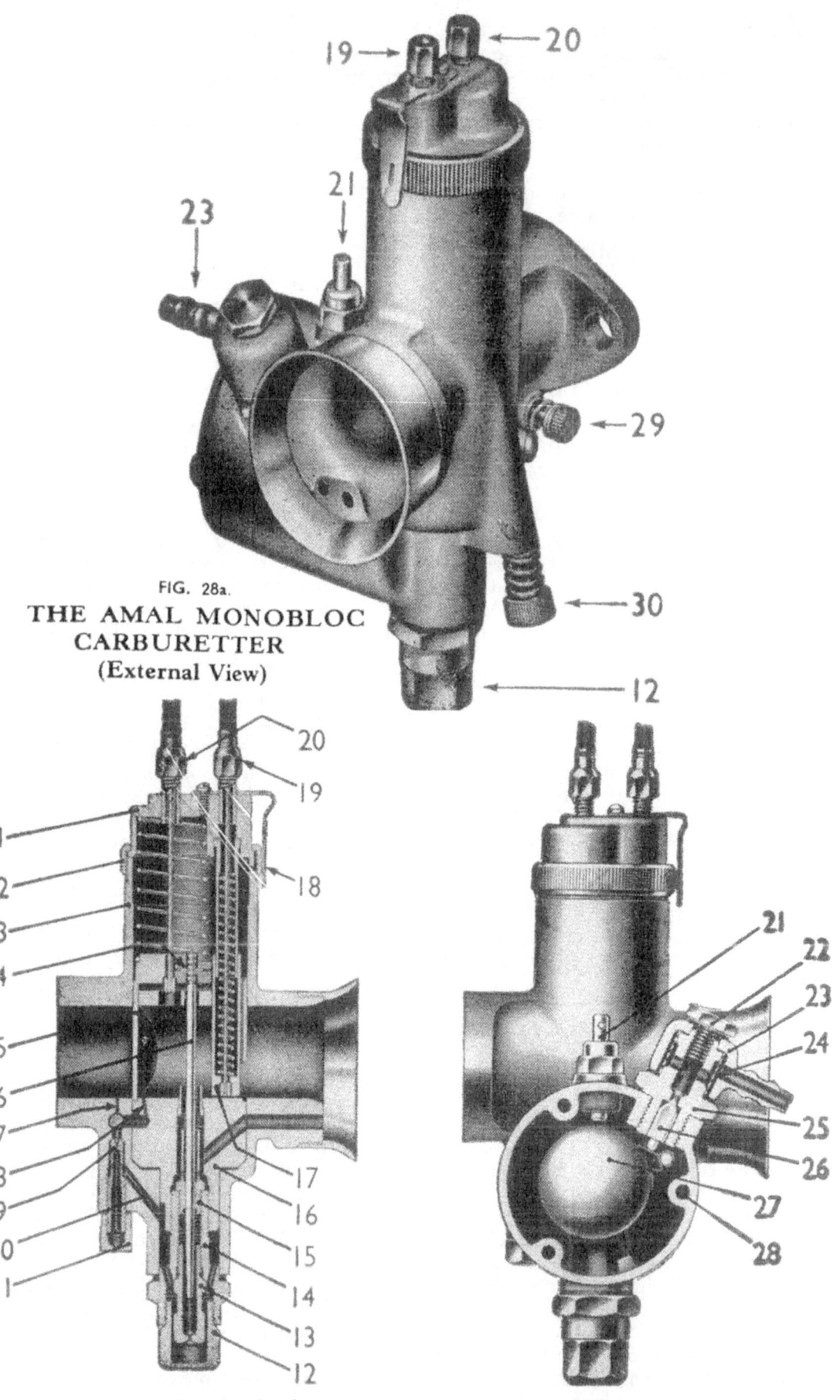

FIG. 28a.
THE AMAL MONOBLOC CARBURETTER
(External View)

Section through mixing chamber, showing air valve and throttle closed.

FIG. 29.

Section through float chamber

60

It is emphasised that this method of setting the rear wheel spindle parallel to the trunnion shaft is for use only when the proper equipment is not available, and must be considered as a less satisfactory expedient. As its accuracy depends on the fit of the bars or mandrels in the frame and fork ends respectively and on the bars being perfectly straight it is necessary to get satisfactory materials for the job, and to be most careful when "sighting" across the mandrels.

THE CARBURETTER. (Figs. 28, 29.)

Description and Explanation of Working.

The illustrations should be referred to for explanation of the following sections. The purpose of the carburetter is to atomise the correct amount of fuel with the air that is induced into the engine, and thus supply a correctly-proportioned mixture at all speeds within the engine's range at all throttle settings.

This is achieved by the selection of the correct size main jet, and main choke bore, in conjunction with the right adjustment or setting of the jet needle and the pilot jet.

The volume of mixture, and therefore the power, is controlled from the handlebar twist grip which causes the throttle valve in the carburetter to be raised or lowered and the correct setting of the carburetter provides the right mixture at all positions of the throttle valve.

The opening of the throttle brings into action first the mixture supply from the pilot system for idling at slow speed, through the pilot outlet The further progressive opening of the throttle admits air via the main intake and reduces the depression on the pilot outlet, but in turn a greater depression is created on the pilot by-pass causing the mixture to flow from the opening as well as from the pilot outlet. At about $\frac{1}{8}$th of the throttle opening more air is admitted and the mixture is augmented from the main jet the throttle valve cut-away governing the mixture strength from this position of the throttle to about $\frac{1}{4}$ open. Proceeding up the throttle range the mixture strength is controlled from about $\frac{1}{4}$ to $\frac{3}{4}$ open by the position of the needle working within the needle jet. The main jet does not directly spray into the mixing chamber, but discharges through the needle jet into the primary air chamber, and the discharge goes from there as a rich fuel-air mixture through the primary air-choke into the main air-choke. This primary air-choke has a compensating action. After about $\frac{3}{4}$ throttle opening the main jet is the only regulation. It will be understood from the foregoing that as the main jet only exercises a regulating effect on the mixture strength after the throttle is opened $\frac{3}{4}$ of its travel or over, the fitting of a smaller main jet for economy purposes is useless, and can only cause overheating due to excessively lean mixtures at high speeds. As the mixture strength over the greatest portion of the throttle range is controlled by the setting of the needle within the needle jet, cases of excessive fuel consumption are usually capable of improvement by adjustment of the needle setting (referred to later) or by replacement of the needle jet and/or needle because of wear on these components.

A separately operated mixture control is also provided by the air valve, operated from the handlebar, for use when starting from cold, and until the engine is warm enough to accept the full air supply. This air control partially restricts the passage of air through the main choke.

Dismantling the Carburetter.

Disconnect the fuel pipe, and unscrew the lock-ring from the mixing chamber. Pull out the throttle and air valves. Remove the carburetter from the engine. Unscrew and take out the float chamber locking bolt, preserving the gaskets from above and below the float chamber banjo. The float chamber is now free for dismantling.

THE CARBURETTER. (*Continued*).

The remainder of the carburetter is dismantled by unscrewing and taking off the mixing chamber nut. Retain the gasket inside the nut. The removal of this nut is best achieved by holding it firmly in a vice (with the jaws protected) and unscrewing the mixing chamber off the nut. As the mixing chamber is fairly easily broken by misuse pass a wooden bar carefully through the choke bore and use the bar as a lever to turn the mixing chamber gently and unscrew it.

The jet block will now be capable of being tapped out from the top using a wooden drift to avoid damaging it. It is most important not to use excessive force. Finally screw out the pilot air adjusting screw keeping the small coil spring which is fitted over it.

The Float Chamber Assembly. (Fig. 30).

To remove the float and float needle first loosen the float chamber lid lock screw and unscrew the lid out of the chamber. Compress the spring bow on the float between finger and thumb and press the float needle down through the float and remove it from the bottom of the float chamber.

Should the carburetter have been flooding check the float for leakage by holding it close to the ear and shaking it. The presence of any petrol inside will be easily detected. Petrol can be removed and the leak traced by immersing the float in boiling water to vaporize the petrol which as it comes out in the form of vapour will show up the leak. Whilst it is possible to repair a leaking float by soldering it is not to be recommended except in a case where a replacement float is unobtainable, as it is impossible not to increase the weight of the float by the addition of solder. A replacement should, therefore, by fitted if a float is found to leak or is damaged.

Flooding may also be caused by a bent or damaged float needle or faulty needle seating. If the needle is bent, or the seat worn hollow, fit a replacement. If the seat is apparently reasonably good push the needle into place, and twist it backward and forward with the finger and thumb whilst holding it upright in the float chamber, and maintainning light pressure on the seating. Do not in any circumstances attempt to grind a needle into the seating.

Before refitting the float chamber lid check the tickler for freedom and make quite certain that the small air vent which is drilled through the edge of the lid is quite clear. Should this hole be obstructed and should the tickler form an airtight seal against the lid (as it often does) this will cause a most baffling fuel shortage, as the engine will repeatedly cut out through the float chamber running dry, but yet the float chamber will refill on the tickler being depressed and relieving the air lock.

Reassembling the Carburetter. (Fig. 30).

Make quite certain that all passages in the mixing chamber are clear. It is advisablle to blow them out with a jet of compressed air. Also blow through all passages in the jet block and clear the jets.

Enter the jet block into the mixing chamber being careful to set it the right way round so that the dowel at the side enters the slot in the bottom edge of the mixing chamber. Tap it home gentlly. Fit the gasket to the mixing chamger nut and hold this firmly in a vice. Screw the mixing chamber into the nut and tighten, using a wooden bar passed carefully through the choke bore. Refit the pilot air adjusting screw with its spring and set it $1\frac{1}{2}$ turns open from the fully screwed in position.

Fit the main jet and needle jet, but when tightening remember that these are easily sheared off so that no excessive force must be used.

Refit the float chamber using a gasket at each side of the banjo, and fit the hollow bolt, but do not tighten it fully at this stage.

Enter the throttle and air valves into the mixing chamber. As the throttle valve enters the mixing chamber the jet needle must be centralized and entered into the hole in the jet block and into the needle jet. Fit and tighten the locking ring.

After the carburetter has been fitted to the machine, not forgetting the special heat insulating flange gasket, the fuel pipe may be connected to the tank and the float chamber lined up to meet the bottom union on the pipe. Connect up the bottom union loosely, tighten the hollow bolt whilst holding the float chamber firmly, and finally tighten the fuel pipe union nuts.

Jet and Throttle Valve Markings.

The jet is marked with figures indicating in cubic centimetres the quantity of petrol which it will pass in one minute under a standard pressure. Hence a smaller number indicates a smaller jet.

The throttle valve is marked with two figures at the top, these being separated by a stroke. The first indicates the type of valve, the second the

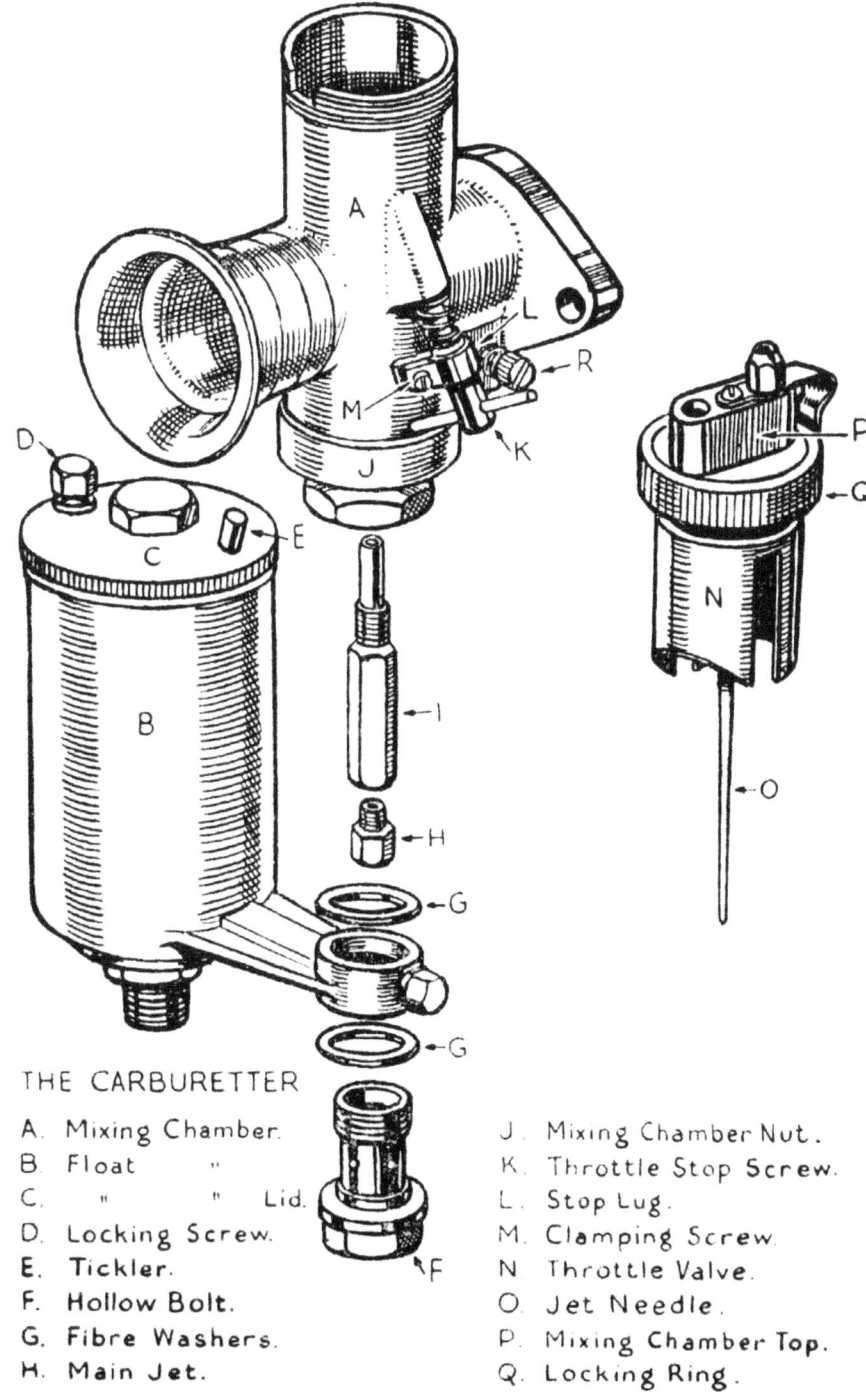

THE CARBURETTER

- A. Mixing Chamber.
- B. Float   "
- C.   "   " Lid.
- D. Locking Screw.
- E. Tickler.
- F. Hollow Bolt.
- G. Fibre Washers.
- H. Main Jet.
- I. Needle Jet.
- J. Mixing Chamber Nut.
- K. Throttle Stop Screw.
- L. Stop Lug.
- M. Clamping Screw.
- N. Throttle Valve.
- O. Jet Needle.
- P. Mixing Chamber Top.
- Q. Locking Ring.
- R. Pilot Adjusting Screw.

FIG. 30.

THE CARBURETTER. (Continued.)

height of the cut-away portion on the atmospheric side of the valve, measured at the centre, in sixteenths of an inch. Hence 6/3 indicates type 6, with $\frac{3}{16}$-in. cut-away, and 6/4 : Type 6 with $\frac{4}{16}$-in., i.e., $\frac{1}{4}$-in. cutaway.

The valve with the larger cut-away will provide a weaker mixture over that part of the throttle opening range that it controls.

Setting and Adjusting.

It is inadvisable to experiment with settings differing from that recommended by us, and given on page 6, but the following information is given as being the standard proceedure advocated by Amal Ltd., and should be followed in the order given and studied in conjunction with the illustration (Fig. 31). By adjusting in the correct order any adjustments already set will not be disturbed.

The carburetter is automatic throughout the throttle range and the air valve should be kept full open in all normal running, and need only be closed for starting and until the engine begins to warm up.

1st—Main Jet with Throttle in Position 1.

Test engine for full throttle running. If power seems better with the air valve slightly closed this indicates too small a main jet.

2nd—Pilot Adjustment with Throttle in Positions 2 and 5.

Time will be saved if before making this test the pilot air adjusting screw is first screwed home fully and then set back $1\frac{1}{2}$ turns.

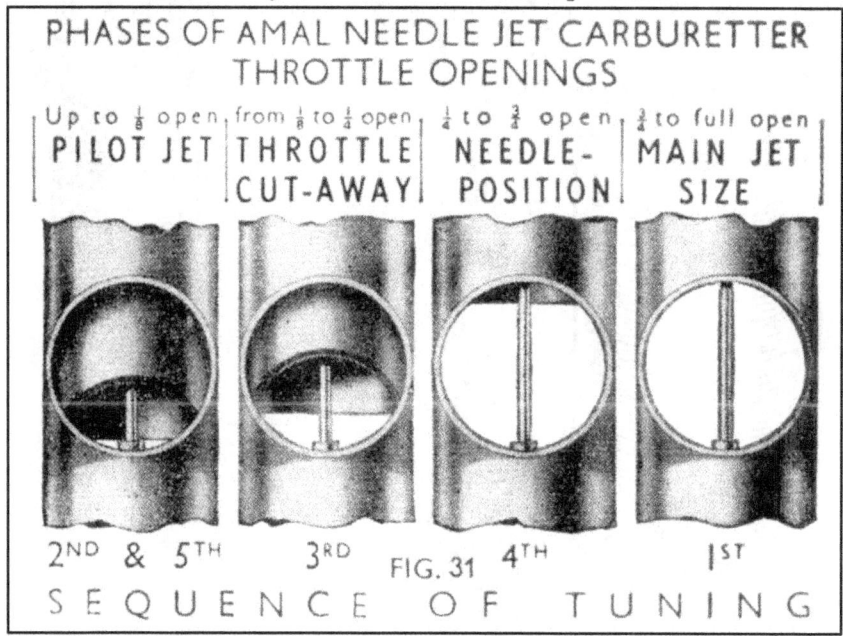

FIG. 31

With the engine idling too fast with the twist grip closed and the throttle valve shut down on to the stop screw (K) (Fig. 30) : Loosen the clamping screw (M) and turn the stop screw down until the engine runs slower and begins to falter, and then adjust the pilot air screw (R) one way or the other to make the engine run regularly. If the idling speed is still too high lower the stop screw a little further and again regulate the pilot screw until even running is obtained. Having obtained the ideal slow running setting by this means set the stop lug (L) to the rear (see position in Fig. 30) without moving the stop screw, and tighten the clamping screw (M).

The throttle stop screw will then be set for the best idling position with a hot engine, and when turned so that the stop lug faces forward to its full extent the correct position for cold starting is obtained.

THE CARBURETTER. (Continued).

3rd—Throttle Cut-away with Throttle in Position 3.

If, on the throttle being opened with the engine idling, there is objectionable spitting back from the carburetter, slightly richen the pilot mixture by screwing in the pilot air adjusting screw about a half turn. If this is not effective reset the screw to its original position and fit a throttle valve with the next smaller cut-away.

Should the running be jerky at this throttle opening and there is no spitting back either the throttle needle is set too high, or a larger cut-away is required to cure richness. After long mileage suspect a worn needle jet.

4th—Needle with Throttle in Position 4.

The needle controls a wide range of throttle opening and also the acceleration. Try the needle set as low as possible, i.e., with the clip in an upper groove. If the acceleration is poor and with the air valve partly closed is better, raise the needle two grooves. If very much better try again with the needle lowered one groove and finally leave it where it is best.

If the mixture is too rich with the clip in the top groove, the needle jet and possibly the needle are worn and must be replaced. The needle is found to wear less than the needle jet.

5th—Finally.

Go over the idling again for final touches.

General Hints.

Occasionally the carburetter may flood on turning on the fuel due to the float needle not seating. This can usually be rectified without extensive dismantling as follows : Turn off the fuel. Loosen the float chamber lid lock screw and remove the float chamber lid. Grasp the top of the float needle between finger and thumb and twist it backwards and forwards with a partly rotary movement, at the same time holding it up lightly in contact with the needle seating. After a few twists turn on the fuel again and if no flooding occurs, refit the lid, finally tightening the lock screw.

Excessive fuel consumption may be due to flooding, leakages from carburetter, pipe, or taps. Heavier consumption than normal may be caused by over-rich pilot air setting, particularly if the machine is used a lot in traffic, or by a worn needle jet and/or jet needle.

It is inadvisable to reduce the main jet size as this will almost certainly cause overheating and possibly pre-ignition. Further, the main jet does not control the mixture strength over that range of throttle opening in most frequent use.

Unsatisfactory running may not be due to carburation. If matters cannot be rectified by alterations to mixture strength, and it is known that the feed is regular and sufficient, or the carburetter is not flooding, the cause must be sought elsewhere. Defective or unsuitable sparking plugs or magneto trouble can in some conditions give similar symptoms to faulty carburation.

Always keep the fuel filters on the taps clear (Fig. 32) and see that the vent holes in the tank cap, and float chamber lid are clear.

THE AIR CLEANER.

Maintenance.

After every 5,000 miles running (approximately) the air cleaner should be removed for cleaning and re-oiling. It should not be dismantled, as if it is taken apart and the wire element is unwound out of position it may not be possible to replace this satisfactorily, so as to get an even flow of air through it.

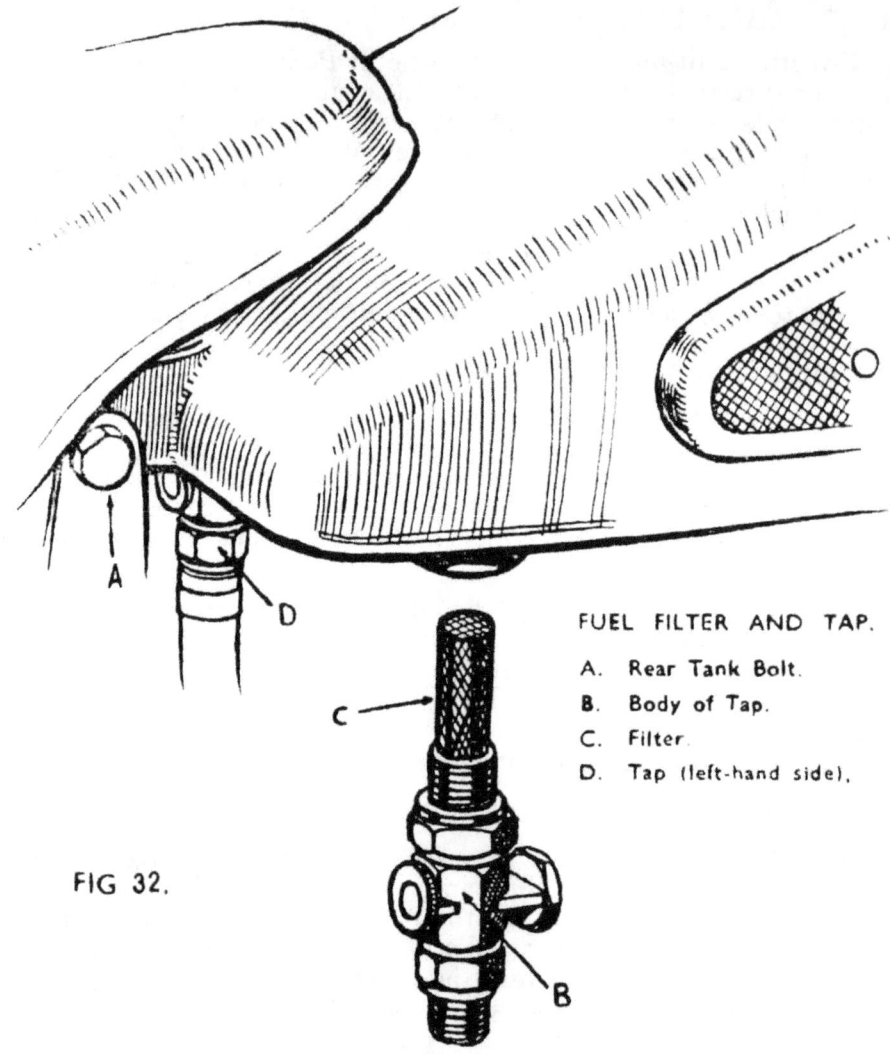

FIG 32.

FUEL FILTER AND TAP.
A. Rear Tank Bolt.
B. Body of Tap.
C. Filter.
D. Tap (left-hand side).

FUEL TAP AND STRAINER.

Removal of Air-cleaner.

Take off the battery, the flexible connecting sleeve between the carburetter and air cleaner, detach the petrol pipes, and remove the carburetter.

Remove the nut from the bolt holding the top lugs of the air-cleaner and oil tank to the frame, and push the bolt through to free the cleaner lug.

Working from the right hand side of the machine, remove the $\frac{1}{4}$-in. B.S.F. bolt that holds the bottom lug of the cleaner to the rear engine plate.

Pull the cleaner away forward and towards the left, springing the battery strap far enough to allow it to clear.

The entire filter should be washed in clean petrol until all accumulated dirt has been removed and should afterwards be dried thoroughly inside and out. Before refitting immerse the filter in clean engine oil (SAE50) and after draining off surplus oil and wiping clean externally refit it to the machine. No other attention is needed.

THE SPARKING PLUG.
Suitable Types.

The type of sparking plug fitted as initial equipment has been selected after exhaustive tests and has the characteristics most suited for general purposes in this type of engine. Sparking plugs are obtainable from several manufacturers who each produce a range of plugs of varying diameters, threads, and reaches (lengths of thread) and each size is usually offered in a range of different heat resistances. At the one extreme, plugs are capable of withstanding very high working temperatures without overheating, and at the other extreme of being able to continue firing in very oily conditions. The first will usually be found to oil up readily, and the second will not work long in a high performance engine before overheating sets in and causes pre-ignition of the charge in the cylinder.

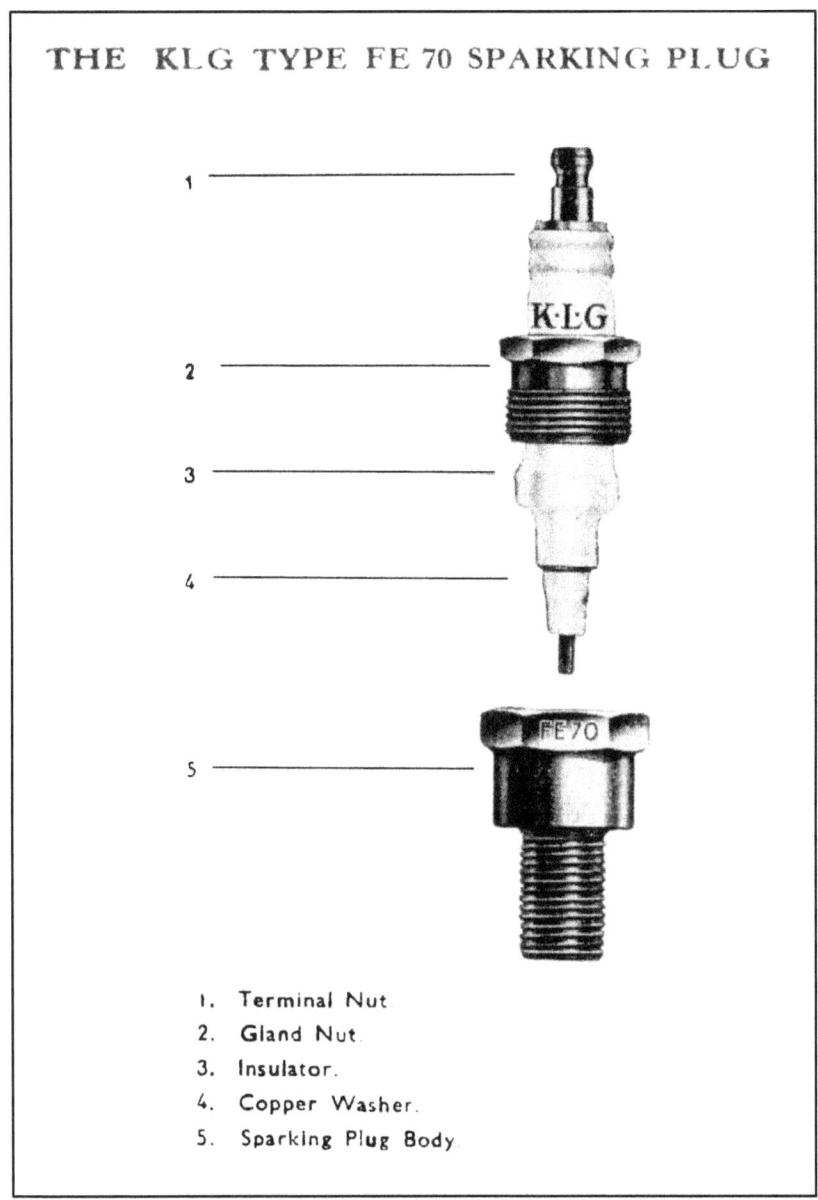

THE KLG TYPE FE 70 SPARKING PLUG

1. Terminal Nut
2. Gland Nut
3. Insulator
4. Copper Washer
5. Sparking Plug Body

FIG. 33.

Thus, if a plug of the same make and type as that originally fitted by us is unobtainable, the replacement must have similar characteristics. This is very important as, whilst a plug of too high internal heat resistance will usually only cause difficult starting, and misfiring, serious harm can be caused to the engine by the use of a " soft " plug, that is one which becomes overheated.

Our recommendations for this machine are KLG type FE70, Lodge type HLN, and Champion type NA8.

The thread diameter is 14 m.m. and the reach 18 m.m. (extra long). In no circumstances whatever must plugs of different reach be fitted.

Maintenance. (Fig. 33.)

The plug will require cleaning from time to time and the method used will depend upon whether the plug is constructed so that it may be taken apart for cleaning or is of the " non-detachable " type.

The " non-detachable " type must be cleaned by brushing the electrodes and the insides of the gas space as far as possible with a wire brush, or by " sand-blasting " on one of the special sparking plug cleaning machines. In either case the plug must afterwards be scrupulously cleaned out by washing in petrol to eliminate all risk of dirt, and more particularly, the sand used in cleaning, from working into the combustion chamber during subsequent service. Do not in any circumstances refit a sparking plug immediately after cleaning on a Plug Service Cleaner employing a sand-blast, but wash it well in petrol and blow out with a compressed air jet.

To clean a " detachable " type plug, this is taken apart as shown in Fig. 33, by holding the gland nut firmly, but not so tightly as to cause damage by crushing, in a vice—the jaws of which have been covered to prevent marking the nut. The plug body is then unscrewed off the gland nut. On removing the central portion take care of the sealing washer which must be refitted on reassembly.

Scrape the electrode, insulator, and the inside of the body clean of carbon with a penknife or clean with a wire-brush. Rinse in petrol before reassembling and make sure that the copper washer is in good condition and smear lightly with thin oil. Refit carefully and put the centre into the plug body, tightening the gland nut fully.

Adjusting the Plug Points.

After cleaning, the firing points will require adjusting to a gap of .018-in. to .023-in. Never adjust by bending the centre electrode as this will crack the insulator and render the sparking plug useless. All adjustments must be made by setting the side electrode.

Refitting to the Engine.

Make certain that the threads are quite clean and, if the sparking plug has been cleaned on a " Sand-blast " cleaner, that there is no sand left inside the plug—this is most important.

Lightly smear the threads of the plug with graphite paste or " Oil Dag," and screw in to the head carefully, being most careful to avoid cross threading.

THE DYNAMO AND LIGHTING SET.

Lamps and Bulbs.

The headlamp is fitted with one Bifocal bulb and one parking (Pilot) bulb. The types used are:

Bifocal Bulb :   6-volt. 24 × 24 watt.   Double filament.   S.B.C. Cap.
Pilot Bulb :   6-volt. 3 watt.   Single filament.   S.C.C. Cap.

To remove the lamp front to change a bulb or for other attention, free the clip below the lamp rim and pull the rim away from the lamp from the bottom first. Note that if it is proposed to do any work to the switch involving any connections, always detach the cables from the positive terminal of the battery.

The bulb holder is detachable from the back of the reflector after springing back the wire clips which hold it, and replacement bulbs may be fitted if required.

To replace a lamp glass or reflector release the four—or more—fixing clips from under the lip of the head lamp rim. The reflector and glass will now come out of the rim.

Do not touch the highly polished inside optical surface of the reflector as this will leave finger marks which it will be most difficult to remove without damaging the surface permanently.

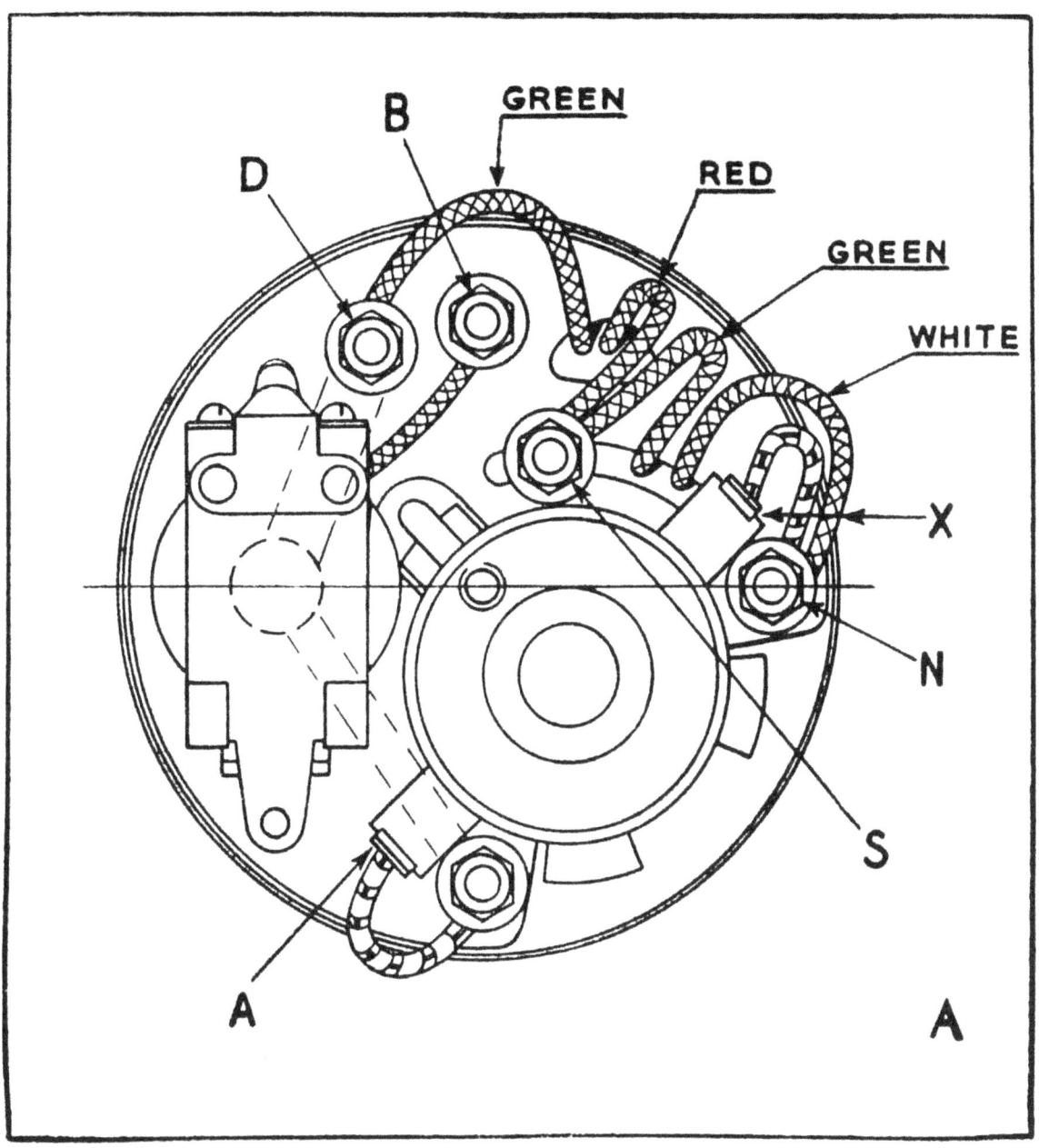

FIG. 34.

When replacing the reflector see that it is fitted correctly with the opening for the pilot bulb underneath. Refit the lamp front at the top first—push it over the lower edge, engage the fixing clip.

The rear lamp and stop lamp are combined in one body and the bulbs used are: 6-volt 3 watt, Single filament, S.C.C. Cap. (The same as the headlamp pilot bulb.)

To reach the bulb, spring out the circlip from under the turned-in lip around the lamp body and take out the plated "fret" and the ruby disc.

Be careful when refitting that the small projection on the fret enters the recess in the edge of the lamp body, and that the circlip is properly seated and cannot spring out accidentally.

The Dynamo. Maintenance.

The commutator and brushes should be inspected occsaionally and should any blackening of the commutator segments be noticed the commutator should be thoroughly cleaned, and all brush dust blown out of the end

The Dynamo (*continued*).

casing. If the charge rate is satisfactory it is best to leave the dynamo and regulator alone and normally no major attention should be required within the first 10,000 miles running.

Before doing any work at all to the dynamo disconnect the leads from the positive terminal (+) of the battery.

The commutator and brushes are exposed by removing the commutator cover (Fig. 35) which is held to the end casting by a single central screw, after pulling out the single pin plug connecting the positive lead to the dynamo.

See that the brushes move freely in their holders. If stiff remove the brush concerned and clean the sides with a cloth moistened in petrol, or rub lightly with fine glasspaper. Always replace brushes in their original positions.

Brushes which have worn so that they do not bear firmly on the commutator, or which expose the embedded end of the flexible lead on the running face must be replaced at once.

The commutator must be clean, true, and free from all traces of oil or dirt. If dirty or blackened it can be cleaned by pressing a cloth against it and turning it round by the kickstart. If very dirty moisten the cloth in petrol, or hold against it a piece of fine glasspaper whilst turning.

Clean away all traces of dust or carbon before refitting the brushes.

Testing. (Fig. 34.)

The dynamo can be checked quickly and with very little trouble by removing the driving belt, and the commutator cover, and pressing the cut-out points together. If the dynamo does not begin to run as a motor from the battery current there is a fault in it.

This is not a 100 per cent check, as in some circumstances a dynamo with a faulty winding may 'motor', but by testing in this way a lot of time can be saved.

The work about to be described should not be undertaken unless the necessary equipment is available and is best entrusted to a Miller Service Agent.

Remove the commutator cover screw, then remove the cover, exposing the commutator and end bracket. Disconnect the three outside leads (Regulator and headlamp) from terminals D.B. and S. Clip the negative lead of a good quality moving coil voltmeter, reading from 0 to 10-volts to a clean earthing point on the dynamo, and clip the voltmeter positive lead to terminal B.

Start the engine and slowly increase its speed. If no reading is shown on the Voltmeter, transfer the positive lead of the voltmeter to terminal D. If a reading is now shown the cut out is at fault and should be adjusted (see page 75). If no reading the fault is in the dynamo.

On no account must the engine speed be increased to such an extent that a reading 8 volts is exceeded during these tests.

If dynamo and cut-out are in order, re-connect the three leads to terminals D. B. & S, and test voltage regulator. (See paragraph on Regulator page 74.)

Removal.

Electrical breakdown of the dynamo is most unusual, and the unit should be tested as described above before assuming that removal is necessary.

The removal of the dynamo is described on page 31.

Dismantling. (Fig. 35.)

Take off the armature shaft nut and washer, and draw the pulley off the tapered end of the armature shaft with a "Claw" extractor, being most careful when using the extractor not to break the thin flange of the pulley.

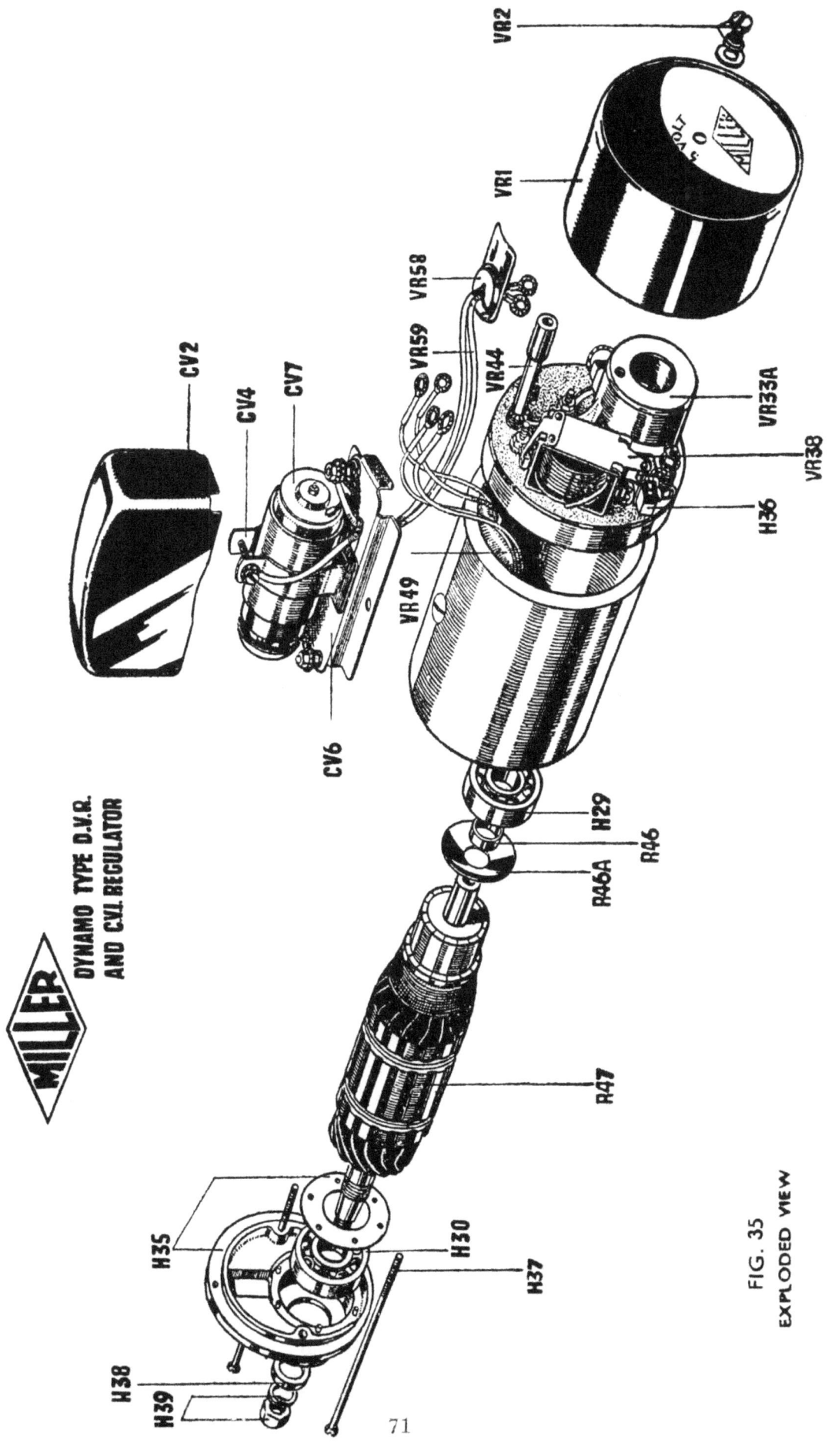

FIG. 35
EXPLODED VIEW

The Dynamo (*continued*).

Remove brushes A and X (Fig. 34) from their holders. Unscrew and remove the two long through bolts (Fig. 35) securing both end castings of the dynamo yoke. The countersunk heads of these screws can be seen at the driving end.

With a ⅜-in. diameter metal punch and hammer, tap the armature shaft at the commutator end. As soon as the ballrace at the commutator end is clear of the casting, the armature with the driving end casing can be withdrawn.

If it is necessary to remove the driving end casting from the armature shaft, first take out the pulley key (if fitted) from the shaft, and then unscrew and remove the bearing lockring (Fig. 35) which is screwed on the armature shaft just behind the tapered portion.

Do not in any circumstances attempt the removal of the lockring by knocking it round with a punch. Always use a special pin spanner as shown (Fig. 36). This spanner is quite easily made from the details given in the illustration.

Support the bearing retaining plate (Fig. 35) firmly and press out the armature shaft. Take care not to damage the threads or bend the shaft when removing it.

To remove the commutator end casting from the yoke, first disconnect the four insulated leads at D, N, & S (one each white and red, and two green) which pass through the end casting to the field coil (Fig. 34).

The end casing can then be pulled away from the yoke, drawing the four leads carefully through the accommodation slots in the casting and being very careful to avoid damaging them.

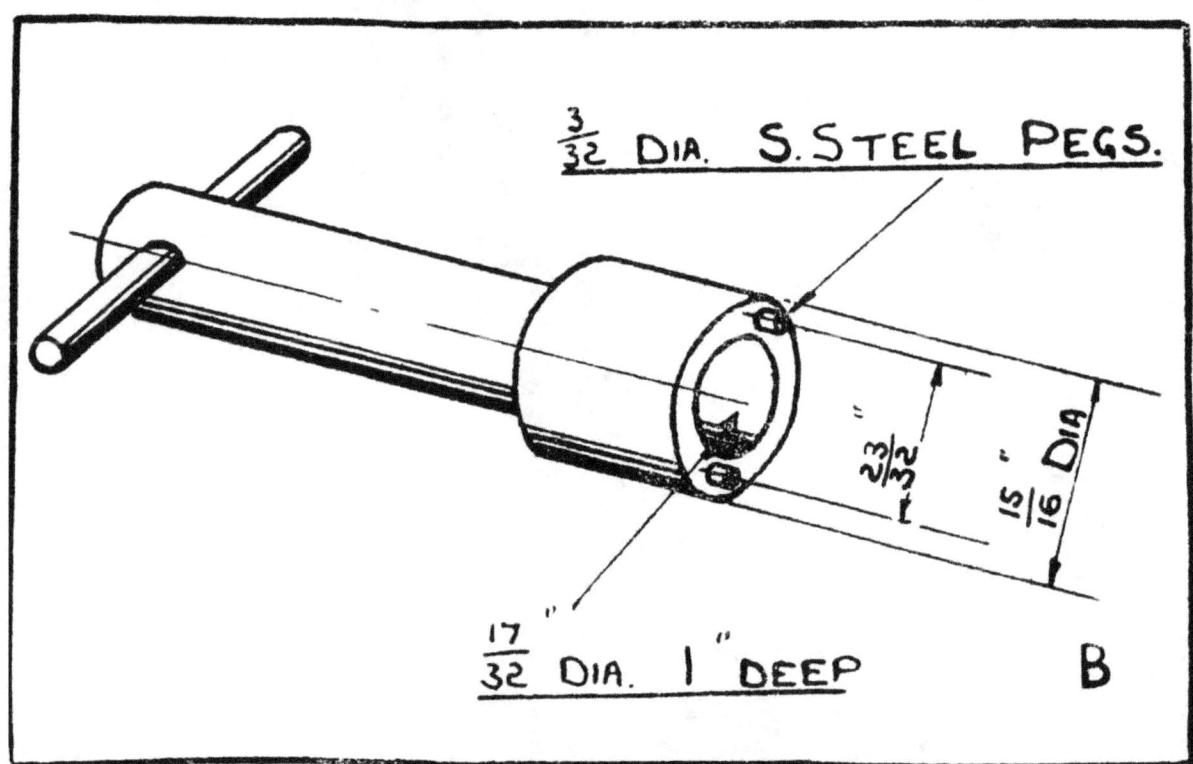

FIG. 36.

Commutator and Brushes.

Check the brushes for cleanliness, condition, and freedom in their holders. If either are stiff, free off as described previously. Inspect the commutator and if not badly worn clean up by polishing with fine glass-

The Dynamo (continued).

paper. To do this whilst the armature is out of the dynamo, it is advisable to rotate the armature in a lathe and hold the glasspaper against the revolving commutator; in this way ensuring that it is true. If required, the commutator micas separating the segments must be undercut afterwards to a depth of approximately .025-in. They must not stand level with the rubbing surfaces of the segments. Clean up carefully afterwards when the armature is ready for refitting.

If new brushes are fitted they must be properly bedded to ensure that they make good contact with the commutator. To do this it is necessary to postpone the fitting until the armature is once more assembled into the dynamo.

To bed the brushes pass a thin strip of superfine glasspaper between the commutator and the brushes with the smooth side of the paper against the commutator. Press each brush in turn lightly on to the glass side of the paper and then pull the paper backwards and forwards several times. This will form the working ends of the brushes to suit the commutator.

Remove the glasspaper and clean out all glass and brush dust—preferably by means of a jet of compressed air.

Dynamo Bearings. (Replacement and Lubrication.)

It is very seldom that the bearings have to be replaced and they should not be removed unless absolutely necessary.

The drive end bearing is retained by a plate rivetted to the end casing (Fig. 35, H35). Only three of the projecting rivets are peened over and these must be filed off flush with the plate to remove it. On refitting the other three projections are used and are peened over to hold the retaining plate.

A small extractor will be needed to draw the commutator end ballrace off the shaft—it is not very tight.

On reassembly the bearings must be carefully packed with a high-melting point grease. Soft grease must not be used. Subsequent lubrication in service may be given by oiling sparingly through the commutator cover fixing screw hole, and to the drive end bearing through the grub screw hole in the top of the bearing housing.

Dynamo Armature. (Testing.)

The resistance of the armature coils measured between two adjacent commutator segments should be .2 ohms $\pm$ .01 ohms. Megger test to earth should not be less than 100,000 ohms.

Dynamo Field Coils. (Testing and Fitting.)

The resistance of the field winding (red and white leads) should be 4 ohms $\pm$ .25 ohm., and of the resistance winding (green leads) 7 ohms. $\pm$ .25 ohms. Megger test to earth and megger test between field and resistance windings should not be less than 100,000 ohms.

When fitting a new field coil, force the yoke and pole on to a mandrel about 8-in. long, the diameter tapering from 1.773-in. to 1.767-in.

Grip the exposed end of the mandrel in a vice, and by using a robust screwdriver tighten the countersunk pole screw (Fig. 35) dead tight to hold the pole shoe firmly to the yoke.

It is most important that there shall be no air gap between the pole shoe and the inner face of the yoke.

The Dynamo (continued).

Voltage Regulator.

As it is very seldom that the regulator gives trouble it is advisable, if it is suspected that it is at fault, to check the dynamo driving belt adjustment before doing anything else. For instance should it be found that the battery becomes discharged, although there is the normal charge reading of about 2 amperes only, it may be assumed incorrectly that the regulator is failing to increase the charge to compensate for the low state of the battery.

All these symptoms are however, also compatible with a slipping belt, which will drive sufficiently at low speeds to provide a 2 ampere charge but will not drive at higher speeds to provide the higher charge rate that the dynamo would give if driven properly.

The result is that the battery, although requiring a temporarily high charge rate to bring it back to a fully charged condition, does not receive it and gradually becomes discharged.

Normally the regulator provides complete automatic control of the charging so that the dynamo output varies according to the calls upon the battery or its state of charge. In the daytime with no lights in use, and with a battery in good condition the dynamo gives only a trickle charge, so that the ammeter readings will seldom exceed 1 or 2 amperes.

Should the lights be left switched on for only a few minutes, with the engine stationary, it will be found that on the engine being started and its speed increased the charge rate will be increased considerably until the battery is brought up to full charge again. Subsequently the charge rate will drop if there are no further calls on the battery.

The Voltage Regulator. (Testing.)

To test accurately special apparatus is necessary so that the work should be entrusted to a main Miller Service Agent who will have the necessary equipment.

If in normal running conditions, it is found that the battery is continually in a low state of charge, and it is established that this is not due to belt slip, or to a defective battery, and if the dynamo has been tested and found satisfactory, and the cut-out in order, the regulator should be tested by substitution if a replacement is handy.

To test whether the regulator is at fault if no replacement is available, disconnect the battery positive (+) lead, and connect a moving-coil voltmeter, to the two regulator base terminals (positive and negative), start the engine, and run it at a speed equivalent to about 20 m.p.h. road speed in top gear (approximately 1450 r.p.m.). If the regulator is in correct adjustment the voltmeter reading should be from 7.5 to 8.2 volts.

The Voltage Regulator. (Adjusting.)

If the voltmeter reading is below 7.5 volts, over regulation is taking place, causing the battery to be continually in a low state of charge. In the absence of a replacement, a purely temporary adjustment may be made by screwing out the negative (—) contact screw (which is visible at the conical end of the regulator cartridge), two complete turns.

Should the voltmeter indicate over 8.2 volts, which would cause overcharging, a temporary adjustment may be made by screwing out the positive contact screw at the other end not more than a quarter of a turn.

Note that these adjustments will not give the correct voltage readings, but will enable the machine to be run with improved results until a replacement regulator can be fitted. Note also that it is quite safe to run temporarily without the regulator cartridge in place. With the cartridge removed and the dynamo leads left in place, that is with the red coloured lead connected to the base plate and the green coloured lead to the clip bolt, the dynamo will give a reduced output with a maximum of about 3.5 amperes. It is advisable to fit a small block of wood or metal 1-in. long by 1¼-in. dia. into the clip temporarily, to allow the clip to be tightened and the lead held firm. Replacement as soon as possible is essential.

MILLER CUT-OUT. (DVR TYPE DYNAMO).

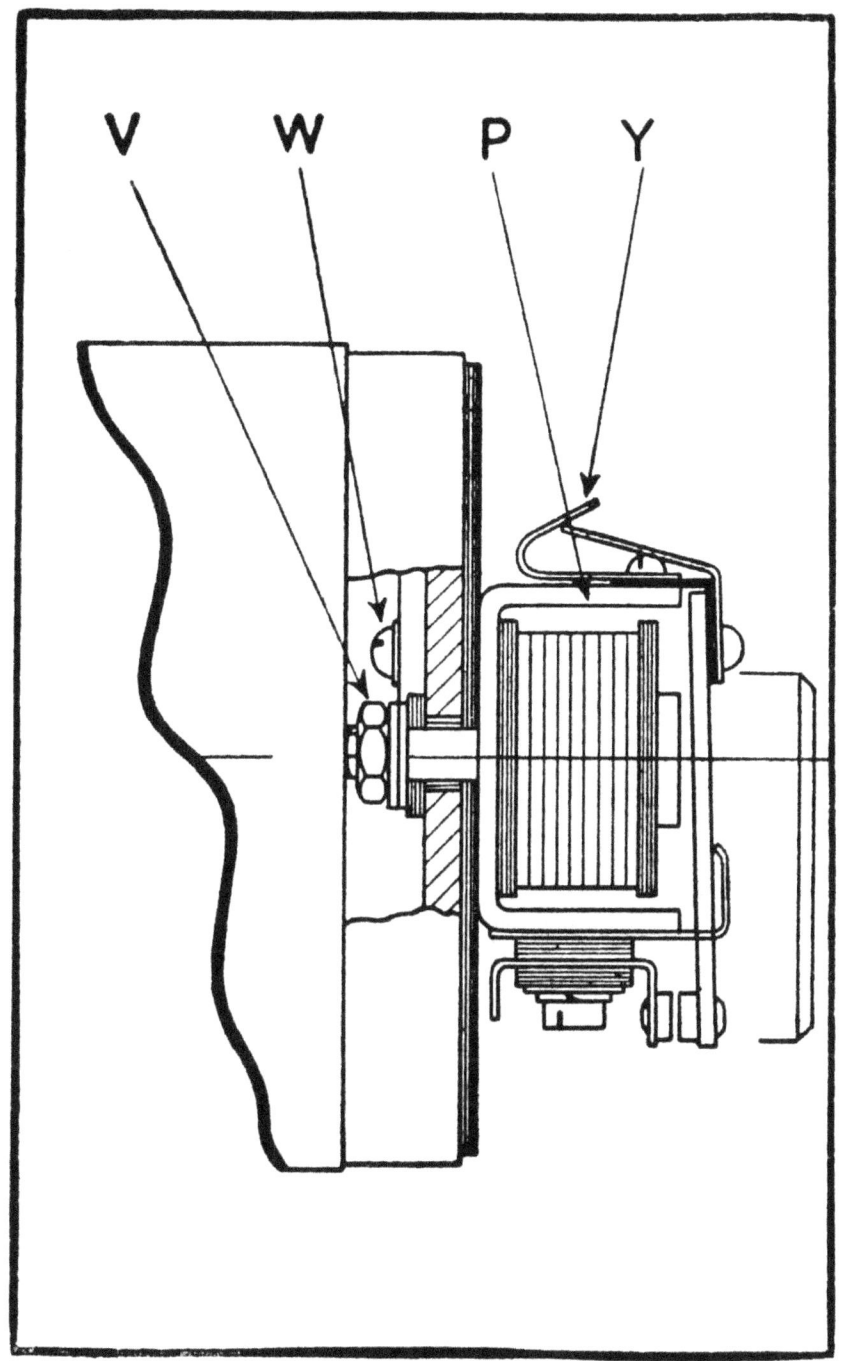

FIG 37.

The Cut-out (Type VR38). (Fig. 37.)

The cut-out (P) is attached to the dynamo commutator end casing by a nut (V) and is removable after taking off the commutator cover, the nut (V) and disconnecting the earth lead which is attached to the end cover by the screw and washer (W) and the lead to the centre one of the three terminals (B), Fig. 34.

The resistance of the series winding is .09 to .1 ohm. Resistance of shunt winding 55 to 56 ohms. The contact clearance is Q-in. (.031-in.). The contacts should close at approximately 6 volts, when a current of from 0 to k ampere is being generated, and open when the current falls from

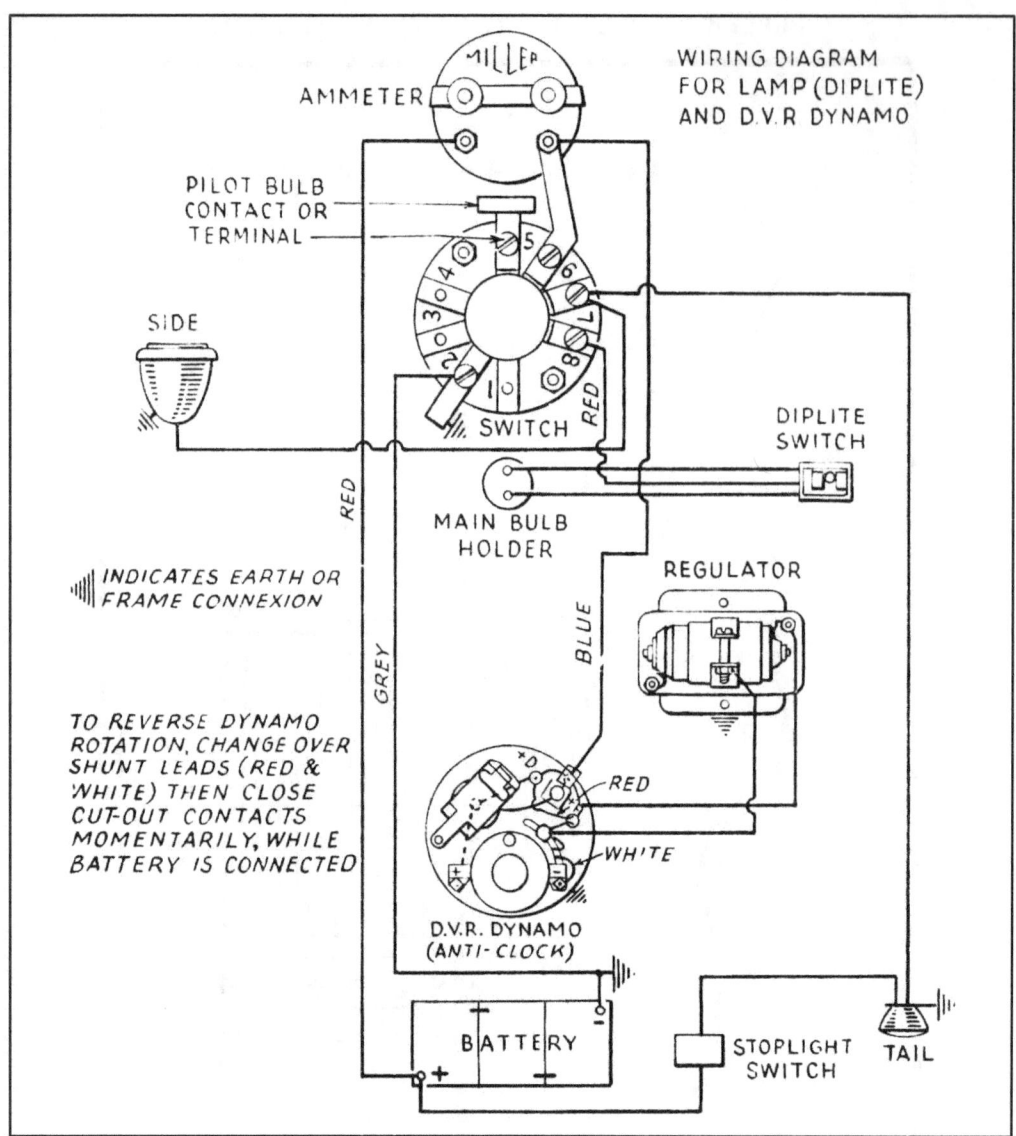

FIG. 38.

0 to ½ ampere discharge. The "off" and "on" tension can be adjusted by bending the brass tensioning bracket (Y).

The Ammeter. (Testing.)

With the engine stationary, switch on the lights. With the headlamp, main bulb, tail lamp bulb, and speedometer bulb the discharge will be 4.8 amperes. On switching off, the needle should swing back freely to zero. If at fault replace as soon as possible.

The Dynamo (Type DVR). Reassembling.

This is broadly a reversal of the process of dismantling already described but the following should be noted.

Attach the commutator end casting to the yoke first. Pass the red lead and the adjacent lead through the triangular slot and connect to terminals S and D respectively (Fig. 34). Pass the white lead and adjacent green lead through the long curved slot and connect to N and S respectively.

Fit the drive end ballrace to the end casting, refit the retaining plate and screws to the end casting. Place the assembly over the tapered end of the armature shaft. Screw on the lockring tightly. With the commutator end bearing already on the shaft push the armature through the yoke, entering

THEORETICAL DIAGRAM : MILLER DYNAMO (DVR) and REGULATOR

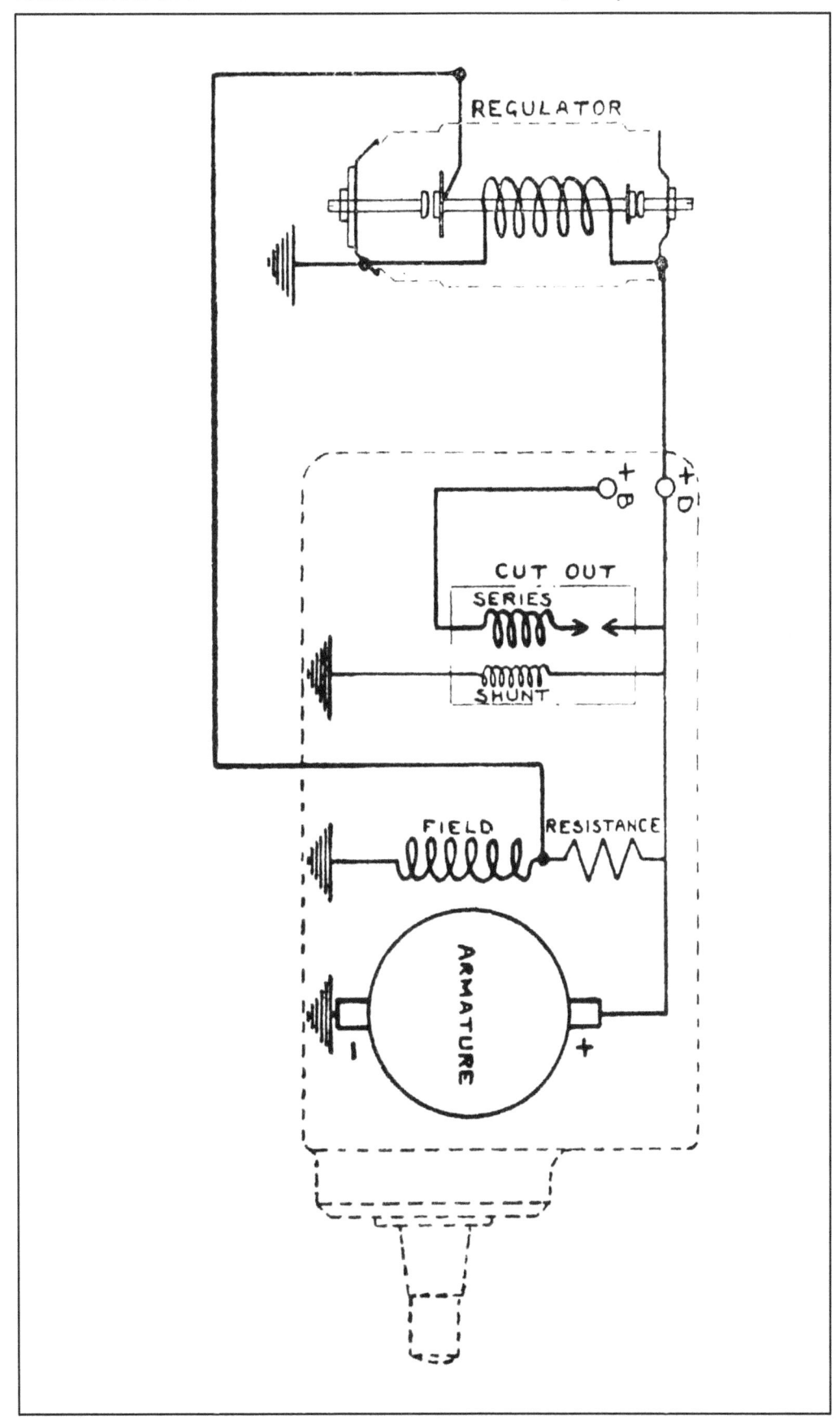

FIG. 39

the ballrace in the commutator end casting and press gently home. Refit the two through bolts securing the ends to the yoke and tighten.

Replace the back half of the belt cover on the dynamo and fit the pulley washer, and nut, finally tightening the nut.

Fit the rubber bush protecting the leads into the commutator cover and connect up the leads : Red coloured lead from voltage regulator to " D ", the plain lead from regulator to terminal " S " and the blue coloured lead from ammeter (in headlamp) to " B."

Replace the brushes, fit the dynamo to the machine, afterwards fitting the commutator end cover.

A full wiring diagram of the installation appears on page 76 (Fig. 38) and a theoretical diagram of the dynamo and regulator on the following page (Fig. 39).

THE BATTERY.

First Charge instructions for Batteries already filled with acid but requiring first charge—Varley Battery.

Normally, machines delivered into the home market leave the works with the battery filled with acid, but uncharged. Correct charging in accordance with the instructions issued by the battery makers is essential. A card of instructions is issued with each new battery.

To make ready for service a filled but uncharged battery, the following instructions should be carried out :

(1) Remove sealing tape, unscrew vent stoppers, and if fitted, break away sealing discs in the vents.

(2) Put on charge for 60 hours at $1\frac{1}{4}$ amps.

(3) During the whole of the first charge period the electrolyte level should be maintained $\frac{1}{4}$-in. above plate/separator block. For this, use distilled water only. Keep vent stoppers in—do not screw down.

(4) This first charge period should be continuous. If for any major reason the current is cut, the open circuit standing time should be allowed for.

(5) The charge is complete when all cells are gassing freely and cell voltages remain constant for five consecutive half-hourly readings.

(6) After charge, allow battery to stand to complete absorption, then, after a period of 30 minutes any electrolyte should be removed. Dry top of battery, screw down vent stoppers and coat terminals and connector bars slightly with vaseline before putting into service.

(7) A fully charged battery should read at least 6.3 volts. on open ci-cuit.

Note that the battery must be wired negative terminal to earth.

Battery Maintenance.

In normal use the dynamo will keep the battery well charged, and the only attention which is usually needed is the periodical topping up with distilled water. This should be done after a run with Varley batteries, but is better carried out just before a run in the case of other makes which contain free liquid.

Check the battery about every 1,000 miles running, or more frequently in hot conditions. Remove the lid and vent plugs and inspect the interior.

The Varley battery should have no free liquid in it, but the filling visible on removing the vent plugs must be moist. If seen to be dry add a small amount of distilled water (about one teaspoonful) and allow time for it to be absorbed. Add a little more if needed, but if after ten minutes standing there is free liquid in the cells shake this out before refitting, or charging the battery.

Other types of battery containing free liquid need topping up until the plates are covered. The separators between the plates which are usually higher than the plates, and often mistaken for them, must not be covered.

Overfilling of any battery will cause flooding of the top of the battery when it is charged and the excess liquid may get out and run over parts of the machine, or the rider's clothes, and will be very destructive due to its corrosive nature. Further, an electrical leakage can take place across a damp or wet battery top causing gradual discharge of the battery when standing.

Never leave a battery standing unused in a partly or fully discharged state. See "Storage."

Battery Storage.

Should a battery have been in use, or have been filled and charged for the first time, and it becomes necessary to store it, it is essential first to see that it is properly topped up, clean, dry externally and the terminals greased. It must also be fully charged.

Do not in any circumstances empty a "wet" battery.

During storage the battery must be given a monthly "livening" charge of 1 ampere for 8 hours.

THE MAGNETO AND AUTOMATIC TIMING UNIT. (LUCAS).

Description.

The magneto is of rotating armature pattern, and is fitted with an automatic timing control. The latter employs a driving gear carrying a plate fitted with two pins; a weight is pivoted on each pin and the movement of the weight is controlled by a spring connected between the pivot of the weight and a toggle lever pivoted at approximately the centre of the weight. (Fig. 17.)

Holes are provided in each toggle lever, which locate with pegs on the underside of a driving plate secured to the magneto spindle. This plate is also provided with stops that limit the range of control.

When the magneto is stationary, the weights are in the closed position and the magneto retarded for starting. When the engine is started and the speed is increased, centrifugal force acting on the weights overcomes the restraint of the springs and the weights move outwards, causing relative movement between the driving gear and the magneto spindle, so advancing the ignition timing.

The characteristics of the control are arranged to conform closely with the engine requirements.

Features of the magneto include a ring cam operated contact breaker, and a high energy magnet cast integral with the magneto body.

The armature ball bearings which are packed with grease during assembly, will not need attention until the motor cycle is dismantled for a general overhaul, when it is advisable to have the magneto inspected at a Lucas Service Depot, or by a Lucas Agent.

Maintenance : Lubrication.

Every 3,000 miles take out the hexagon-headed screw from the centre of the contact breaker (Fig. 40) and pull the mechanism off the tapered shaft to which it is fitted. Push aside the rocker arm retaining spring, loosen the two small screws to free the spring—prise the rocker arm off its pivot and smear the bearing lightly with clean engine oil.

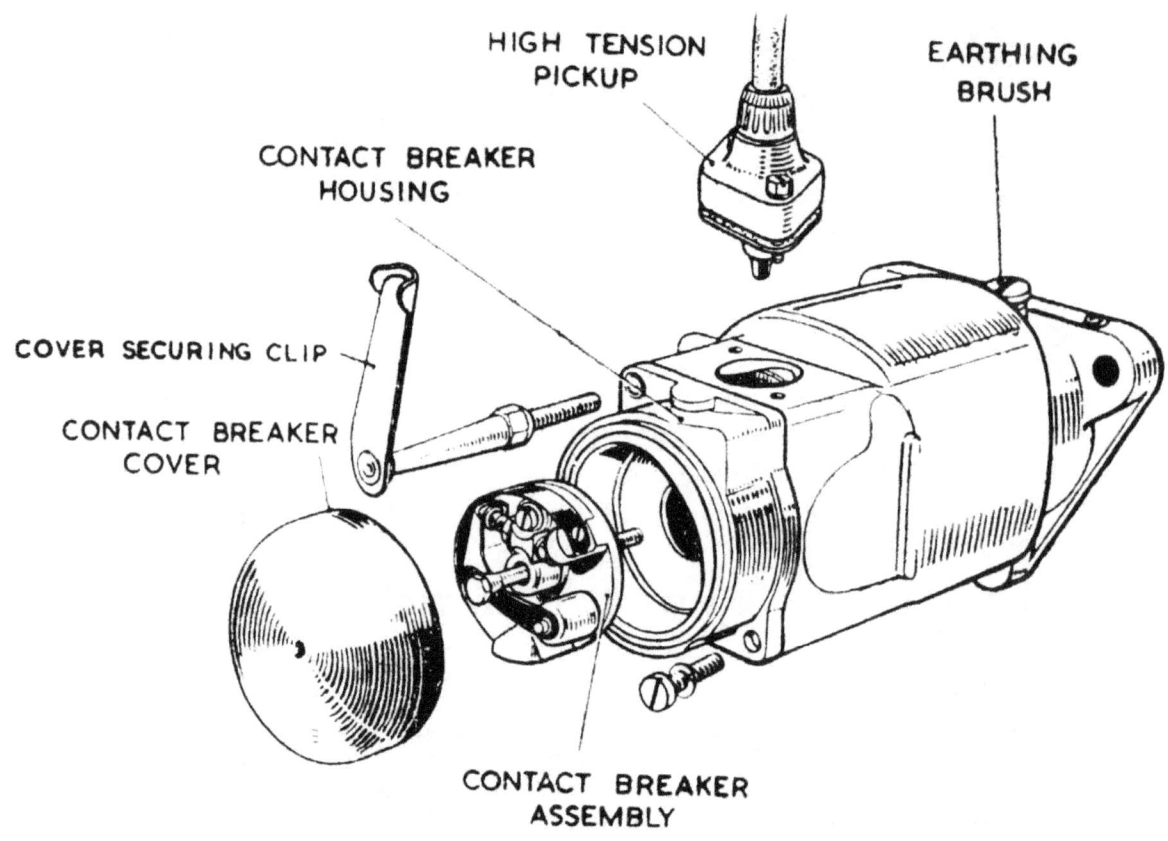

FIG. 40.

LUCAS TYPE KIF MAGNETO.
Showing H.T. Brush and Contact Breaker Mechanism, dismantled.

The cam is lubricated from a felt pad contained in a pocket in the contact breaker housing. A small hole in the cam is fitted with a wick which enables the oil to reach the surface of the cam. Add a few drops of thin oil (SAE10) to the wick. **Do not allow any oil to get on the contacts.**

When refitting the contact breaker, be sure that the projecting key on the tapered part of the contact breaker base engages with the keyway cut in the magneto spindle, otherwise the timing will be upset.

Tighten the hexagon headed screw carefully. It must not be slack, but no undue force must be used. Check the contact point gap: see below.

Maintenance. Adjustment.

Every 3,000 miles check the contact point gap, after turning the engine until the contacts are fully opened. The correct gap is .012-in. If the setting is correct, the .012-in. gauge will be a sliding fit between the contacts, but if too tight or too loose the gap must be adjusted.

To adjust, keep the contact breaker in the position giving the maximum opening of the contacts, slacken the lock-nut on the adjustable contact screw, and turn the screw by its hexagon head until the gap is set to the gauge. Tighten the lock-nut and re-check the setting in case there has been alteration when tightening the lock-nut.

Maintenance. Cleaning.

Every 6,000 miles examine the contacts for signs of burning or blackening. Clean them with a fine carborundum stone, or with superfine emery cloth. Wipe away all dust and dirt afterwards with a petrol-moistened cloth.

It is easier to attend to the contacts if the contact breaker is removed.

Remove the high tension pick-up—held to the magneto body by two screws—wipe it clean and polish with a fine dry cloth. The pick up brush must move freely in the holder. If it is dirty, clean with a petrol-moistened cloth. Should the brush be worn to within $\frac{1}{8}$-in. of the shoulder it must be renewed.

While the pick-up is removed, clean the slip ring track and flanges by holding a soft cloth against the ring with a wedge of wood suitably shaped to conform to the included angle of the slip ring flanges, and turn the engine slowly. Remove the rag, and repeat the cleaning with another piece until all dirt is cleaned from the slip ring.

Testing the Magneto for Causes of Misfiring, or Failure of Ignition.

Disconnect the high tension cable from the sparking plug and hold it so that the terminal end is about $\frac{1}{8}$-in. from some metal part of the engine, such as the edge of one of the fins on cylinder or head.

(1) Rotate the engine smartly by means of the kick-start and note the spark that jumps from the terminal to the engine. If the spark is strong and regular the fault lies with the sparking plug which should be removed for inspection and attention.

(2) Examine the high-tension cable. After long service or if oil has been allowed to get on to and remain on it, the insulation may have become perished or cracked. Instructions for fitting a new one follow.

(3) If the magneto has been replaced recently or removed and refitted it may be incorrectly timed. Refer to page 47 for timing instructions.

(4) If the performance of the magneto is still unsatisfactory the contacts may need cleaning and adjustment, or the rocker arm may be sticking and working sluggishly. Badly worn or burned contacts should be replaced by a new Lucas contact set. Should the contact breaker be in good order check the pick-up and high tension pick-up brush. Failing this being responsible there may be an internal fault in the magneto. If this is suspected the advice of a Lucas Service Agent should be sought.

Removal of Magneto.

Remove the timing cover, and engage first gear to hold the crankshaft stationary. Unscrew the hexagon headed centre screw in the automatic timing unit. The screw will loosen and then, almost at once, tighten again. This tightening is caused by the extraction thread coming into operation, and another turn will free the timing unit from the magneto spindle, enabling it to be taken out.

Take off the three nuts and washers holding the triangular flange of the magneto to the crankcase. If the cylinder is in position a waisted $\frac{3}{16}$-in. box spanner will be needed to reach the upper nut nearest the crankcase. Either of the standard spanners, LE479 or KA228/2 may be modified quite easily to suit. A gasket is fitted between the magneto and the crankcase.

Refitting the Magneto.

Place the automatic timing unit in position meshing the gear with the intermediate gear, and with the hexagon head screw held against the unit, and the magneto flange gasket in place, push the magneto over the studs, entering the magneto shaft in the centre of the timing unit.

Screw the hexagon headed centre screw on to the magneto shaft holding the head firmly against the mechanism, and allowing the magneto to locate itself under the influence of the screw.

Fit the three flange washers and nuts and tighten fully. See remarks in preceding section *re* spanner.

Retime the magneto—see page 47, and finally refit the timing cover.

CHAINS.

Maintenance.

The primary chain case will require the addition of oil from time to time and it is usually convenient to squirt a little over the chain from a force-feed oil can whilst the chain is moved forward by the kickstart. The chain cover small inspection cover (Fig. 7, page 21) is removed for lubrication purposes.

It is best to remove the rear chain for attention, including thorough washing in paraffin—several changes being used to ensure removal of all dirt.

After draining and drying off, relubrication by soaking the chain in molten grease or tallow, preferably containing graphite, is the best method.

The lubricant must be liquid enough to get into the bearings of the chain, but must in no circumstances be boiling. After being satisfied that the lubricant has penetrated the bearings properly, and allowing it to cool off until it begins to solidify, remove the chain and wipe off surplus lubricant.

Adjustment of Primary Chain. (Fig. 16.)

The correct adjustment of the primary chain is $\frac{1}{2}$-in. free up and down movement on one run of the chain midway between the sprockets. In this case the checking is done through the inspection opening in the cover.

The tension must be checked in several different positions so that there is freedom in the tightest place, and the chain must be moved forward by the kickstart and several checks carried out.

Adjustment is by pivoting the gearbox on its bottom-fixing bolt, after freeing off this bolt and the two top ones. To take up excess slack turn the forward one of the two adjusting nuts (Fig. 16, page 36) forward on the adjuster and then turn the rear nut in the same direction thus drawing the adjuster, which is attached to the fixing bolt, through the eye-bolt fixed to the engine plate.

When the correct setting is obtained tighten the three fixing bolts and make certain that the adjuster nuts are tight against the eye-bolt.

Adjustment of Rear Chain. (Fig. 41.)

On all spring frame machines the tension of the rear chain constantly alters when the springing is working, due to the very slight difference between the actual arc of movement of the rear wheel axis from the theoretical arc, which it would traverse if the rear fork was pivoted on the same axis as the final drive sprocket.

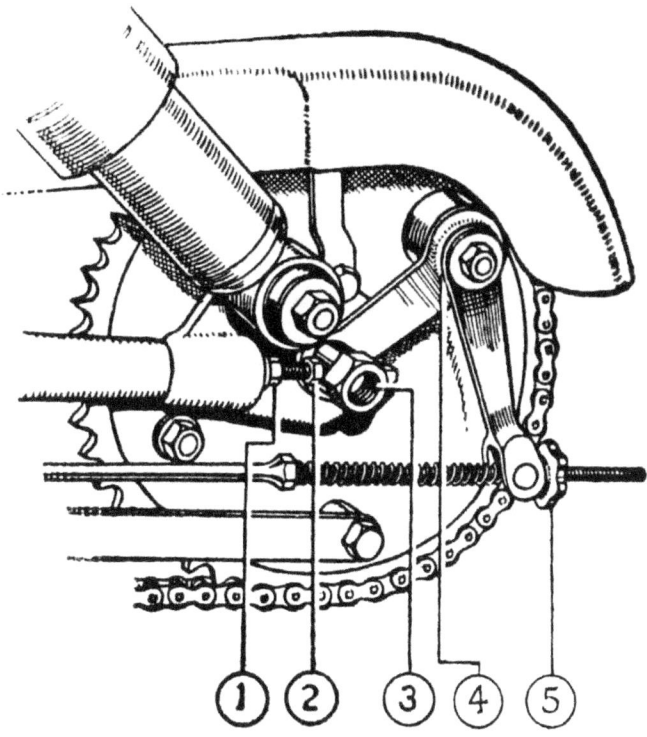

REAR BRAKE AND REAR CHAIN ADJUSTMENT (Fig. 41)

    (1) Chain Adjuster Lock Nut.
    (2) Chain Adjuster.
    (3) Rear Brake Plate Locking Bolt Nut.
    (4) Rear Brake Cam Felt Washer.
    (5) Rear Brake Adjusting Nut.

Never check the chain tension when the chain is in motion—this is highly dangerous.

On swinging fork designs the chain is tightest with the fork in mid-position, and becomes slacker as the fork swings either up on compression or down on extension of the springs. The adjustment must, therefore, be set to give ½-in. free up and down movement on one run of the chain midway between the sprockets with the struts compressed to 11½-in. centres. (Fig. 25, page 55.)

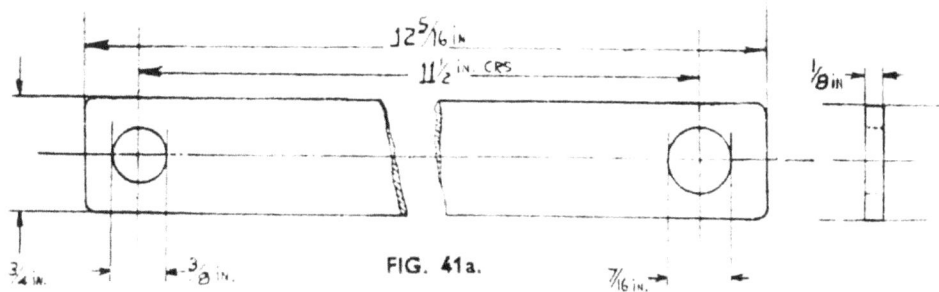

FIG. 41a.

To hold the swinging fork as described above a simple strap (Fig. 41a) can easily be made.

As it would be difficult when working alone to hold the struts compressed without a special tool, the adjustment can be made with the fork at its lowest position, but the setting must allow for the chain becoming tighter when the springing is working. If this alternative method is used support the machine on the centre stand, allowing the tyre to clear the floor—this is important.

Now adjust the chain to give 1¼-in. free up and down movement on one run midway between the sprockets.

Whichever method is adopted check the chain in several different positions, turning the rear wheel between checks, to allow the specified freedom in the tightest place.

The alternative method is not so satisfactory as the first one, and if used, the first opportunity should be taken to make a recheck, with the struts held compressed to 11½-in. centres.

FIXING TRANSFERS.

The transfers are printed on duplex paper, i.e., one sheet as a guide to place the transfer in position, and the other as a support for the transfer. These two sheets must be separated before transferring. They can be divided by rubbing a corner of the transfer.

Before complete separation is made apply a very thin and even coat of adhesive varnish to the face of the transfer. Keep as closely as possible to the outlines of the design so as not to overlap. Allow the varnish to set until it becomes very tacky, whilst it is setting clean the surface to be occupied by the transfer of all dirt and be sure that it is free from grease. Separate the thin paper from the support.

Apply the transfer in the desired position and press it down very firmly and evenly, driving out all air bubbles, by rubbing with a soft cloth rolled into a ball. Work outwards from the centre to the edges. Then with a damp (not wet) sponge or washleather press down again, taking care not to shift the transfer. It is absolutely essential for the transfer to be in **direct contact with the surface in every part.** When this is certain apply water freely from a wet sponge, and when the paper is well soaked, lift up by one corner and peel or slide it off. Press the transfer down again to make sure that it is fully in contact.

After doing this, sponge with clean water to remove the composition remaining on the surface of the transfer. This is an extremely important detail, as unless it is properly done the transfer will crack.

To remove traces of surplus adhesive varnish from around the transfer, use a wet sponge to which a little paraffin has been added. Then quickly wipe it off with a damp washleather, **away from the centre.**

When the transfer is perfectly dry on the article (usually in about twenty-four hours) it can be varnished to add to its lustre.

It must not be varnished directly it is transferred.

INSTRUCTIONS FOR FITTING PANNIERS.

We can supply, as additional equipment, Pannier frames and bags designed to suit the MAC model. As these are made to fit the Velocette and are not intended to be suitable for all other makes they are more easily fitted and look much better than proprietary fittings which, because they have to be adaptable to a variety of different frames usually suit none of them very well.

The Velocette Panniers are easily fitted as follows:—

Remove both rear mudguard stay bolts, distance pieces, and the inner end caps from the rear suspension brackets on the main frame. The distance pieces are not refitted. Also remove the two pillion footrest pivot bolts.

On some earlier machines the aluminium end caps—inner and outer—have to be filed to clear the pannier frame tubes that are attached to the suspension brackets by the mudguard stay bolts. By offering up each pannier frame in turn it is easy to mark the end caps so that the turned over edge can be filed to clear the pannier frame tube.

Mark the inner end-caps in the same way and file out as needed.

A six inch half-round file is best for the job.

Fit both frames in position bolting them into the rear suspension brackets at the top in place of the distance pieces that were discarded, and at the bottom to the pillion footrest eye-bolts with the pivot bolts.

Attach the cross bracing tube to the frames with the bolts provided and finally tighten all bolts fully.

REAR CARRIER.

This is another useful addition for attachment to the Pannier frames at the back and to the dual seat mounting at the front.

Designed specially for the MAC it enables extra luggage to be carried behind the pillion passenger and is easily fitted.

TYRE INFLATION PRESSURE CHART.

The minimum pressures for 3.25×19 tyres are 16-lbs. front and 18-lbs. rear, and are sufficient for a solo rider of average weight.

The carrying of a pillion passenger will make additional pressure in the rear tyre essential, and also the adjustment of the rear suspension should be altered.

Pressures for extra loads are as follows :

Load in Pounds.	Pressure in Pounds per sq. inch.
200	16
240	18
280	20
350	24
400	28
440	32

TYRES.

Maintenance.

Regular checking of tyre pressures is essential for good mileage to be obtained from the tyres. Under inflation, particularly, is very destructive to the casings, and by increasing the rolling resistance tends to increase the fuel consumption.

It should be noted when refitting a cover, or fitting a new one that on some makes the walls are marked to indicate how the cover should fit in relation to the rim. A white spot on the wall must line up with the valve to keep the wheel in balance.

Periodically the tyres should be inspected with the object of removing from the treads any sharp flints or other foreign bodies which may have become embedded in the rubber. Their removal is made easier if the tyre is partly deflated before attempting to prise them out.

Damage to the tyre casing and the tube may often be avoided by the removal of these potential puncture makers.

CLEANING THE MACHINE.
(Enamelled and Bare Metal Parts.)

Accumulated road dirt and mud must never be rubbed or brushed off dry from enamelled parts as the abrasive nature of the dirt will scratch and dull the surface of the enamel.

Always wash off dirt by means of liberal supplies of water, if possible from a hose pipe, but do not employ a high pressure jet.

The water should be set to run at a slow rate so that it does not penetrate where it can do harm, such as into the brakes or items of the electrical equipment and carburetter.

Use a soft cloth or sponge to mop off the dirt when it is properly loosened by the water.

If water is used from a bucket a little household detergent washing powder (such as " Tide ") may be mixed with the water and will help to remove oil or grease.

Dry off with a leather and polish with one of the many polishes now on the market. Chemico " 49 " will give a high finish which remains waterproof for quite a good time. Proprietary polishes, however, are not a substitute for cleaning and will not give a proper finish unless the surface is properly cleaned first.

Aluminium parts, such as the engine and gearbox, may be cleaned with paraffin and a stiff brush, and afterwards with petrol. These parts are best cleaned before the enamel is tackled.

Care of Plated Parts.

All plating is porous, and although chromium is rustless, the surfaces of plated ferrous parts will deteriorate if neglected and left exposed to the weather, due to rusting of the metal underneath the plating.

Whilst still clean therefore, the plated parts of a new machine should be wiped over with a rust preventative which will penetrate the pores in the plating. To prevent the attraction of dust through leaving the surface ' greasy' it can be wiped clear after application. We recommend ' Rus-Veto Amber X ' obtainable from the Service Department. Ordinary grease or oil are not as effective and in some circumstances can cause rusting.

Do not use anything abrasive, or ordinary metal polish, to clean the plating, and do not wipe off dirt that has dried on. Wash clean with soap and water, dry thoroughly afterwards, and then polish with F.L.P. (Supplier, G. H. White, Lowestoft Road, Gorleston, Norfolk).

Apply " Rust-Veto ' as described above.

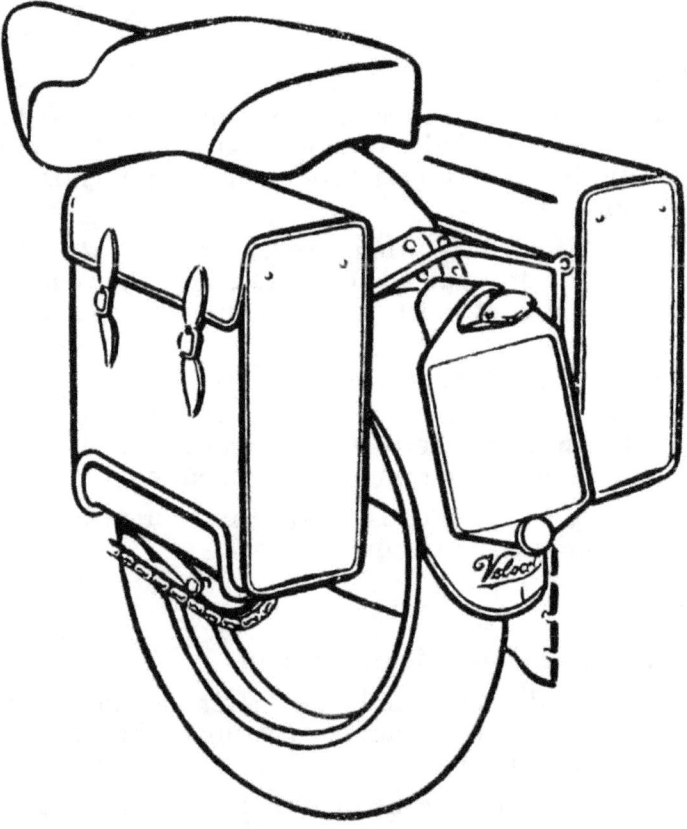

FIG. 42.

PANNIERS AND LUGGAGE GRID.

The panniers that are obtainable from the Service Department have tubular frames specially designed to fit the Velocette frame, and they do not depend for security upon clip fixings. The illustration Fig. 42 shows them fitted.

To fit, remove both rear mudguard stay bolts, distance pieces, and aluminium end caps from the rear suspension brackets. Remove pillion footrests. The distance pieces are discarded.

Offer up one pannier frame into place pushing the tube into the end of the bracket. On early models the aluminium cap will require filing to clear the pannier frame tube and allow it to fit flush against the bracket with the pannier tube in position. Secure the tube by fitting the mudguard stay bolt and attach the bottom of the pannier to the pillion footrest lugs with the footrest pivot bolts, or if pillion footrests are not fitted, by the silencer fixing bolt on the right and an extra similar bolt SL111/2 on the left. A nut SL56/27 will also be needed.

Fit the other frame and attach the cross bracing tube with the bolts provided and finally tighten up all bolts securely.

The luggage grid (also obtainable as an extra) fits to the pannier frames and cannot of course be used without them.

NOTES

SPARE PARTS LIST

FOR

MAC (SPRING FRAME) MODEL 350 c.c.

VELOCE LIMITED

: HALL GREEN WORKS :
YORK RD., HALL GREEN
BIRMINGHAM, 28

TELEphone: SPRingfield 1145/6/7
TELEgrams: "Veloce, Birmingham."

INDEX

Section or Group.	Page.	Illus.
A.		
Air-cleaner assembly	35	I
Air control	37	J
B.		
Ball valve assembly	34	I
Battery carrier	23	E
Brake control—Front	37	J
Brake control—Rear	24	E
Brake assembly—Front	28	G
Brake assembly—Rear	40	K
Brake torque arm—Rear	24	E
C.		
Cable assemblies	37	J
Cam gear	13	B
Chains—Driving	32	H
Chain adjuster—Primary	17	C
Chain adjuster—Rear	22	E
Chain case—Primary	16	C
Chain guard—Rear	32	H
Clutch	20	D
Clutch control	37	J
Connecting rod assembly	11	B
Crankcase assembly	8	A
Cylinder	7	A
Cylinder head assembly	7	A
D.		
Dynamo belt and cover	31	H
Dynamo mounting	8	A
Dynamo pulley	12	B
E.		
Engine-plates—Front	23	E
Engine plates—Rear	16	C
Engine steady	24	E
Exhaust pipe and clips	38	J
Exhaust lifter control	37	J
F.		
Footrests	24	E
Flywheel assembly	12	B
Fork. Front	26	F
Fork. Rear swinging	22	E
Frame	22	E
G.		
Gears. Timing	13	B
Gears. Transmission	19	D
Gear control mechanism	20	D
Gear pedal and rocker shaft	15	C
Gearbox bearings	19	D
Gear box housing and cover	15	C
Gear box shafts	19	D

Section or Group.	Page.	Illus.
H.		
Handlebar and controls	37	J
Horn mounting	31	H
Hub assembly. Front	28	G
Hub assembly—Rear	40	K
K.		
Kickstart crank	19	D
Kickstart ratchet assembly	19	D
M.		
Main bearings—Engine	8	A
Mudguards and stays	31	H
N.		
Number plates and mountings	31	H
O.		
Oil filter and tank assembly	34	I
Oil pipe assemblies	35	I
Oil pump assembly	13	B
P.		
Petrol tank, pipe, and taps	34	I
Pillion footrests	24	E
Piston assembly	11	B
R.		
Rocker gear assembly	11	B
Rims and spokes	28 & 40	G & K
S.		
Seat	35	I
Shock absorber assembly	12	B
Silencer	38	J
Speedometer and drive	38	J
Spokes and rims	28 & 40	G & K
Stand assemblies	23	E
Steering head bearings	22	E
T.		
Tanks. Petrol and oil	34	I
Timing gear	13	B
Tools	38	J
Toolbox	35	I
Torque tube assemblies	22	E
Trunnion shaft and bearings	22	E
V.		
Valves and springs	12	B
Wheel assembly—Front	28	G
Wheel assembly—Rear	40	K

INTRODUCTION

HOW TO ORDER SPARE PARTS.

As the prompt despatch of spare parts depends to a great extent upon the orders for them being accurately and clearly made out, we ask for the co-operation of customers in the following requirements:

(1) The printing in block letters of the name and address of the consignee. (We receive quite a number of orders which cannot be executed because forwarding addresses are omitted or are unreadable).

(2) The inclusion of the engine and frame numbers of the machine for which the parts are required. (These should be taken from the engine and frame. Do not rely on the Registration Book.)

(3) The accurate quoting of part numbers—*not illustration references*—and brief descriptions of the parts. As we work to part numbers these are the more important.

(4) The use of separate sheets for orders, which should be written on one side of the paper only. If technical or other information is needed at the time of ordering please ask for this in a separate letter which may be posted with the order.

(5) Clear directions for despatch, which should state whether parts shall be posted C.O.D., or whether against a remittance with order. If the latter please state amount enclosed, and please do not send coin unless the envelope is registered. Postal Orders, Money Orders, or Cheques, crossed "& Co.," and made payable to Veloce Ltd., are advised.

If the spares are to be sent to an address other than that from which the order is sent, this must be clearly stated. In such cases unless the person ordering is sure that a C.O.D. parcel will be paid for on presentation, remittances must always be sent.

EXAMPLE OF ORDER. The following is an example of an order correctly set out:

Please despatch per C.O.D. (*or*) Please despatch against remittance enclosed value .... to :

NAME AND ADDRESS (*In block letters*).

FOR MAC MODEL. FRAME No. RS/1001. ENGINE No. MAC/20001
    1   M220.   Cylinder head gasket.
    1   K180/3   Carburetter gasket.
    1   M256   Rocket cover gasket.

(*Signed*) ....

TELEGRAPHED ORDERS. The code on page 4 should be used when ordering by telegram. If orders are not to be sent C.O.D. remittances may be sent by Telegraphed Money Order. It is essential, however, to instruct the telegraph clerk to include the sender's name and address in the message space, otherwise this will not be transmitted.

EXAMPLE OF TELEGRAPHED ORDER.
VELOCE, BIRMINGHAM.
VELOD ONE M 220, ONE K 180/3, ONE M 256.
NAME AND ADDRESS.

TERMS. Strictly nett cash before despatch, except in the case of our appointed Agents and Spares Stockists.

All Spares Invoices will be surcharged 2½% to cover postage, or packing and carriage charges—subject to a minimum surcharge of 6d. C.O.D. fees are charged extra.

Cases and Crates, etc., are charged for on despatch, the charge being recoverable from us upon receipt by us of the returned empty container in good condition if returned within 21 days from the date of Invoice.

The return of empties must be advised and Invoice numbers quoted.

C.O.D. ORDERS. These can be executed by parcels post only. The maximum weight acceptable by the Post Office is 15-lbs., and there are certain limitations as to size. The minimum parcel post charge and C.O.D. fee makes it uneconomical to send orders less than 5/- value by this means. Remittances should, therefore, be sent with any very small or very large orders.

PATTERNS. Old parts may be sent as patterns, but must be cleaned thoroughly before packing, and must be labelled clearly with sender's name and address in block letters and marked " Pattern(s) to order herewith (or under separate cover)." Do not include coin, Notes, Cheques, or Money Orders with patterns.

REPAIRS. We are usually able to test customers' machines without previous arrangements being made, but it is seldom possible to start repairs and complete them within a specified time, unless an appointment has been made beforehand for the motorcycle to be taken in on a fixed day. Appointments will be arranged on request.

Whilst all reasonable care is taken, customers' motorcycles and property are received, stored, and driven at owners' sole risk. We do not accept responsibility for loss or damage arising from accident, fire, theft, or other causes.

Customers' wishes as to delivery will be met as far as is practicable, but no responsibility can be accepted for delays in the carrying out of any repairs, or for the quality of, or delays in procuring any replacements that are not of our manufacture.

Parts removed and replaced during repairs will be disposed of at once, unless we are instructed before beginning the work that they are to be retained for return to the customer.

ORDERS FOR REPAIRS. The term " overhaul " is capable of different meanings to different people. Customers should, therefore, state exactly and in detail the work required. Otherwise work may have to be stopped for us to obtain sanction to supply and fit parts found to be necessary.

It is particularly important to be specific in the case of engine and transmission units which on being stripped and examined may be found to need more than the owner has authorized.

ESTIMATES. We can prepare Estimates if desired for repairs needed to machines, or component assemblies sent us. In such cases we do not begin repairs until the Estimate is accepted. Estimates are prepared as accurately as possible, but are subject to slight revision if, when repairs are progressing, additional work or parts are required.

In the event of the non-acceptance of an Estimate a charge will be made for stripping, cleaning and assembling. Parts detailed for renewal will be kept available for inspection until the Estimate is accepted, but will be disposed of immediately on acceptance unless instructions are received for their return.

No guarantee is given with any repair if the Estimate is not accepted in full.

NOTIFICATION OF COMPLETION. Customers will be advised by post unless we are instructed otherwise. This notification will normally take the form of an Invoice for the work done and parts fitted.

PAYMENT FOR REPAIRS. Payment is required before despatch, or on collection at the works.

HOURS OF BUSINESS. Mondays to Fridays inclusive : 9 a.m. to 12-15 p.m. and 2 p.m. to 5 p.m. Closed Saturdays. Bank Holidays and special occasions excepted.

VELOCE LTD.,
SERVICE DEPARTMENT.

F.473/5M/5/53.

CODE

For the convenience of customers, to ensure accuracy, and to save cost of telegraphing, we draw your attention to the following Code Words and their meanings :—

VEL	Despatch immediately per passenger train to address below.
VELAIR	Despatch immediately per Air.
VELO	Despatch immediately per passenger train to station to be called for.
VELOD	Despatch C.O.D.
VELOR	Despatch immediately per parcels post.
VELOX 1715	Expedite delivery of our Order No. 1715.
VELOC	Send immediately by goods train to address below.
VELORIS	Send immediately by goods train to station to be called for.
VELORUM	Send immediately by registered post.

We strongly advise the use of above Code Words when telegraphing.

When remittance is sent by Telegraphic Money Order, unless NAME and ADDRESS are given in the space provided for a Private Message, the Post Office will not give this information in the Telegram.

PROPRIETARY ARTICLES

Customers are requested to deal direct with the manufacturers of Proprietary Articles for any technical information or claims under guarantee. Overseas owners should obtain the above information either from the Velocette Agent or the Proprietary Manufacturer's Representative in their Territory.

For our Customers' convenience we give the addresses of our suppliers below :—

CARBURETTER EQUIPMENT :—
Amal Ltd., Holford Road, Witton, Birmingham, 6.

LAMPS AND SWITCHES :—
H. Miller & Co., Ltd., Aston Brook Street, Birmingham, 6.

GENERATOR :—
B.T.H. Co., Ltd., Alma Street, Coventry.
H. Miller & Co., Ltd., Aston Brook Street, Birmingham, 6.

SPARKING PLUGS :—
K.L.G. Sparking Plugs, Ltd., Robinhood Eng. Works, Putney Vale, London, S.W.15.
Lodge Plugs Ltd., Rugby.
Champion Sparking Plugs, Feltham, Middlesex.

ELECTRIC HORNS :—
Clear Hooters Ltd., Hampton Street, Birmingham, 19.

TYRES :—
Dunlop Rubber Co. Ltd., Fort Dunlop, Birmingham.
Goodyear Tyre Co., Bushbury, Wolverhampton.

BATTERIES :—
Chloride Electrical Storage Co., Dale End, Birmingham.
Varley Dry Accumulators Ltd., By-Pass Road, Barking, Essex.
J. Lucas Ltd., Gt. King Street, Birmingham, 18.

SPEEDOMETERS :—
S. Smith & Sons (M.A.) Ltd., Cricklewood Works, Cricklewood, London, N.W.12.

SUSPENSION UNITS :—
Jonas-Woodhead & Sons, Ltd., Kirkstall Road, Leeds, 4.

ILLUSTRATION A

ORDER BY PART NUMBERS—DO NOT QUOTE ILLUSTRATION REFERENCES.

FOR PART NUMBERS AND DESCRIPTIONS OF ITEMS
{ 1 to 40 see page **7**
41 to 73 ,, ,, **8**
74 to 93 ,, ,, **9** }

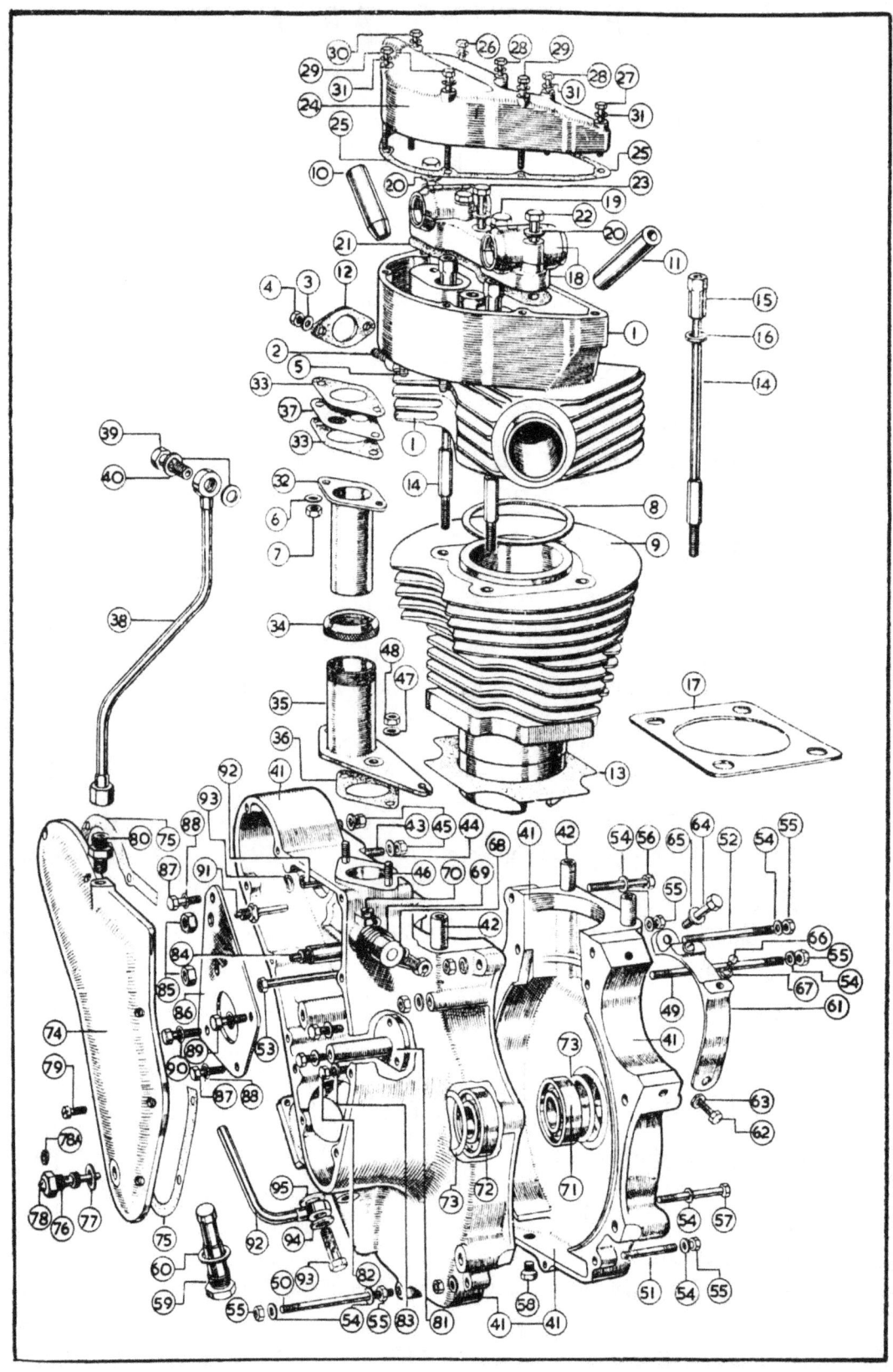

6

ENGINE SECTION. See Illustration "A" page 6.
Cylinder Head and Cylinder Group.

Note.—Quote Part Numbers when ordering—
NOT Illustration Reference Numbers.

Ref.	Part No.	Description.	Qty. Off.
1	MAS32	Cylinder head assembly. Includes items indicated §	1
2	SL103/2	§Cylinder head stud. $\frac{3}{16}''$ B.S.F. $1\frac{3}{16}''$. Carburetter fixing	2
3	SL6/40	Cylinder head stud washer. $\frac{3}{16}''$. Carburetter fixing	2
4	SL56/38	Cylinder head stud nut. $\frac{3}{16}''$ B.S.F.	2
5	SL102/11	§Cylinder head stud. $\frac{1}{4}''$ B.S.F. $\frac{7}{8}''$. Push rod cover fixing	2
6	SL6/32	Cylinder head stud washer. $\frac{1}{4}''$. Push rod cover fixing	2
7	SL56/4	Cylinder head stud nut. $\frac{1}{4}''$ B.S.F. Push rod cover fixing	2
8	M220	Cylinder head gasket	1
9	M22/11	Cylinder barrel	1
10	M3/6	§Cylinder head valve guide. Inlet	1
11	M3/4	§Cylinder head valve guide. Exhaust	1
12	K180/3	Carburetter gasket	1
13	M70	Cylinder barrel gasket—Cylinder base joint	1
14	M249	Cylinder holding down stud	4
15	M208	Cylinder stud nut	4
16	M251	Cylinder stud washer	4
17	{ M203	Compression plate, .031" thick	As required
	{ M203/4	Compression plate, .010" thick	As required
18	MAS17	Rocker bearing bracket assembly. Includes items marked †	1
19	SL109/4	†Rocker bearing cap bolt, $\frac{5}{16}''$ B.S.F. $\times 1''$ U/H	2
20	SL6/40	†Rocker bearing cap, and bracket bolt washer	5
21	M250	Rocker bearing bracket gasket	1
22	SL109/7	Rocker bearing bracket bolt, $\frac{5}{16}''$ B.S.F. $\times 2\frac{1}{16}''$ U/H	2
23	SL109/8	Rocker bearing bracket bolt, $\frac{5}{16}''$ B.S.F. $\times 1\frac{7}{16}''$ U/H. Centre	1
24	M247/2	Rocker cover	1
25	M256	Rocker cover gasket	1
26	SL107/3	Rocker cover bolt, 2BA $\times 1\frac{1}{8}''$ U/H	1
27	SL107/6	Rocker cover bolt, 2BA $\times 1\frac{5}{8}''$ U/H	1
28	SL107/7	Rocker cover bolt, 2BA $\times 1\frac{13}{16}''$ U/H	2
29	SL107/8	Rocker cover bolt, 2BA $\times 2\frac{1}{4}''$ U/H	3
30	SL107/9	Rocker cover bolt, 2BA $\times 2\frac{11}{16}''$ U/H	1
31	LE366	Rocker cover bolt lock washer, $\frac{3}{16}''$	8

Push Rod Cover and Rocker Oil Pipe Group.

Ref.	Part No.	Description.	Qty. Off.
32	M50AS	Push rod cover assembly—top	1
33	M120	Push rod cover flange gasket—top	2
34	M52	Push rod cover gland nut	1
35	M50/2AS	Push rod cover assembly—bottom	1
36	M120/2	Push rod cover flange gasket—bottom	1
37	M234	Push rod guide plate	1
38	MAS18	Rocker oil-pipe assembly	1
39	M214	Rocker oil-pipe hollow bolt	1
40	A37	Oil pipe hollow bolt gasket	2

Engine Section—*continued*.

Crankcase Group.

Ref.	Part No.	Description.	Qty. Off.
41	MAS29	Crankcase assembly. Two halves with studs. Includes items marked *	1
42	M56/2	*Crankcase stud. Cylinder base	4
43	SL31/3	*Crankcase stud, $\frac{5}{16}''$ 18×18 T.P.I.×$1\frac{11}{32}''$. Magneto fixing	3
44	SL6/40	Crankcase stud washer, $\frac{5}{16}''$. Magneto fixing	3
45	SL56/13	Crankcase stud nut, $\frac{5}{16}''$ 18 T.P.I. Magneto fixing	3
46	SL30/21	*Crankcase stud, $\frac{1}{4}''$ B.S.F.×$\frac{13}{16}''$. Push rod cover fixing	2
47	SL6/32	Crankcase stud washer, $\frac{1}{4}''$. Push rod cover fixing	2
48	SL56/4	Crankcase stud nut, $\frac{1}{4}''$ B.S.F. Push rod cover fixing	2
49	SL30/1	*Crankcase stud, $\frac{1}{4}''$ B.S.F.×$4\frac{1}{4}''$. Through crankcase	1
50	SL30/2	*Crankcase stud, $\frac{1}{4}''$ B.S.F.×$3\frac{1}{2}''$. Through crankcase	1
51	SL30/14	Crankcase stud, $\frac{1}{4}''$ B.S.F.×$1\frac{3}{4}''$. Through crankcase	1
52	SL30/23	*Crankcase stud, $\frac{1}{4}''$ B.S.F.×$2\frac{5}{8}''$. Through crankcase	1
53	SL30/24	Crankcase stud, $\frac{1}{4}''$ B.S.F.×$4\frac{1}{16}''$. Through crankcase	1
54	SL6/32	Crankcase stud and bolt washer, $\frac{1}{4}''$	11
55	SL56/4	Crankcase stud nut, $\frac{1}{4}''$ B.S.F.	10
56	SL8/11	Crankcase bolt, $\frac{1}{4}''$ 20 T.P.I.×$1\frac{1}{2}''$ U/H ..	1
57	SL8/24	Crankcase bolt, $\frac{1}{4}''$ 20 T.P.I.×2″ U/H ..	1
58	B38	Crankcase drain plug, $\frac{1}{8}''$ B.S.P. ..	1
59	K246/5	Crankcase filter plug	1
60	KA115/2	Crankcase filter plug gasket	1
61	MAS44	Dynamo strap assembly	1
62	SL8/2	Dynamo strap bolt, $\frac{1}{4}''$ 20 T.P.I.×$\frac{9}{16}''$ U/H..	1
63	SL6/32	Dynamo strap bolt washer, $\frac{1}{4}''$	1
64	SL9/21	Dynamo strap clamp bolt, $\frac{5}{16}''$ B.S.F.×$1\frac{1}{8}''$ U/H	1
65	SL6/40	Dynamo strap clamp bolt washer, $\frac{5}{16}''$ ..	1
66	SL80/21	Voltage control box screw, 2BA×$\frac{1}{4}''$ U/H ..	2
67	LE366	Voltage control box lock washer, $\frac{3}{16}''$ ..	2
68	M11	Exhaust lifter lever	1
69	M155/2	Exhaust lifter lever spring	1
70	K76	Exhaust lifter lever screw	1

Crankcase Bearing Group.

Ref.	Part No.	Description.	Qty. Off.
71	K87/2	Driving shaft roller bearing	1
72	K87	Timing shaft ball bearing	1
73	{ K174	Timing or driving side bearing shim, .005″ thick .. ..As required	
	K174/2	Timing or driving side bearing shim, .002″ thick .. ..As required	
	K174/3	Timing or driving side bearing shim, .010″ thick .. ..As required	

Engine Section—*continued.*

Ref.	Part No.	Description.	Qty. Off.
		Timing Cover, Steady Plate, and Timing Spindle Group.	
74	M45/7	Timing cover	1
75	M68	Timing cover gasket	1
76	M212	Timing cover oil jet	1
77	A37/2	Timing cover oil jet gasket	1
78	SL80/22	Timing cover oil jet screw, 2BA × ⅜" U/H	1
78A	A37/6	Timing Cover oil jet screw gasket	1
79	K55	Timing cover fixing screw	10
80	K119	Timing cover oil union, ⅛" × ¼" B.S.P.	1
81	M200/4	Intermediate gear spindle	1
82	SL8/5	Intermediate gear spindle bolt, ¼" B.S.F. × ¾" U/H	3
83	SL6/32	Intermediate gear spindle washer, ¼"..	3
84	M15/2	Cam wheel spindle	1
85	M244	Cam wheel spindle, and steady plate oil jet nut	2
86	M199/2	Timing gear steady plate	1
87	M210	Steady plate bolt, ¼". Plate to spindles	2
88	LE367	Steady plate bolt lock washer, ¼"	2
89	M211	Steady plate bolt, 5⁄16". Plate to crankcase	2
90	LE368	Steady plate lock washer, 5⁄16"	2
91	M259	Steady plate oil jet. Cam feed	1
92	M10	Bottom rocker spindle	1
93	M216	Bottom rocker thrust washer	1

§ These parts are included in MAS32 cylinder head assembly.

† These parts are included in MAS17 Rocker bearing bracket assembly.

* These parts are included in MAS29 Crankcase assembly.

ILLUSTRATION B

ORDER BY PART NUMBERS—**DO NOT** QUOTE ILLUSTRATION REFERENCES.

FOR PART NUMBERS AND DESCRIPTIONS OF ITEMS { 1 to 21 see page 11 / 22 to 48 ,, ,, 12 / 49 to 67 ,, ,, 13

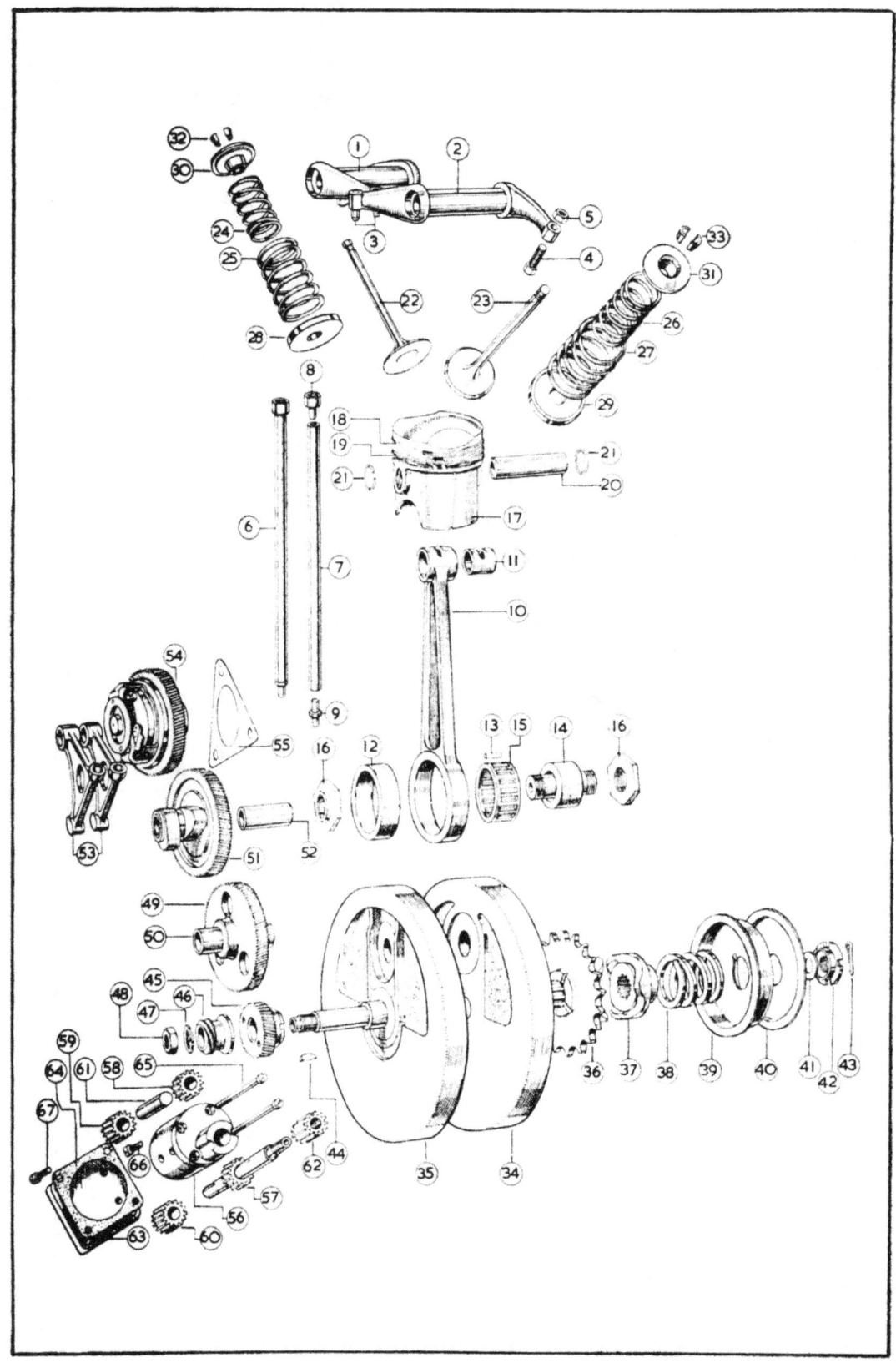

ENGINE SECTION—continued. See Illustration "B," page 10.

Rocker Assembly and Push Rod Group.

Note.—Quote Part Numbers when ordering.
NOT Illustration Reference Numbers.

Illus. Ref.	Part No.	Description.	Qty. Off.
1	M9/4AS	Rocker assembly—Inlet. (Includes item marked §)	1
2	M9/2AS	Rocker assembly. Exhaust. (Includes item marked §)	1
3	M41	§Rocker end	2
4	M139	Rocker tappet	2
5	SL56/33	Rocker tappet locknut, ₃⁄₈" 26 T.P.I. .447 Hexagon	2
6	M196/6AS	Push rod assembly. (Assembly of items marked *)	2
7	M196/6	*Push rod	2
8	M194	*Push rod end—top	2
9	M195	*Push rod end—bottom	2

Connecting Rod and Piston Group.

Illus. Ref.	Part No.	Description.	Qty. Off.
10	M28/2ASM	Connecting rod assembly. (Includes small end bush M29)	1
11	M29	Connecting rod small end bush. (Included in assembly M28/2ASM)	1
12	K190	Connecting rod outer race	1
13	K191	Connecting rod roller. Standard diameter	16
	K191/3	Connecting rod roller, .0004" oversize	As required
	K191/4	Connecting rod roller, .0002" oversize	As required
14	K192AS	Crankpin assembly. (Includes crankpin nuts)	1
15	K193	Connecting rod roller cage	1
16	K62/4	Crankpin nut. (Included in assembly K192AS)	2
17	M27/4	†Piston. Standard diameter	1
	M27/5	†Piston. First oversize +.020" on diameter	As reqd.
	M27/6	†Piston. Second oversize +.040" on diameter	As reqd.
	M27/7	†Piston. Third oversize +.060" on diameter	As reqd.
18	SL3/18	†Piston ring—compression. Standard diameter	2
	SL3/20	†Piston ring—compression. First oversize, +.020" on diameter	As required
	SL3/33	†Piston ring—compression. Second oversize, +.040" on diameter	As required
	SL3/51	†Piston ring—compression. Third oversize, +.060" on diameter	As required
19	SL3/53	†Piston ring—scraper. Standard diameter	1
	SL3/54	†Piston ring—scraper. First oversize, +.020" on diameter	As required
	SL3/55	†Piston ring—scraper. Second oversize, +.040" on diameter	As required
	SL3/56	†Piston ring—scraper. Third oversize, +.060" on diameter	As required
20	M31	†Gudgeon pin. Standard diameter	1
	M31/2	Gudgeon pin. Plus .001" on diameter	As required
21	K149	†Gudgeon pin circlip	2

Engine Section—*continued.*

Valve, Valve Spring, and Collar Group.

Illus. Ref.	Part No.	Description.	Qty. Off.
22	M2/8	Valve—Inlet	1
23	M2/8	Valve—Exhaust	1
24	K7/6	Valve spring—Inner, inlet ⎫ Supplied	1
25	K6/7	Valve spring—Outer, inlet ⎭ together only	1
26	K7/6	Valve spring—Inner, exhaust ⎫ Supplied	1
27	K6/7	Valve spring—Outer, exhaust ⎭ together only	1
28	M38/3	Valve spring washer—bottom, inlet	1
29	M38/3	Valve spring washer—bottom, exhausts	1
30	K4/5	Valve spring collar—Inlet	1
31	K4/5	Valve spring collar—Exhaust	1
32	K5/4	Valve spring cotter—Inlet	1
33	K5/4	Valve spring cotter—Exhaust	1

Flywheel, Pump Drive, and Shock Absorber Group.

34	M25/4AS	Flywheel and shaft assembly—Driving side	1
35	M23/4AS	Flywheel and shaft assembly—Timing side	1
36	M89/7	Engine sprocket, 21 teeth	1
37	M91/3	Shock absorber clutch	1
38	M90	Shock absorber spring	1
39	E19/4	Dynamo driving pulley	1
40	E19/5	Dynamo driving pulley flange	1
41	SL6/67	Shock absorber spring washer	1
42	M93	Shock absorber spring collar	1
43	SL71/1	Split cotter. $\frac{3}{32}'' \times 1''$	1
44	K36/2	Timing shaft key	1
45	M32/4	Timing pinion	1
46	M206/2	Oil pump driving worm	1
47	K127	Timing shaft washer	1
48	SL56/32	Timing shaft nut. $\frac{1}{2}''$ 20 T.P.I., L/H thread	1

Engine Section—*continued.*

Timing Gear, Timing Unit, and Oil Pump Group.

Illus. Ref.	Part No.	Description.	Qty. Off.
49	MAS1	Intermediate gear assembly. Includes bush M202/4	1
50	M202/4	Intermediate gear bush. Included in assembly MAS1	1
51	MAS19/2	Camwheel assembly. Includes bush M12/2	1
52	M12/2	Camwheel bush. Included in assembly MAS19/2	1
53	M9/3	Bottom rocker	2
54	MAS40	Magneto gear assembly. (Auto-timing unit)	1
55	M260	Magneto flange gasket	1
56	M78/2AS	‡Oil pump body and cover assembly	1
57	M80/2	‡Oil pump spindle	1
58	M82	‡Oil pump feed gear	1
59	K81	‡Oil pump return gear—loose	1
60	K83	‡Oil pump return gear—fixed	1
61	K98	‡Oil pump fixed spindle	1
62	M217/2	‡Oil pump driven gear	1
63	M207	‡Oil pump base plate	1
64	M226	Oil pump base plate gasket	1
65	M97	‡Oil pump fixing screw	4
66	K55	Oil pump fixing screw—Short	3
67	K95	Oil pump fixing screw—long—Inner front corner	1

* These parts are included in M196/6AS Push rod assembly.

§ These parts are included in M9/2AS and M9/4AS Rocker assemblies.

† Pistons with rings, gudgeon pins, and circlips may be ordered assembled as :

    M27/4AS   Piston assembly. Standard diameter.
    M27/5AS   Piston assembly. Plus .020"
    M27/6AS   Piston assembly. Plus .040"
    M27/7AS   Piston assembly. Plus .060"

‡ The oil pump, comprising these items, may be ordered assembled as :
    MAS47   Oil pump assembly.

ILLUSTRATION C

ORDER BY PART NUMBERS—DO NOT QUOTE ILLUSTRATION REFERENCES.

FOR PART NUMBERS AND DESCRIPTIONS OF ITEMS { 1 to 39 see page 15
40 to 81 „   „   16
82 to 93 „   „   17

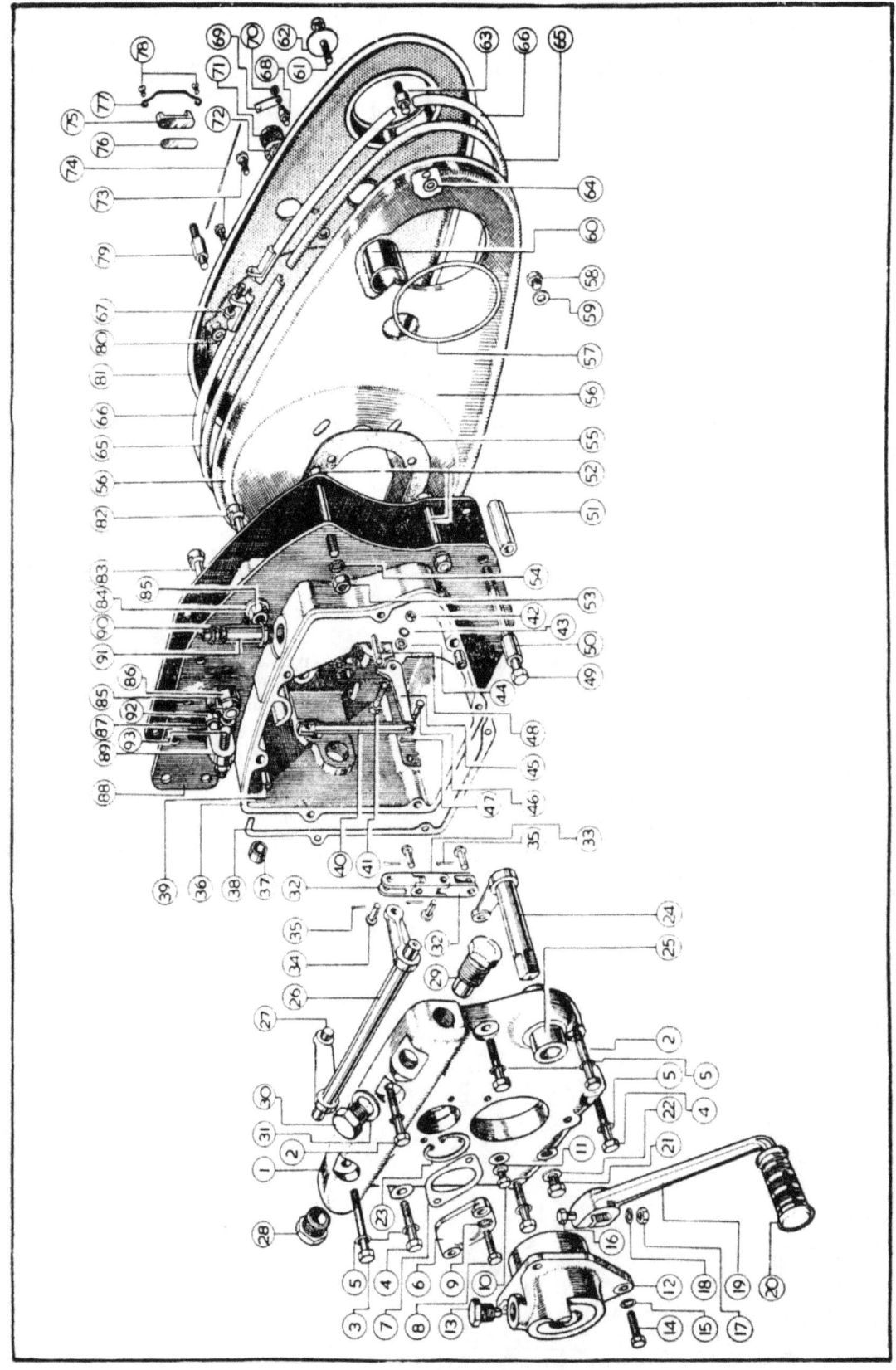

14

GEARBOX AND CLUTCH SECTION.

See Illustration " C," page 14.

Gearbox housing, End Cover, Kickstart Bearing and Gear Lever Group.

Note.—Quote Part Numbers when ordering.
NOT Illustration Reference Numbers.

Illus. Ref.	*Part No.*	*Description.*	*Qty. Off.*
1	MAS55	Gearbox end cover assembly	1
2	SL108/3	Gearbox end cover bolt, $\frac{1}{4}$" B.S.F. × $1\frac{3}{8}$" U/H	2
3	SL108/4	Gearbox end cover bolt, $\frac{1}{4}$" B.S.F. × $1\frac{1}{2}$" U/H	1
4	SL108/5	Gearbox end cover bolt, $\frac{1}{4}$" B.S.F. × $1\frac{3}{32}$" U/H	4
5	LE367	Gearbox end cover bolt lockwasher, $\frac{1}{4}$"	7
6	B97	Gearbox end cover plate	1
7	B98	Gearbox end cover plate gasket	1
8	SL108/2	Gearbox end cover plate bolt, $\frac{1}{4}$" B.S.F. × $\frac{5}{8}$" U/H	2
9	LE367	Gearbox end cover plate lockwasher $\frac{1}{4}$"	2
10	SL8/1	Gearbox oil level plug, $\frac{1}{4}$" B.S.F. × $\frac{3}{8}$" U/H	1
11	A37/5	Gearbox oil level plug gasket	1
12	BK4	Kickstart bearing	1
13	BK73/2	Kickstart return spring anchor peg	1
14	SL108/2	Kickstart bearing fixing bolt, $\frac{1}{4}$" B.S.F. × $\frac{5}{8}$" U/H	3
15	LE367	Kickstart bearing fixing bolt lockwasher, $\frac{1}{4}$"	3
16	SL108/3	Foot lever clamp bolt, $\frac{1}{4}$" B.S.F. × $1\frac{3}{8}$" U/H	1
17	SL56/4	Foot lever clamp bolt nut, $\frac{1}{4}$" B.S.F.	1
18	LE367	Foot lever clamp bolt lock washer, $\frac{1}{4}$"	1
19	GC4/21	Gear change foot lever	1
20	B60/4	Gear change foot lever rubber	1
21	B38	Gearbox oil drain plug, $\frac{1}{8}$" B.S.P.	1
22	A37	Gearbox oil drain plug gasket	1
23	B100	Gearbox end cover circlip	1
24	GC55	Gearchange foot lever shaft	1
25	GC42/3†	Gearchange foot lever shaft bush	1
26	MAS46	Gearchange rocker shaft assembly. (Includes GC60 Rocker shaft pin)	1
27	GC60	Gear change rocker shaft pin. (Included in MAS46 assembly)	1
28	GC53	Rocker shaft bush—rear, short	1
29	GC54	Rocker shaft bush—front, long	1
30	BK40	Gearbox oil filler	1
31	LE75	Gearbox oil filler plug gasket	1
32	GC56	Gear change yoke end	2
33	GC58	Gear change connecting link	1
34	GC59	Gear change clevis pin	4
35	SL71/2	Gear change clevis pin split cotter, $\frac{1}{16}$" × $\frac{1}{2}$"	4
36	MAS53	Gearbox housing (bushed). Includes BK36/2 Bush	1
37	BK36/2	Gearbox housing bush. Included in MAS53 assembly	1
38	B43/2	Gearbox end cover gasket	1
39	LE333	Gearbox housing dowel	2

† Included in MAS55 End Cover Assembly.

Gearbox and Clutch Section—*continued.*

Clutch Operation, Chain Case and Rear Engine Plate Group.

Illus. Ref.	Part No.	Description.	Qty. Off.
40	CK34/4	Clutch operating plunger	1
41	SL8/13	Clutch operating lever bolt, $\frac{1}{4}$" B.S.F. × $1\frac{1}{16}$" U/H	1
42	SL56/4	Clutch operating lever bolt nut, $\frac{1}{4}$" B.S.F.	1
43	LE367	Clutch operating lever bolt lock washer, $\frac{1}{4}$"	1
44	SL6/32	Clutch operating lever bolt washer, $\frac{1}{4}$"	1
45	C31/3	Clutch operating lever	1
46	S32	Clutch operating plunger clevis pin	1
47	SL71/2	Clutch operating plunger split cotter, $\frac{1}{16}$" × $\frac{1}{2}$"	1
48	{ C30	Clutch operating thrust pin, 1.328" long	*
	{ C30/2	Clutch operating thrust pin, 1.343" long	*
		* One off used per gearbox—the length used being determined by selective assembly.	
49	SL11/2	Rear engine plate fixing bolt (long), $\frac{3}{8}$" 26 T.P.I. × $3\frac{7}{8}$" U/H	1
50	FK221/3	Rear engine plate distance piece. (Outside right-hand plate)	1
51	F305	Rear engine plate distance piece. (Between plates)	1
52	SL11/1	Rear engine plate and bottom gearbox bolt, $\frac{3}{8}$" 26 T.P.I. × $2\frac{3}{4}$" U/H	5
53	SL56/8	Rear engine plate and bottom gearbox bolt nut, $\frac{3}{8}$" 26 T.P.I.	5
54	LE369	Rear engine plate and bottom gearbox bolt lock washer, $\frac{3}{8}$"	5
55	A179/6	Chaincase packing	1
56	F45/5	Chaincase rear half	1
57	F285	Chaincase oil seal	1
58	B38	Chaincase drain plug, $\frac{1}{8}$" B.S.P.	1
59	A37	Chaincase drain plug gasket	1
60	FK205	Chaincase bolt distance piece	1
61	SL109/3	Chaincase bolt, $\frac{5}{16}$" B.S.F. × $1\frac{3}{16}$" U/H	1
62	SL6/42	Chaincase bolt washer, $\frac{5}{16}$" × $1\frac{3}{16}$" O/D	1
63	FK207	*Chaincase stud. (Dynamo cover)	1
64	SL6/32	*Chaincase stud washer	1
65	F284/2	Chaincase joint moulding	1
66	MAS16/2	Chaincase strap assembly	1
67	SL107/4	Chaincase strap fixing pin, 2BA × 1"	1
68	T95/2	*Chaincase stud. (Inspection cap)	1
69	T72/19	*Chaincase inspection cap clip	1
70	SL6/8	*Chaincase stud washer, $\frac{3}{32}$" × $\frac{9}{32}$" O/D	1
71	T71/19K	Chaincase inspection cap	1
72	KA244	Chaincase inspection cap pad	1
73	F201	Chaincase fixing pin	4
74	FK210	Chaincase fixing pin locking wire	2
75	BK70	Clutch operating thrust pad	1
76	BK97	Clutch operating thrust pad shim	As required
77	BK52	Clutch operating thrust cup wire clip	1
78	B34	Clutch operating thrust cup screw, $\frac{1}{8}$" (Whit.) 40 T.P.I., C/S H/D	2
79	FK207/2	*Chaincase stud (Rear chain cover)	2
80	SL6/32	*Chaincase stud washer—inside $\frac{1}{4}$"	2
81	MAS50	Chaincase front half assembly. (Includes items marked *)	1

Gearbox and Clutch Section—continued.

Illus. Ref.	Part No.	Description.	Qty. Off.
82	FK81/2	Gearbox fixing bolt top. (Short)	1
83	FK81	Gearbox fixing bolt top (long)	1
84	SL6/48	Gearbox fixing bolt washer (top), $\frac{3}{8}''$	1
85	SL56/8	Gearbox fixing bolt nut, $\frac{3}{8}''$, 26 T.P.I.	2
86	FK19/2	Gearbox adjuster	1
87	LE369	Gearbox adjuster stop lock washer, $\frac{3}{8}''$	1
88	F110/17	Rear engine plate	2
89	FK228	Gearbox adjuster stop	1
90	CK14/2	Clutch cable stop	1
91	CK21/2	Clutch cable stop holder	1
92	SL56/8	Gearbox adjuster stop nut, $\frac{3}{8}''$, 26 T.P.I.	1
93	SL56/13	Gearbox adjuster nut, $\frac{5}{16}''$, 18 T.P.I.	2

* Items included in MAS50 assembly.

ILLUSTRATION D

ORDER BY PART NUMBERS—**DO NOT** QUOTE ILLUSTRATION REFERENCES.

FOR PART NUMBERS AND DESCRIPTIONS OF ITEMS { 1 to 42 see page 19
43 to 86 ,, ,, 20

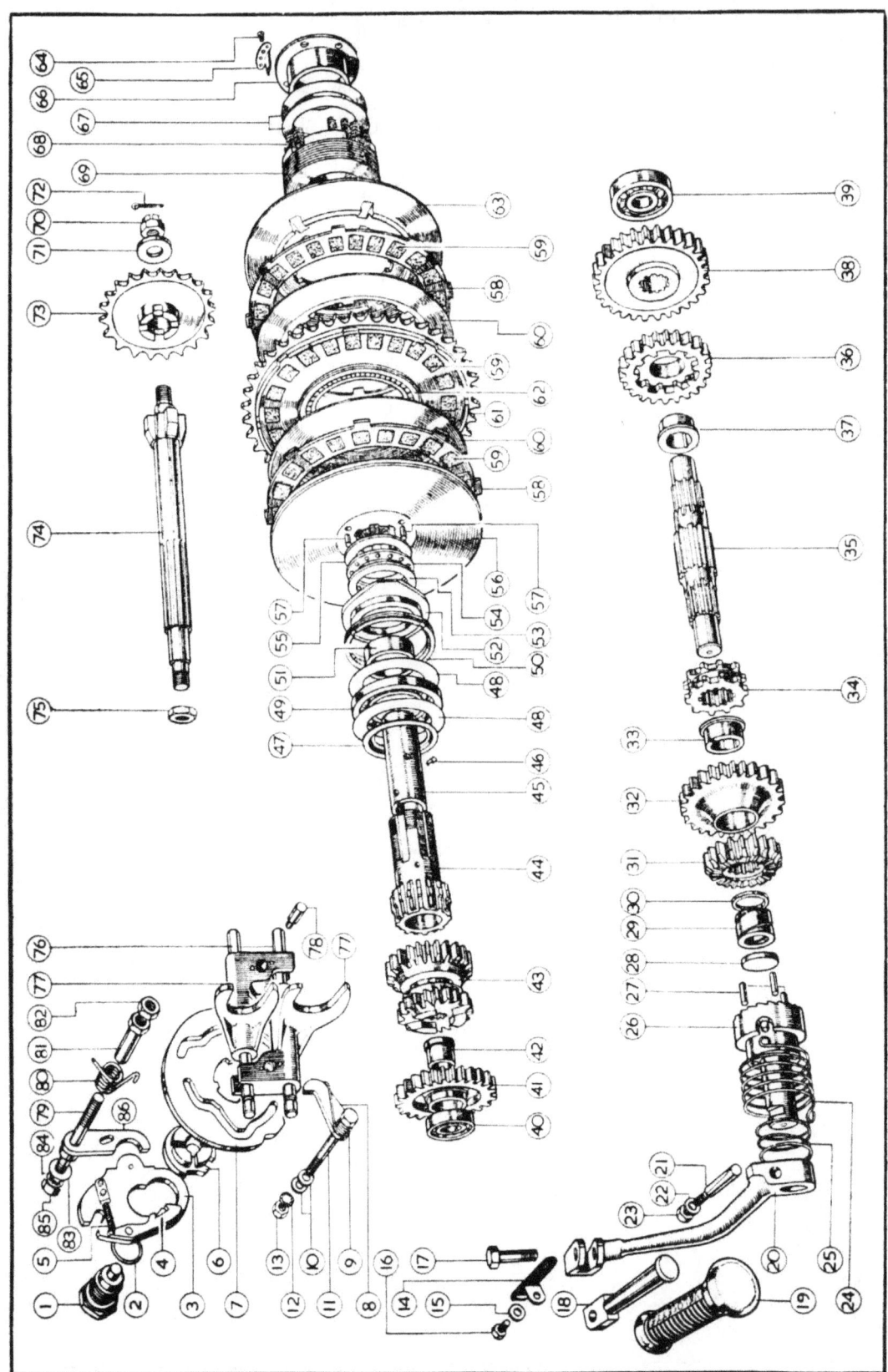

GEARBOX SECTION—continued. See Illustration "D," page 18.
Camplate, Striking Plate, and Indexing Mechanism Group.
Note.—Quote Part Numbers when ordering.
NOT Illustration Reference Numbers.

Illus. Ref.	Part No.	Description.	Qty. Off.
1	BK64/3	Camplate pivot	1
2	BK96	Camplate pivot shim	As required
3	MAS45	Striking plate assembly	1
4	GC23/2	Striking pawl	1
5	GC24/2	Striking pawl spring	1
6	BK98/2	Camplate ratchet plate	1
7	BK80/5	Camplate	1
8	BK66	Indexing pawl	1
9	BK68	Indexing pawl spring	1
10	SL6/32	Indexing pawl washer, ¼"	2
11	BK83/2	Indexing pawl pivot	1
12	LE367	Indexing pawl pivot lock washer, ¼"	1
13	SL56/4	Indexing pawl pivot nut, ¼" B.S.F.	1

Kickstart Ratchet, Spring, and Crank Group.

14	A254/3	Kickstart foot-piece retaining spring	1
15	SL6/32	Kickstart retaining spring washer, ¼"	1
16	SL8/1	Kickstart retaining spring bolt, ¼" B.S.F. × ⅜" U H	1
17	SL11/15	Kickstart foot piece bolt, ⅜", 26 T.P.I. × 1 1/16" U H	1
18	BK18	Kickstart footpiece	1
19	B60/5	Kickstart rubber	1
20	BK12/5	Kickstart crank	1
21	LE242	Kickstart crank cotter pin	1
22	SL6/32	Kickstart crank cotter pin washer, ¼"	1
23	SL56/4	Kickstart crank cotter pin nut, ¼" B.S.F.	1
24	BK19	Kickstart return spring	1
25	BK19/2	Kickstart spring (engaging)	1
26	BK14	Kickstart ratchet	1
27	K191	Kickstart bearing thrust pin (3/16" × 9/16" Bearing roller)	3
28	BK82	Kickstart layshaft thrust washer	1
29	BK85/2	Kickstart bearing bush	1

Shafts, Gears, Clutch Plate, and Bearing Group.

30	BK95	Layshaft washer	1
31	B87	Layshaft first gear wheel	1
32	B89AS	Layshaft third gear wheel assembly. (Includes B91 Bush)	1
33	B91	Layshaft third gear wheel bush. (Included in B89AS assembly)	
34	BK77	Layshaft sliding dog	1
35	B10/6	Layshaft	1
36	B88AS	Layshaft second gear wheel assembly. (Includes B91 Bush)	1
37	B91	Layshaft second gear wheel bush. (Included in B88AS assembly)	
38	B86	Layshaft driving gear	1
39	B22/3	Gearbox housing ball bearing (for layshaft)	1
40	B23	Gearbox end cover ball bearing	1
41	B9/4AS	Gearshaft first gear wheel assembly. (Includes bush B75)	1
42	B75	Gearshaft first gear wheel bush. (Included in B9/4AS assembly)	1

Gearbox and Clutch Section—*continued.*

Illus. Ref.	Part No.	Description.	Qty. Off.
43	B78	Gearshaft sliding gear	1
44	B6/2AS	Sleeve gear assembly. (Includes B7/4 Bush and B101 Peg)	1
45	B7/4	Sleeve gear bush. (Included in B6/2AS assembly)	1
46	B101	Sleeve gear peg. (Included in B6/2AS Assembly)	1
47	BK33	Sleeve gear oil thrower	1
48	B31/2	Gearbox housing oil retaining shim	2
49	B22	Gearbox housing ball bearing	1
50	B39/26	Gearbox bearing retaining ring	1
51	B35/3	Sleeve gear distance piece	1
52	C29/26	Clutch operating thrust cup	1
53	C28	Clutch spherical thrust ring	1
54	MAS57	Clutch thrust bearing assembly	1
55	C7/26	Clutch thrust ring	1
56	KC1/25	Clutch back plate	1
57	C6/3	Clutch back plate thrust pin	3
58	C23AS	Clutch plate assembly. (Includes C25 insert—22 off)	2
59	C25	Clutch plate insert. (Included in C23AS and KC3/25AS assemblies)	44
60	C24	Clutch spacing plate	2
61	KC3/25AS	Clutch chain wheel assembly. (Includes C25 insert—22 off)	1
62	C26AS	Clutch ballrace assembly	1
63	KC2/25	Clutch front plate	1
64	B34	Sleeve gear locking plate screw, $\frac{1}{8}''$ Whit., c s head	1
65	C32/2	Sleeve gear nut locking plate	1
66	C5/2	Sleeve gear nut	1
67	C8	Sleeve gear shim	2
68	C12/4	Clutch spring	16
69	KC40/2AS	Clutch spring holder assembly	1
70	BK50	Gearshaft nut. (Sprocket end), $\frac{1}{2}''$, 20 T.P.I., castellated	1
71	SL6/65	Gearshaft washer $\frac{1}{2}'' \times 1\frac{1}{8}''$ O/D	1
72	SL71/1	Gearshaft split cotter, $\frac{3}{32}'' \times 1''$	1
73	SL94/1	Gearbox sprocket, 21 teeth, $\frac{1}{2}''$ P. $\times$ .305"	1
74	B5/5	Gearshaft	1
75	SL56/21	Gearshaft nut. (Cover end). $\frac{1}{2}''$ 20 T.P.I., $\frac{3}{8}''$ thick	1

Selector Fork and Centralizing Mechanism Group.

76	B90/2	Selector fork rod	2
77	MAS43	Selector fork assembly. (Includes BK32 Selector fork pin)	2
78	BK32	Selector fork pin	2
79	BK100/3	Centralizing lever pivot	1
80	BK101/2	Centralizing lever spring	1
81	BK102	Centralizing lever pivot sleeve	1
82	SL56/17	Centralizing lever pivot lock nut, $\frac{3}{8}'' \times 26$ T.P.I., $\frac{1}{4}''$ thick	1
83	BK103	Centralizing lever pivot shim	As required
84	LE369	Centralizing lever pivot lock washer, $\frac{3}{8}''$	1
85	SL56/8	Centralizing lever pivot nut, $\frac{3}{8}''$ 26 T.P.I.	1
86	BK99/2	Centralizing lever	1

ILLUSTRATION E

ORDER BY PART NUMBERS—DO NOT QUOTE ILLUSTRATION REFERENCES.

FOR PART NUMBERS AND DESCRIPTIONS OF ITEMS
- 1 to 26 see page 22
- 27 to 66 ,, ,, 23
- 67 to 101 ,, ,, 24

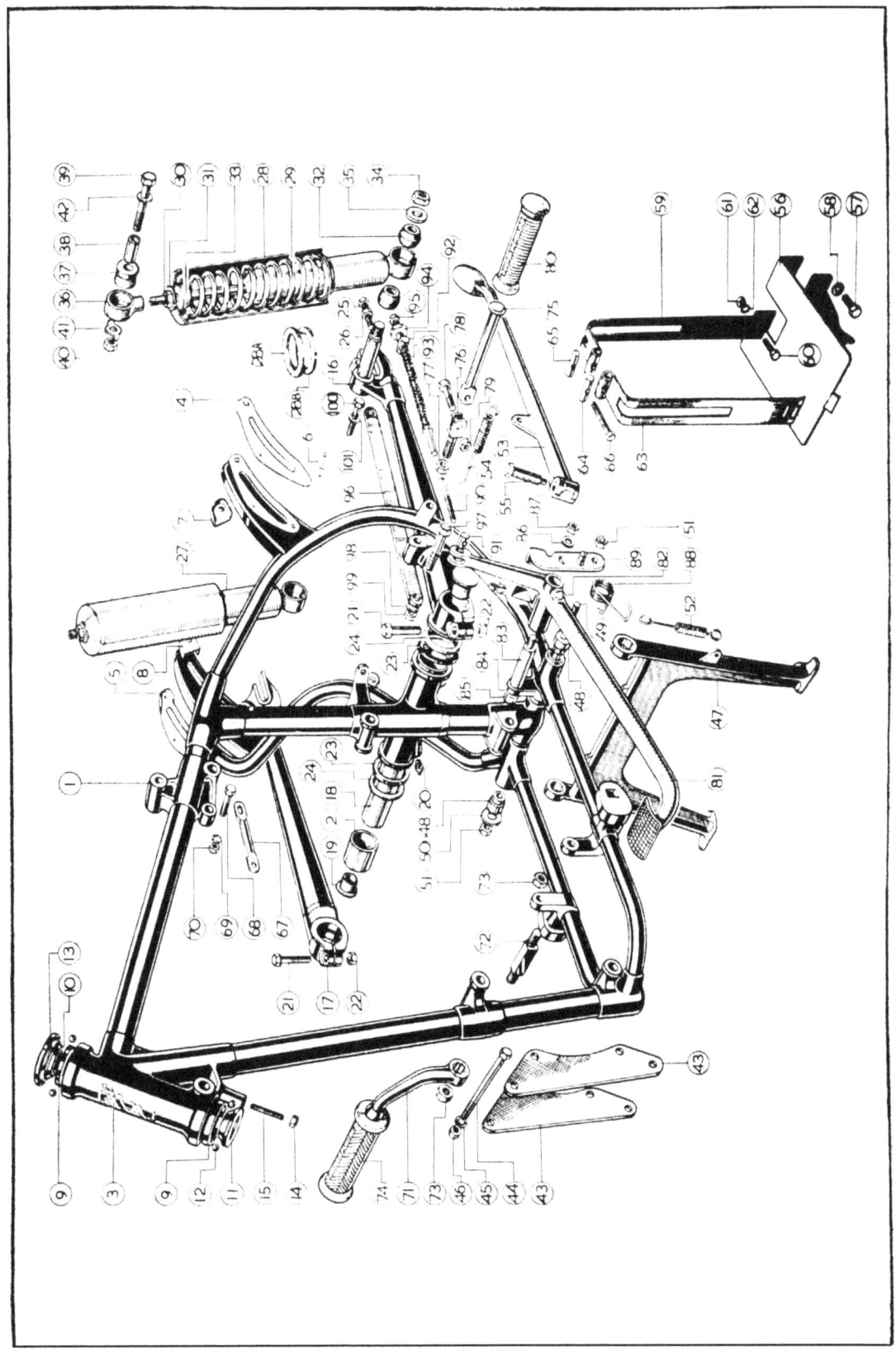

FRAME SECTION. See Illustration "E," page 21.

Main Frame, Torque Tube, Trunnion Bearing, Head Bearing, and Chain Adjuster Group.

Note.—Quote Part Numbers when ordering.
NOT Illustration Reference Numbers.

Illus. Ref.	Part No.	Description.	Qty. Off.
1	MAS31	Frame assembly. Includes steering head, transfer, outer rear suspension end caps, and trunnion shaft bushes	1
2	FA3/5*	Trunnion shaft bush. (Included in assembly MAS31)	2
3	A133*	Steering head transfer. (Included in Assembly MAS31)	1
4	FA104*	rear suspension bracket end cap — Outer, left-hand	1
5	FA105*	Rear suspension bracket end cap—Outer, right-hand	1
6	LE380/4*	Rear suspension bracket end cap rivet.. ..	4
7	FA106	Rear suspension bracket end cap—Inner left-hand	1
8	FA107	Rear suspension bracket end cap—Inner, right-hand	1
9	LE532*	Steering head cup	2
10	F32/3	Steering head cone—top	1
11	F32/4	Steering head cone—bottom	1
12	K100	Steering head ball, $\frac{1}{4}$"	38
13	F165	Steering head dust cap	1
14	SL56/6	Steering damper stud nut $\frac{5}{16}$" 26 T.P.I. ..	2
15	FK239	Steering damper stud	1
16	MAS35	Torque tube assembly—left-hand	1
17	MAS36	Torque tube assembly—right-hand	1
18	FA1/3	Trunnion shaft	1
19	F302	Trunnion shaft end plug	2
20	KA46	Trunnion shaft lug grease nipple	2
21	SL111/1	Trunnion lug clamp bolt, $\frac{7}{16}$" B.S.F. × $1\frac{3}{8}$" U/H	2
22	SL56/27	Trunnion lug clamp bolt nut, $\frac{7}{16}$" B.S.F. ..	2
23	F300	Trunnion lug felt washer housing	2
24	F301	Trunnion lug felt washer	2
25	FA47	Rear chain adjuster	2
26	SL56/4	Rear chain adjuster lock nut, $\frac{1}{4}$" B.S.F. ..	2

* Included in assembly No. MAS31

Frame Section—*continued.*

Rear Suspension Unit and Mounting Group.

Illus. Ref.	Part No.	Description.	Qty. Off.
27	MAS33	Rear suspension unit. Includes next eight items	2
28	A314	Rear suspension unit dust cover. Included in assembly MAS33	2
28a	A319	Rear suspension unit felt washer. Included in MAS33	2
28b	A320	Rear suspension unit felt washer retainer. Included in MAS33	2
29	A315	Rear suspension unit spring. Included in assembly MAS33	2
30	SL56/27	Rear suspension unit dust cover nut, $\frac{7}{16}$" B.S.F. Included in assembly MAS33	2
31	SL6/57	Rear suspension unit dust cover washer, $\frac{7}{16}$". Included in assembly MAS33	2
32	A316	Rear suspension unit grommet. Included in assembly MAS33	4
33	A317	Rear suspension unit stop buffer. Included in assembly MAS33	2
34	SL56/27	Rear suspension pivot pin nut, $\frac{7}{16}$" B.S.F.	2
35	SL6/60	Rear suspension pivot pin washer $\frac{7}{16}$"	2
36	F294	Rear suspension unit fixing lug	2
37	F295	Rear suspension unit fixing sleeve	2
38	F296	Rear suspension unit fixing distance piece	2
39	SL110/3	Rear suspension unit fixing bolt, $\frac{3}{8}$" B.S.F. $\times 1\frac{5}{8}$" U/H	2
40	SL56/7	Rear suspension unit fixing bolt nut, $\frac{3}{8}$"	2
41	F297	Rear suspension unit fixing bolt tabwasher	2
42	SL6/50	Rear suspension unit fixing bolt washer, $\frac{3}{8}$"	2

Front Engine Plate, Stand and Battery Mounting Group.

Illus. Ref.	Part No.	Description.	Qty. Off.
43	F174/4	Front engine plate	2
44	SL11/2	Front engine plate bolt, $\frac{3}{8}$" 26 T.P.I., $3\frac{7}{8}$" U/H	4
45	LE369	Front engine plate bolt lock washer, $\frac{3}{8}$"	4
46	SL56/8	Front engine plate bolt nut, $\frac{3}{8}$" 26 T.P.I.	4
47	F293	Centre stand	1
48	F292	Centre stand pivot	2
49	SL31/17	Centre stand stud, $\frac{5}{16}$" B.S.F. $\times 10\frac{1}{8}$" long	1
50	SL6/39	Centre stand stud washer, $\frac{5}{16}$" $\times 1$" O/D	1
51	SL56/38	Centre stand stud nut, $\frac{5}{16}$" B.S.F.	2
52	F69/5	Centre stand spring	1
53	FK29/11	Prop. stand	1
54	F69/5	Prop stand spring	1
55	F4/10	Prop stand pivot pin	1
56	E8/8	Battery platform	1
57	SL9/3	Battery platform bolt, $\frac{5}{16}$" 26 T.P.I. $\times \frac{1}{2}$" U/H	3
58	SL6/40	Battery platform bolt washer, $\frac{5}{16}$"	3
59	E9/6	Battery strap—rear	1
60	SL8/3	Battery strap bolt, $\frac{1}{4}$" B.S.F. $\times \frac{9}{16}$" U/H	1
61	SL56/4	Battery strap bolt nut, $\frac{1}{4}$"	1
62	LE367	Battery strap bolt lockwasher, $\frac{1}{4}$"	1
63	E9/5	Battery strap front	1
64	E51	Battery strap trunnion—plain hole	1
65	E51/2	Battery strap trunnion—threaded hole	1
66	E53	Battery strap clamp bolt, 2BA	1

Frame Section—*continued.*

Engine Steady, Footrest, Brake Pedal, Brake Rod and Torque Arm Group.

Illus. Ref.	Part No.	Description.	Qty. Off.
67	FK75/14	Engine steady	1
68	SL109/3	Engine steady bolt, $\frac{5}{16}$" B.S.F. × $1\frac{3}{16}$" U/H	2
69	LE368	Engine steady bolt lockwasher, $\frac{5}{16}$"	2
70	SL56/38	Engine steady bolt nut, $\frac{5}{16}$" B.S.F.	2
71	F126/6	Footrest hanger	2
72	FK23/14	Footrest rod	2
73	SL56/27	Footrest rod nut $\frac{7}{16}$" B.S.F.	4
74	KA76/2	Footrest rubber	2
75	BK18	Pillion footrest footpiece	2
76	F298	Pillion footrest eye bolt	2
77	SL56/27	Pillion footrest eye bolt nut, $\frac{7}{16}$" B.S.F.	2
78	SL110/2	Pillion footrest bolt (Pivot), $\frac{3}{8}$" B.S.F. × $1\frac{1}{4}$"	2
79	SL56/7	Pillion footrest bolt nut, $\frac{3}{8}$" B.S.F.	2
80	B60/5	Pillion footrest rubber	2
81	F39/11	Brake pedal	1
82	KA46	Brake pedal grease nipple	1
83	F130/14	Brake pedal support	1
84	SL6/57	Brake pedal support washer, $\frac{7}{16}$"—Inner	1
85	SL56/27	Brake pedal support nut, $\frac{7}{16}$" B.S.F.—Inner	1
86	SL6/40	Brake pedal support washer, $\frac{5}{16}$"—Outer	1
87	SL56/38	Brake pedal support nut, $\frac{5}{16}$" B.S.F.—Outer	1
88	F233/5	Brake pedal return spring	1
89	MAS38	Brake pedal stop	1
90	MAS41	Rear brake rod assembly	1
91	FK43	Rear brake rod trunnion—threaded hole	1
92	FK43/2	Rear brake rod trunnion—plain hole	1
93	KS43/2	Rear brake rod spring	1
94	KS44	Rear brake rod adjusting nut	1
95	SL56/4	Rear brake rod locknut, $\frac{1}{4}$" B.S.F.	1
96	S55/3	Rear brake torque stay	1
97	SL110/3	Rear brake torque stay bolt—front, $\frac{3}{8}$" B.S.F. × $1\frac{5}{8}$" U/H	1
98	LE369	Rear brake torque stay lockwasher, $\frac{3}{8}$"	1
99	SL56/7	Rear brake torque stay nut, $\frac{3}{8}$" B.S.F.	1
100	SL110/2	Rear brake torque stay bolt—rear, $\frac{3}{8}$" B.S.F. × $1\frac{1}{4}$" U/H	1
101	SL6/50	Rear brake torque stay bolt washer, $\frac{3}{8}$"	1

ILLUSTRATION F

ORDER BY PART NUMBERS—**DO NOT** QUOTE ILLUSTRATION REFERENCES.

FOR PART NUMBERS AND DESCRIPTIONS OF ITEMS see page 26

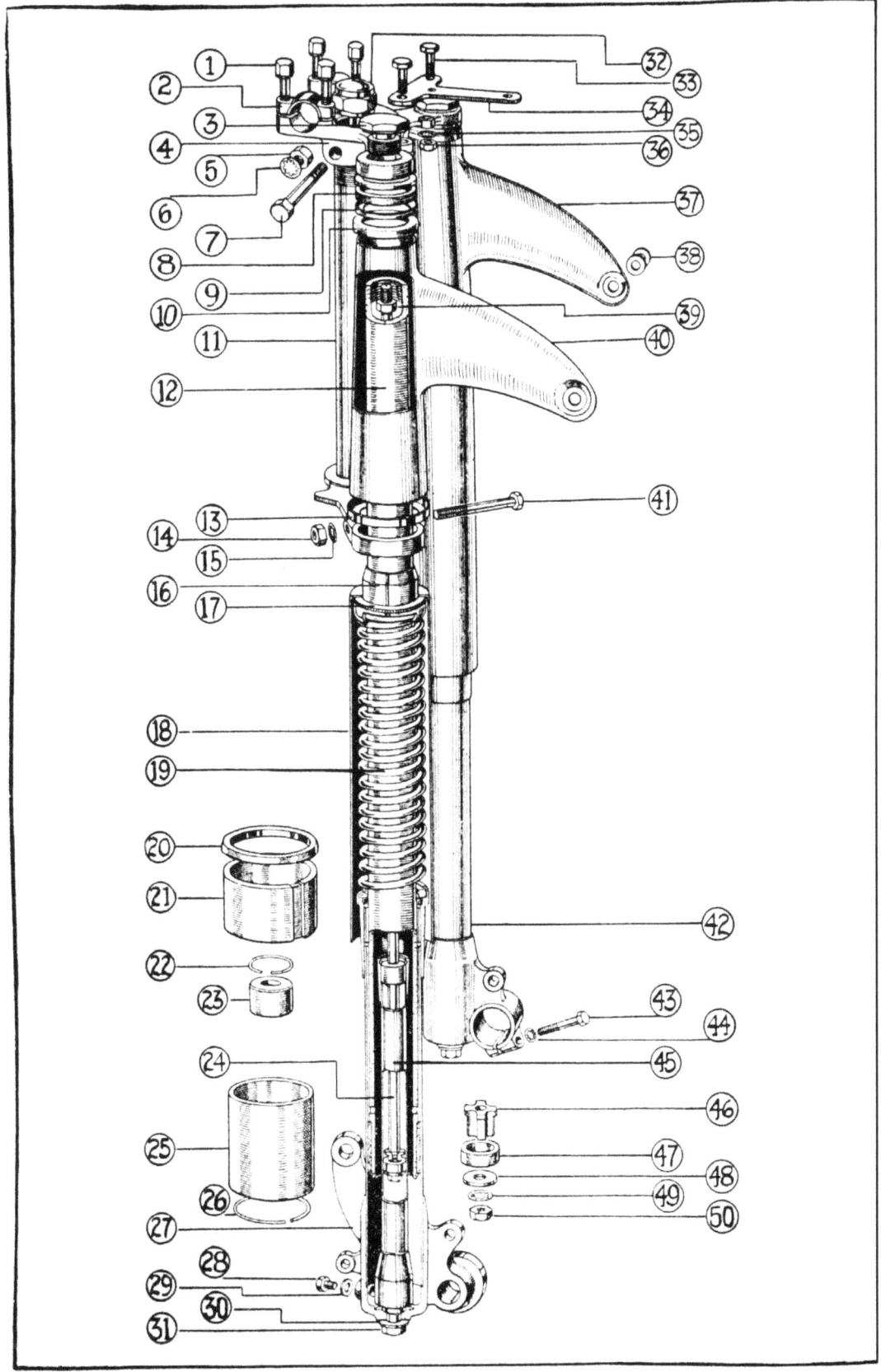

FRONT FORK SECTION. See Illustration "F," page 25.

Note.—Quote Part Numbers when ordering.
NOT Illustration Reference Numbers.

Illus. Ref.	Part No.	Description	Qty. Off.
1	F269	Handlebar clip bolt	4
2	F268	Handlebar clip	2
3	F253	Fork damper piston rod adaptor	2
4	F249/2	Fork cross member—top	1
5	SL56/7	Fork cross member nut, $\tfrac{3}{8}''$ B.S.F.	1
6	LE369	Fork cross member lockwasher, $\tfrac{3}{8}''$	1
7	SL110/4	Fork cross member clamp bolt, $\tfrac{3}{8}''$ B.S.F. $\times 1\tfrac{29}{32}''$ U/H	1
8	F272	Headlamp bracket sleeve—Rubber buffer	2
9	F278	Headlamp bracket sleeve housing—top	4
10	F271	Headlamp bracket locating cup	2
11	MAS7/2	Steering column assembly. (Column and bottom cross member)	1
12	F246	Front fork tube	2
13	F257	Headlamp bracket locating cup. Bottom	2
14	SL56/38	Fork cross member nut, $\tfrac{5}{16}''$ B.S.F.	2
15	LE368	Fork cross member lockwasher, $\tfrac{5}{16}''$	2
16	F262	Front fork tube (split) sleeve	2
17	F282	Front fork dust cover washer. Rubber	2
18	F245	Front fork spring dust cover	2
19	F252	Front fork spring	2
20	LE335/2	Fork slider tube oil seal	2
21	F256	Fork slider tube bush	2
22	F267	Fork damper bush circlip	2
23	F260	Fork damper bush	2
24	F259	Fork damper piston rod	2
25	LE216	Front fork tube bush	2
26	LE191	Front fork tube circlip	2
27	MAS4	Fork slider tube assembly. Right-hand, brake side	1
28	SL8/1	Fork oil drain bolt, $\tfrac{1}{4}''$ B.S.F. $\times \tfrac{3}{8}''$ U/H	2
29	A37/5	Fork oil drain bolt gasket	2
30	SL6/50	Fork damper tube adaptor washer, $\tfrac{3}{8}''$	2
31	SL56/7	Fork damper tube adaptor nut, $\tfrac{3}{8}''$ B.S.F.	2
32	MAS6	Steering column lock nut assembly	1
33	SL109/2	Speedometer bracket bolt, $\tfrac{5}{16}''$ B.S.F. $\times \tfrac{7}{8}''$ U/H	2
34	KA269/3	Speedometer bracket	1
35	LE368	Speedometer bracket bolt lockwasher, $\tfrac{5}{16}''$	2
36	SL56/38	Speedometer bracket bolt nut, $\tfrac{5}{16}''$ B.S.F.	2
37	MAS8	Headlamp bracket assembly. Left-hand side	1
38	F274	Headlamp washer—for licence holder fixing	1
39	SL56/38	Fork damper piston rod locknut, $\tfrac{5}{16}''$ B.S.F.	2
40	MAS9	Head lamp bracket assembly. Right-hand side	1
41	SL109/6	Fork cross member clamp bolt, $\tfrac{5}{16}''$ B.S.F. $\times 1\tfrac{31}{32}''$ U/H	2
42	MAS3	Fork slider tube assembly. Left-hand side	1
43	SL109/3	Front wheel spindle clamp bolt, $\tfrac{5}{16}''$ B.S.F. $\times 1\tfrac{3}{16}''$	1
44	LE368	Front wheel spindle clamp bolt lockwasher, $\tfrac{5}{16}''$	1
45	MAS5	Fork damper tube assembly	2
46	F251	Fork damper valve	2
47	F265	Fork damper piston	2
48	F266	Fork damper piston rod washer	2
49	LE366	Fork damper piston rod lockwasher $\tfrac{3}{16}''$	2
50	SL56/2	Fork damper piston rod nut, 2BA	2
		The front fork may be ordered fully assembled less speedometer bracket and bolts as:	
	MAS10/2	Front fork assembly	

ILLUSTRATION G

ORDER BY PART NUMBERS—DO NOT QUOTE ILLUSTRATION REFERENCES.

FOR PART NUMBERS AND DESCRIPTIONS OF ITEMS ON THIS PAGE see page 28

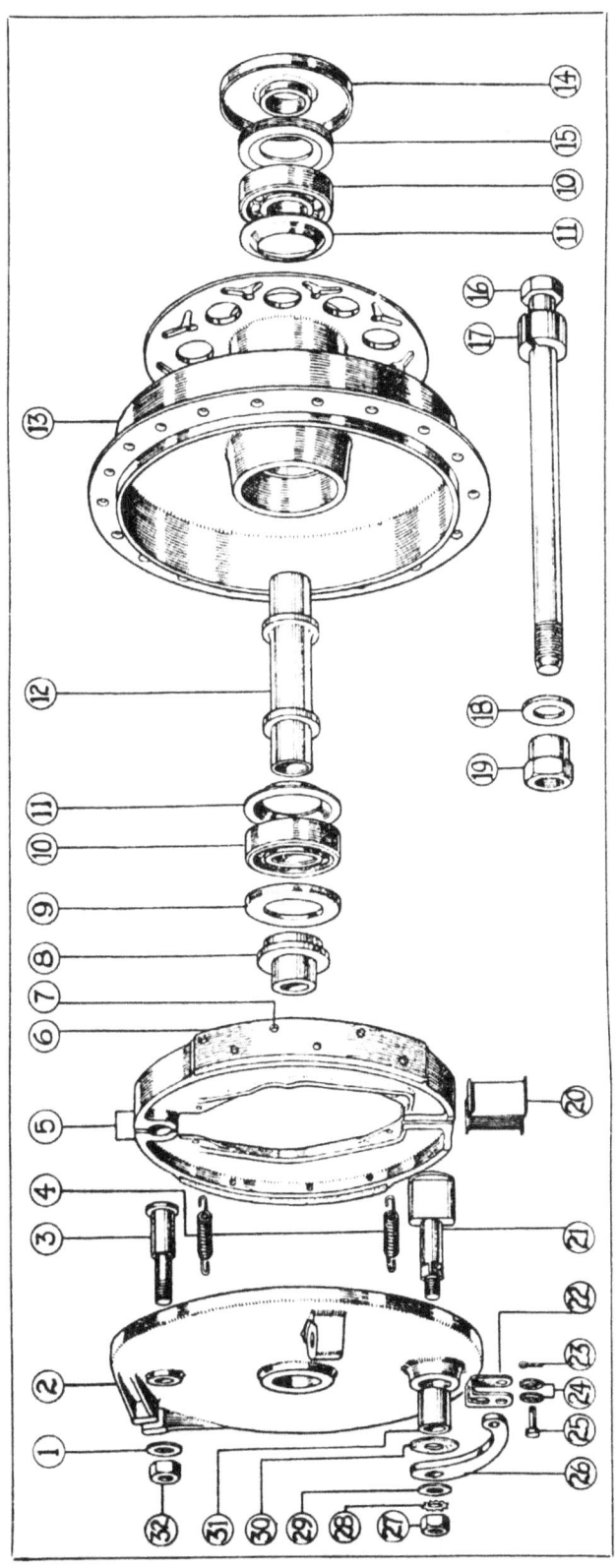

FRONT WHEEL AND BRAKE SECTION.
See Illustration "G," page 27.

Note.—Quote Part Numbers when ordering.
NOT Illustration Reference Numbers.

Illus. Ref.	Part No.	Description.	Qty. Off.
1	SL6/50	‡Front brake shoe fulcrum pin washer, $\frac{3}{8}$"	1
2	MAS72	‡Front brake plate assembly. Includes W71 bush	1
3	W10/4	‡Front brake shoe fulcrum pin	1
4	S27/2	‡Brake shoe spring	2
5	MAS74/75	‡Brake shoe assembly. Left and right-hand Includes lining and rivets .. pair	1
6	KS19/2	Brake shoe lining. Included in assemblies MAS74 and MAS75	2
7	KS31	Brake shoe lining rivet. Included in assemblies MAS74 and MAS75	12
8	W52/3	‡Front brake plate distance-piece	1
9	KS11/4	*Front hub inner dust cap	1
10	KS18/3	*Front hub ball bearing	2
11	KS57/3	*Front hub grease retainer	2
12	W62/2	*Front hub hollow spindle	1
13	MAS70	*Front hub shell assembly	1
14	MAS73	*Front hub outer dust cover assembly	1
15	KS61	*Front hub lockring	1
16	W21/6	Front wheel spindle	1
17	W64/2	Front wheel spindle distance piece	1
18	KS51/2	Front wheel spindle washer	1
19	W65/2	Front wheel spindle nut	1
20	KS16/2	Brake shoe slipper. Included in assemblies MAS74 and MAS75	2
21	MAS76	‡Front brake cam assembly	1
22	FB54	‡Front brake cable shackle	1
23	SL71/2	‡Clevis pin split cotter, $\frac{1}{16}$" × $\frac{1}{2}$"	1
24	FB61	‡Cable shackle felt washer	2
25	S32	‡Cable shackle clevis pin	1
26	FB11/5	‡Front brake cam lever	1
27	SL56/6	‡Front brake cam nut, $\frac{5}{16}$" 26 T.P.I.	1
28	LE368	‡Front brake cam lock washer, $\frac{5}{16}$"	1
29	FB60	‡Front brake cam lever washer	1
30	W12/2	‡Front brake cam felt washer	1
31	W71	Front brake cam bush. Included in assembly MAS72	1
32	SL56/8	‡Brake shoe fulcrum pin nut	1

Parts not illustrated—

	A17/8	†Front wheel rim, WM2 × 19" (36 holes)	1
	KA18/5	†Front wheel spoke, 10 S.W.G. × $6\frac{5}{8}$" long. Brake side	18
	KA18/26	†Front wheel spoke, 10 S.W.G. × $7\frac{1}{4}$" long. Left side	18
	KA19	†Front wheel spoke nipple, 10 S.W.G.	36

*These items may be ordered assembled as :
| | MAS69 | Front hub assembly. | |

†These items plus MAS69 may be ordered assembled as :
| | MAS67 | Front wheel assembly. | |

‡These items may be ordered assembled as :
| | MAS71 | Brake plate and shoe assembly. | |

ILLUSTRATION H

ORDER BY PART NUMBERS—**DO NOT** QUOTE ILLUSTRATION REFERENCES.

FOR PART NUMBERS AND DESCRIPTIONS OF ITEMS { 1 to 37 see page 30
38 to 71 ,, ,, 31
72 to 82 ,, ,, 32 }

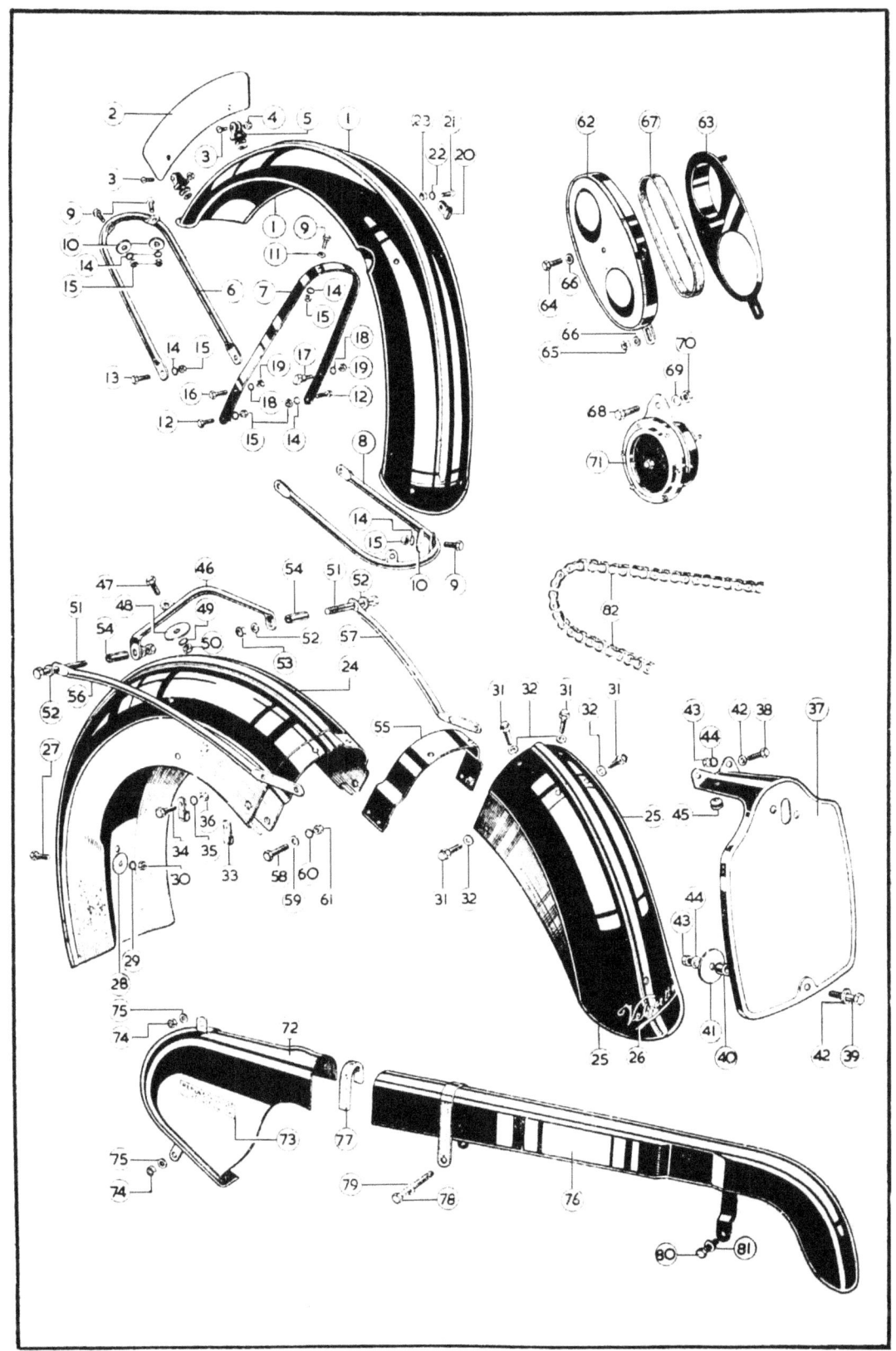

MUDGUARD, DYNAMO DRIVE COVER, CHAIN GUARD, CHAIN AND HORN SECTIONS.

See Illustration "H," page 29.
Front Mudguard Section.

Note.—Quote Part Numbers when ordering. NOT Illustration Reference Numbers.

Illus. Ref.	Part No.	Description.	Qty. Off.
1	KA16/9	Front mudguard. Includes A283 (2 off)	1
2	A23	Front number plate	1
3	SL80/22	Front number plate screw, 2BA × $\frac{3}{8}$" U/H	2
4	SL56/2	Front number plate screw nut, 2BA	2
5	A283	Front number plate clip assembly. Included in KA16/9	2
6	FK157/14AS	Front mudguard stay—front	1
7	FK157/15	Front mudguard stay—centre	1
8	FK157/16AS	Front mudguard stay—rear	1
9	SL8/3	Front mudguard stay fixing bolt, $\frac{1}{4}$" B.S.F. × $\frac{9}{16}$" U/H. (Stays to mudguard)	6
10	KA145/2	Front mudguard stay strengthening washer	4
11	SL6/32	Front mudguard stay washer, $\frac{1}{4}$"	2
12	SL8/14	Front mudguard stay fixing bolt, $\frac{1}{4}$" B.S.F. × 1" U/H. (Centre and rear stays to fork end)	2
13	SL8/29	Front mudguard stay fixing bolt, $\frac{1}{4}$" B.S.F. × $\frac{3}{4}$" U/H. (Front stay to fork end)	2
14	LE367	Front mudguard stay lock washer, $\frac{1}{4}$"	10
15	SL56/4	Front mudguard stay nut, $\frac{1}{4}$" B.S.F.	10
16	SL9/6	Front mudguard stay fixing bolt, $\frac{5}{16}$" 26 T.P.I. × $\frac{13}{16}$" U/H. (Centre stay to fork end)	1
17	FK50/2	Brake torque bolt. (Centre stay to fork end—R H)	1
18	LE368	Front mudguard stay lock washer, $\frac{5}{16}$"	2
19	SL56/6	Front mudguard stay nut, $\frac{5}{16}$" 26 T.P.I.	2
20	LE201/2	Front brake cable clip. Cable assembly to mudguard	1
21	SL8/26	Front brake cable clip bolt, $\frac{1}{4}$" B.S.F. × $\frac{7}{16}$" U/H	1
22	LE367	Front brake cable clip lock washer, $\frac{1}{4}$"	1
23	SL56/4	Front brake cable clip nut, $\frac{1}{4}$" B.S.F.	1

Rear Mudguard Section. Mudguard, Extension and Number Plate Group.

Illus. Ref.	Part No.	Description.	Qty. Off.
24	A15/12	*Rear mudguard	1
25	MAS85	*Rear mudguard extension assembly. Includes A131 transfer	1
26	A131	Rear mudguard transfer. Included in A15/12	1
	MAS84	*These two items may be ordered together as: Rear mudguard assembly	1
27	SL8/3	Rear mudguard bolt, $\frac{1}{4}$" B.S.F. × $\frac{9}{16}$" U/H. (Guard to seat tube lug)	2
28	KA145/2	Rear mudguard bolt washer	2
29	LE367	Rear mudguard bolt lock washer, $\frac{1}{4}$"	2
30	SL56/4	Rear mudguard bolt nut, $\frac{1}{4}$" B.S.F.	2
31	KA303	Rear mudguard extension bolt. (Extension to mudguard)	4
32	SL6/32	Rear mudguard extension bolt washer, $\frac{1}{4}$"	4
33	F306	Rear mudguard clip. Tail lamp cable fixing	2
34	SL8/26	Rear mudguard clip bolt, $\frac{1}{4}$" B.S.F. × $\frac{7}{16}$" U/H	1
35	LE367	Rear mudguard clip lock washer, $\frac{1}{4}$"	1
36	SL56/4	Rear mudguard clip nut, $\frac{1}{4}$" B.S.F.	1
37	A22/20	Rear number plate	1

Mudguard, Dynamo Drive Cover, Chain Guard, Chain and Horn Sections—*continued.*

Illus. Ref.	*Part No.*	*Description.*	*Qty. Off.*
38	SL8/26	Rear number plate bolt, top, $\frac{1}{4}''$ B.S.F. × $\frac{7}{16}''$ U/H	1
39	SL8/14	Rear number plate bolt—bottom, $\frac{1}{4}''$ B.S.F. × 1″ U/H	1
40	A181	Rear number plate bolt buffer..	1
41	KA145/2	Rear number plate bolt washer	1
42	SL6/32	Rear number plate bolt washer, $\frac{1}{4}''$	3
43	SL56/4	Rear number plate bolt nut, $\frac{1}{4}''$ B.S.F. ..	3
44	LE367	Rear number plate bolt lock washer, $\frac{1}{4}''$ ..	3
45	A20	Rear number plate grommet (for Tail lamp cable)	1

Bridge, Stay and Lifting Handle Group.

46	MAS60	Rear mudguard stay assembly	1
47	SL8/3	Rear mudguard stay bolt, $\frac{1}{4}''$ B.S.F. × $\frac{9}{16}''$ U/H. (Stay to guard)	2
48	KA145/2	Rear mudguard stay washer	2
49	LE367	Rear mudguard stay lock washer, $\frac{1}{4}''$ ..	2
50	SL56/4	Rear mudguard stay nut, $\frac{1}{4}''$ B.S.F.	2
51	SL109/6	Rear mudguard stay bolt, $\frac{5}{16}''$ B.S.F. × $1\frac{31}{32}''$ U/H. (Stay to frame)	2
52	SL6/40	Rear mudguard stay bolt washer, $\frac{5}{16}''$ ..	2
53	SL56/38	Rear mudguard stay bolt nut, $\frac{5}{16}''$ B.S.F. ..	2
54	F303	Rear mudguard stay distance piece	2
55	MAS61	Rear mudguard bridge assembly	1
56	FK58/62	Lifting handle, L/H	1
57	FK58/63	Lifting handle, R/H	1
58	SL8/3	Lifting handle bolt, $\frac{1}{4}''$ B.S.F. × $\frac{9}{16}''$ U/H. (Lifting handle to guard)	2
59	SL6/32	Lifting handle bolt washer, $\frac{1}{4}''$..	2
60	LE367	Lifting handle bolt lock washer, $\frac{1}{4}''$	2
61	SL56/4	Lifting handle bolt nut, $\frac{1}{4}''$ B.S.F.	2

Dynamo Belt and Cover Section.

62	KA93/3AS	Dynamo belt cover assembly—Front ..	1
63	KA93/6AS	Dynamo belt cover assembly—Rear	1
64	SL8/26	Dynamo belt cover bolt, $\frac{1}{4}''$ B.S.F. × $\frac{7}{16}''$ U/H	1
65	SL56/4	Dynamo belt cover nut, $\frac{1}{4}''$ B.S.F.	1
66	SL6/32	Dynamo belt cover washer, $\frac{1}{4}''$	2
67	E16/2	Dynamo belt	1

Electric Horn and Mounting Section.

68	SL109/1	Horn fixing bolt, $\frac{5}{16}''$ B.S.F. × $\frac{5}{8}''$ U/H ..	1
69	SL6/40	Horn fixing bolt washer, $\frac{5}{16}''$	1
70	SL56/38	Horn fixing bolt nut, $\frac{5}{16}''$ B.S.F.	1
71	E21/4	Electric horn assembly	1

Mudguard, Dynamo Drive Cover, Chain Guard, Chain and Horn Sections—*continued.*

Chain and Chainguard Section.

Illus. Ref.	Part No.	Description.	Qty. Off.
72	MAS24	Rear chain cover assembly. Includes A253 transfer	1
73	A253	Rear chain cover transfer. Included in MAS24	1
74	SL56/4	Chain case fixing nut, $\frac{1}{4}''$ B.S.F. To primary chain case	2
75	SL6/32	Chain case fixing nut washer, $\frac{1}{4}''$	2
76	MAS95	Rear chain guard and felt assembly. Includes F291 Joint strip	1
77	F291	Rear chain guard joint strip. Included in MAS25	1
78	SL108/4	Rear chain guard bolt—front, $\frac{1}{4}''$ B.S.F. × $1\frac{1}{2}''$ U/H	1
79	SL6/32	Rear chain guard bolt washer, $\frac{1}{4}''$	1
80	SL109/5	Rear chain guard bolt—Rear, $\frac{5}{16}''$ B.S.F. × $\frac{1}{2}''$ U/H	1
81	SL6/40	Rear chain guard bolt washer, $\frac{5}{16}''$	1
82	{ KA27/4	Primary chain, $\frac{1}{2}'' \times .305'' \times 67$ Pitches	1
	A28/8	Rear chain, $\frac{1}{2}'' \times .305'' \times 124$ Pitches	1

ILLUSTRATION I

ORDER BY PART NUMBERS—DO NOT QUOTE ILLUSTRATION REFERENCES.

FOR PART NUMBERS AND DESCRIPTIONS OF ITEMS { 1 to 43 see page 34
44 to 80 ,, ,, 35

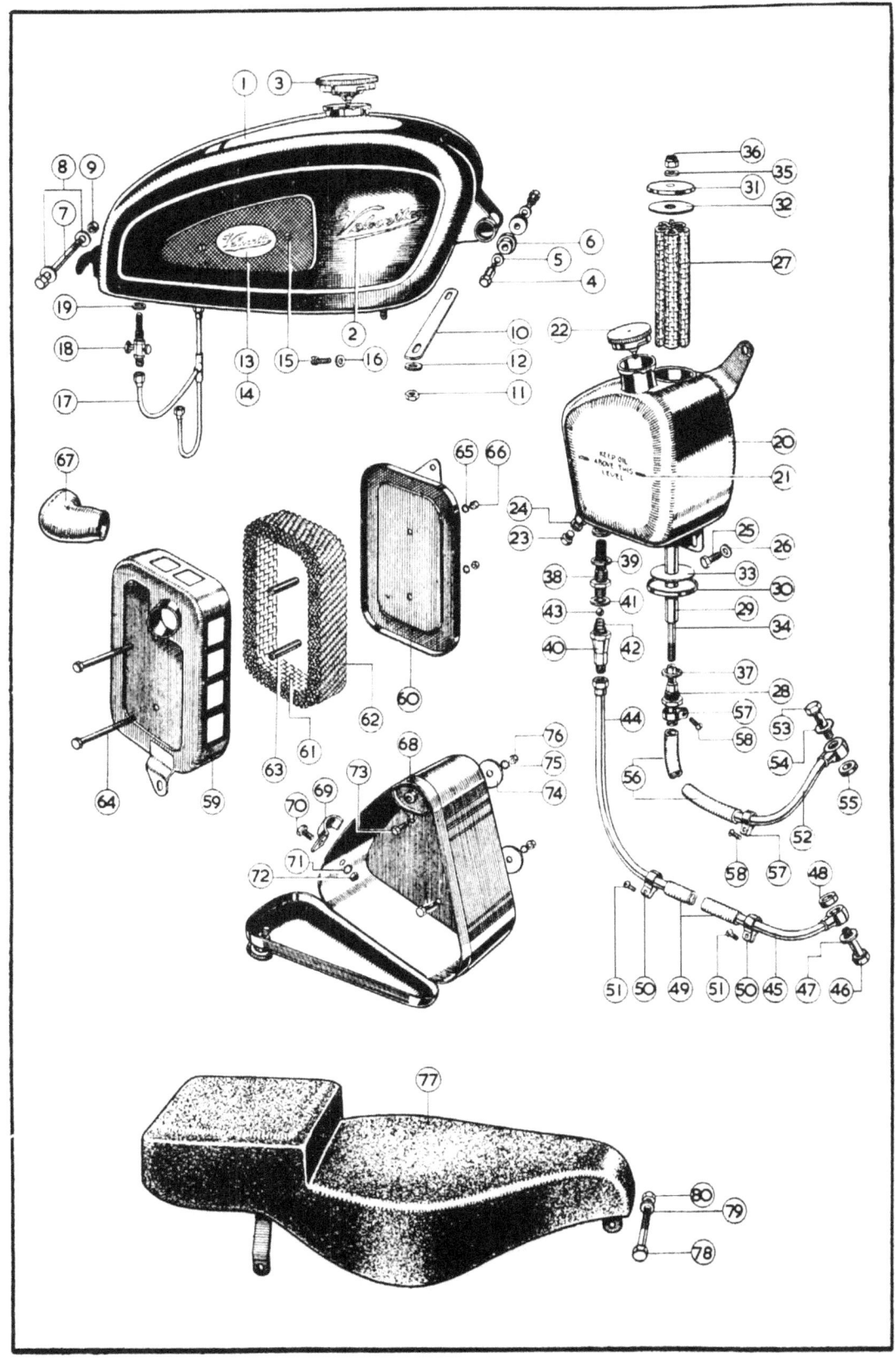

PETROL TANK, OIL TANK, OIL FILTER, OIL PIPE, AIR CLEANER TOOL BOX AND SEAT SECTIONS.

See Illustration "I," page 33.

Petrol Tank Section—Tank and Mounting Group.

Note.—Quote Part Numbers when ordering.
NOT Illustration Reference Numbers.

Illus. Ref.	Part No.	Description.	Qty. Off.
1	MAS63	Petrol tank—Enamelled, lined, and transferred	1
2	A132	Petrol tank transfer	2
3	KA4/9	Petrol tank cap	1
4	FK152/2	Petrol tank fixing bolt—front	2
5	SL6/57	Petrol tank fixing bolt washer, $\frac{7}{16}'' \times \frac{7}{8}''$ O/D	2
6	FK151/4	Petrol tank fixing bolt buffer	2
7	SL9/18	Petrol tank fixing bolt—rear, $\frac{5}{16}''$ 26 T.P.I. $\times 2\frac{11}{16}''$ U H	1
8	SL6/43	Petrol tank fixing bolt washer, $\frac{5}{16}'' \times 1''$ O/D	2
9	SL56/6	Petrol tank fixing bolt nut, $\frac{5}{16}''$ 26 T.P.I.	1
10	A276/2	Petrol tank strap	1
11	SL56/4	Petrol tank strap nut, $\frac{1}{4}''$ B.S.F.	2
12	SL6/32	Petrol tank strap washer, $\frac{1}{4}''$	2

Petrol Pipe, Tap, and Knee Grip Group.

13	KA70/5AS	Petrol tank knee grip—Right-hand side	1
14	KA70/6AS	Petrol tank knee grip—Left-hand side	1
15	KA287	Petrol tank knee grip screw	4
16	SL6/32	Petrol tank knee grip washer, $\frac{1}{4}''$	4
17	MAS27	Petrol pipe assembly	1
18	A2/5	Petrol tap	2
19	KA115	Petrol tap gasket	2

Oil Tank, Oil Filter, and Ball Valve Section.

20	MAS13/2	Oil tank assembly. Enamelled and transferred	1
21	A134/2	Oil tank transfer	1
22	KA6/6	Oil tank filler cap	1
23	B38	Oil tank drain plug, $\frac{1}{8}''$ B.S.P.	1
24	A37	Oil tank drain plug gasket	1
25	SL9/3	Oil tank fixing bolt—bottom, $\frac{5}{16}''$ 26 T.P.I. $\times \frac{1}{2}''$ U H	1
26	SL6/40	Oil tank fixing bolt washer, $\frac{5}{16}''$	1
27	A288	Oil tank filter element	1
28	A292	*Oil tank filter cap adaptor	1
29	A293/2	*Oil tank filter centre tube	1
30	LE543	Oil tank filter cap—Bottom	1
31	LE570	Oil tank filter cap—Top	1
32	LE572	Oil tank filter cap gasket—top	1
33	A287	Oil tank filter cap gasket—bottom	1
34	SL102/13	Oil tank stud, $\frac{1}{4}''$ B.S.F. $\times 7\frac{3}{4}''$ long	1
35	A37/5	Oil tank stud gasket	1
36	A291	Oil tank stud nut. (Simmonds NP/F.082), $\frac{1}{4}''$ B.S.F.	1
37	LE573	Oil tank filter cap adaptor gasket	1
38	MAS14	Ball valve union assembly	1
39	KA115/2	Ball valve union gasket	1
40	M253	Ball valve body	1
41	KA115/3	Ball valve body gasket	1
42	M255	Ball valve spring	1
43	W15/2	Ball valve ball	1

* May be ordered together as MAS94/2 Oil filter centre tube assembly.

Petrol Tank, Oil Tank, Oil Filter, Oil Pipe, Air Cleaner, Tool Box, and Seat Sections—*continued.*

Oil Pipe Section.

Illus. Ref.	Part No.	Description.	Qty. Off.
44	MAS15/2	Oil feed pipe assembly—Tank end	1
45	MAS26	Oil feed pipe assembly—Engine end	1
46	M214	Oil feed pipe hollow bolt—for banjo union	1
47	A37	Oil feed pipe banjo gasket—Outer	1
48	A37/4	Oil feed pipe banjo gasket—Inner. (Between banjo and crankcase)	1
49	KA264/2	†Oil feed pipe hose, $\frac{3}{8}$" bore × $8\frac{1}{2}$" long	1
50	KA100/16	Oil feed pipe hose clip ⎫ These supplied ⎫	2
51	LE433	Oil feed pipe hose clip screw ⎭ together only. ⎭	2
52	MAS90	Oil return pipe assembly	1
53	M214	Oil return pipe hollow bolt	1
54	A37	Oil return pipe banjo gasket—Outer	1
55	A37/4	Oil return pipe banjo gasket—Inner. (Between banjo and crank case)	1
56	KA221/14	‡Oil return pipe hose, $\frac{5}{16}$" bore × 19" long	1
57	KA100	Oil return pipe hose clip ⎫ Supplied ⎫	2
58	LE433	Oil return pipe hose clip screw ⎭ together only ⎭	2

† May be ordered by the foot as part number KA264.
‡ May be ordered by the foot as part number KA102.

Air Cleaner Section.

59	MAS59	*Air cleaner body assembly	1
60	MAS62	*Air cleaner cover assembly	1
61	A303	*Air cleaner element gauze	1
62	A304	*Air cleaner element. (Knitted steel wire)	1
63	A305	*Air cleaner distance piece	2
64	SL107/6	*Air cleaner pin, 2BA × $1\frac{5}{8}$"	2
65	LE366	*Air cleaner pin lockwasher, $\frac{3}{16}$"	2
66	SL56/2	*Air cleaner pin nut, 2BA	2
67	A297	Air cleaner connecting elbow—to carburetter	1
—	MAS51	Air cleaner assembly. Assembly of items marked *	1

* These items may be ordered assembled as MAS51 Air cleaner assembly.

Toolbox Section.

68	MAS37	Toolbox with knob assembly	1
69	A153/2	Toolbox fixing clip	1
70	SL8/3	Toolbox fixing clip bolt, $\frac{1}{4}$" B.S.F. × $\frac{9}{16}$" U/H	1
71	LE367	Toolbox fixing clip bolt lockwasher, $\frac{1}{4}$"	1
72	SL56/4	Toolbox fixing clip bolt nut, $\frac{1}{4}$" B.S.F.	1
73	SL8/26	Toolbox fixing bolt $\frac{1}{4}$" B.S.F. × $\frac{7}{16}$" U/H	2
74	KA145/2	Toolbox fixing bolt washer	2
75	LE367	Toolbox fixing bolt lockwasher, $\frac{1}{4}$"	2
76	SL56/4	Toolbox fixing bolt nut, $\frac{1}{4}$"	2

Dual Seat Section.

77	MAS89	Dual Seat	1
78	SL11/18	Dual Seat fixing bolt, $\frac{3}{8}$" 26 T.P.I. × $2\frac{1}{16}$" U/H	1
79	SL6/50	Dual Seat fixing bolt washer, $\frac{3}{8}$"	1
80	SL56/17	Dual Seat fixing bolt nut, $\frac{3}{8}$" 26 T.P.I.	1

ILLUSTRATION J

ORDER BY PART NUMBERS—**DO NOT** QUOTE ILLUSTRATION REFERENCES.

FOR PART NUMBERS AND DESCRIPTIONS OF ITEMS { 1 to 17 see page 37
18 to 45 ,, ,, 38

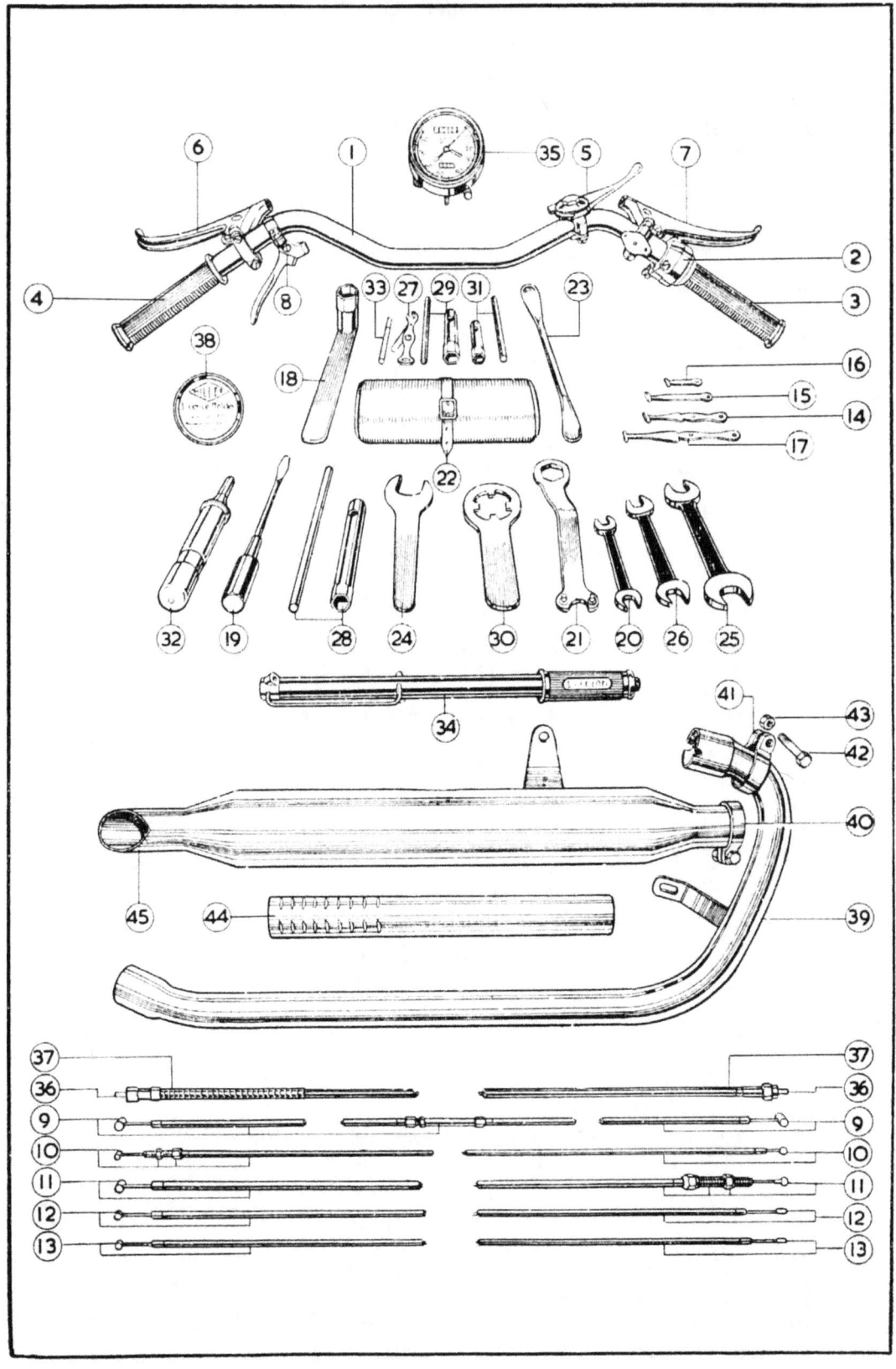

HANDLEBAR, CONTROLS, CABLES, TOOL KIT, SPEEDOMETER, LICENCE HOLDER, AND EXHAUST SYSTEM SECTIONS.

See Illustration "J," page 36.

Handlebar and Control Section. Handlebar, Twist Grip, and Lever Group.

Note.—Quote Part Numbers when ordering. NOT Illustration Reference Numbers.

Illus. Ref.	Part No.	Description.	Qty. Off.
1	{ FK61/8	Handlebar bend. Standard	1
	{ F61/5	Handlebar bend. Special American style upswept	1
2	A211/2	Twist grip assembly. Includes twist grip rubber A220/2	1
3	A220/2	Twist grip rubber. Included in assembly A211/2	1
4	A225/2	Handlebar grip. (Amal No. 16/069)	1
5	A36/3	Handlebar air control lever (Amal No. 12/120)	1
6	KC16/3	Handlebar clutch or brake lever. (Amal No. 18/582)	2
7	KC16/4	Handlebar brake lever. With platform clip for flange fitting horn push	1
8	A72/3	Handlebar exhaust lifter lever (Amal. No. 18/453)	1

Cable Assembly and Cable Clip Group.

Illus. Ref.	Part No.	Description.	Qty. Off.
9	{ KC17/9AS	Clutch cable assembly—standard	1
	{ KC17/10AS	Clutch cable assembly. Special length for use with American style bar	1
10	{ A125/4AS	Exhaust lifter cable assembly—Standard	1
	{ A125/5AS	Exhaust lifter cable assembly. Special length for use with American style bar	1
11	{ W33/6AS	Front brake cable assembly—Standard	1
	{ W33/8AS	Front brake cable assembly. Special length for use with Americal style bar	1
12	{ A237/3AS	Air cable assembly—Standard	1
	{ A237/4AS	Air cable assembly. Special length for use with American style bar	1
13	{ A234/10AS	Throttle cable assembly—Standard	1
	{ A234/11AS	Throttle cable assembly. Special length for use with American style bar	1
14	A256	Cable clip—Rubber. (John Bull type 'S')	1
15	A256/2	Cable clip—Rubber. (John Bull type 'C')	4
16	A256/3	Cable clip—Rubber. (John Bull type 'D')	1
17	A256/4	Cable clip—Rubber. (John Bull type 'A')	2

Handlebar Controls, Cables, Tool Kit, Speedometer, Licence Holder and Exhaust System Sections—*continued*.

Tool Kit and Inflator Section.

Illus. Ref.	Part No.	Description.	Qty. Off.
18	A55/4	*Sparking plug and suction filter plug spanner	1
19	A57	*Screwdriver	1
20	A58	*Double open-ended spanner, $\frac{1}{8}'' \times \frac{3}{16}''$ Whit.	1
21	A61/2AS	*Peg spanner	1
22	A63	*Tool roll	1
23	A64	*Tyre lever	1
24	A65/2	*Steering head locknut spanner	1
25	A101	*Double open-ended spanner, $\frac{3}{8}'' \times \frac{7}{16}''$ Whit.	1
26	A102	*Double open-ended spanner, $\frac{1}{4}'' \times \frac{5}{16}''$ Whit.	1
27	A154/2	*Magneto spanner	1
28	A227	*Tubular spanner, $\frac{3}{8}''$ Whitworth—and tommy bar	1
29	A228	*Tubular spanner, $\frac{1}{4}''$ Whitworth—and tommy bar	1
30	A229	*Shock absorber nut spanner	1
31	A248	*Tubular spanner, $\frac{3}{16}''$ Whitworth—and tommy bar	1
32	KA51	*Grease gun	1
33	KA62/2	*Clutch adjusting tool	1

* **Note.**—The sixteen items above may be ordered as :

—	MAS88	Toolkit assembly. Includes all items in the section marked *	
34	A25/3	Tyre inflator	1

Speedometer and Drive Section.

35	KA268/5	Speedometer. Calibrated in miles per hour	1
36	KA270/4	†Speedometer drive cable	1
37	KA271/4	†Speedometer drive cable casing	1

†These may be ordered together as :

—	MAS58	Speedometer drive cable assembly. Comprising items marked †	

Licence Holder Section.

38	A157	Licence holder	1
—	LE458	§Licence holder glass	1
—	LE459	§Licence holder rubber ring	1
—	LE460	§Licence holder rim	1

§ These items, which are included in A157 Licence holder can only be supplied together.

Exhaust Pipe and Silencer Section.

39	MAS28	Exhaust pipe assembly	1
40	A141/2	Exhaust pipe clip—Silencer end	1
41	A141/3	Exhaust pipe clip. Engine end	1
42	SL108/3	Exhaust pipe clip bolt, $\frac{1}{4}''$ B.S.F. $\times 1\frac{3}{8}''$ U/H	2
43	SL56/4	Exhaust pipe clip nut, $\frac{1}{4}''$ B.S.F.	2
44	KA142/4	Silencer baffle	1
45	MAS30	Silencer assembly	1

ILLUSTRATION K

ORDER BY PART NUMBERS—DO NOT QUOTE ILLUSTRATION REFERENCES.
FOR PART NUMBERS AND DESCRIPTIONS OF ITEMS ON THIS PAGE see page 40

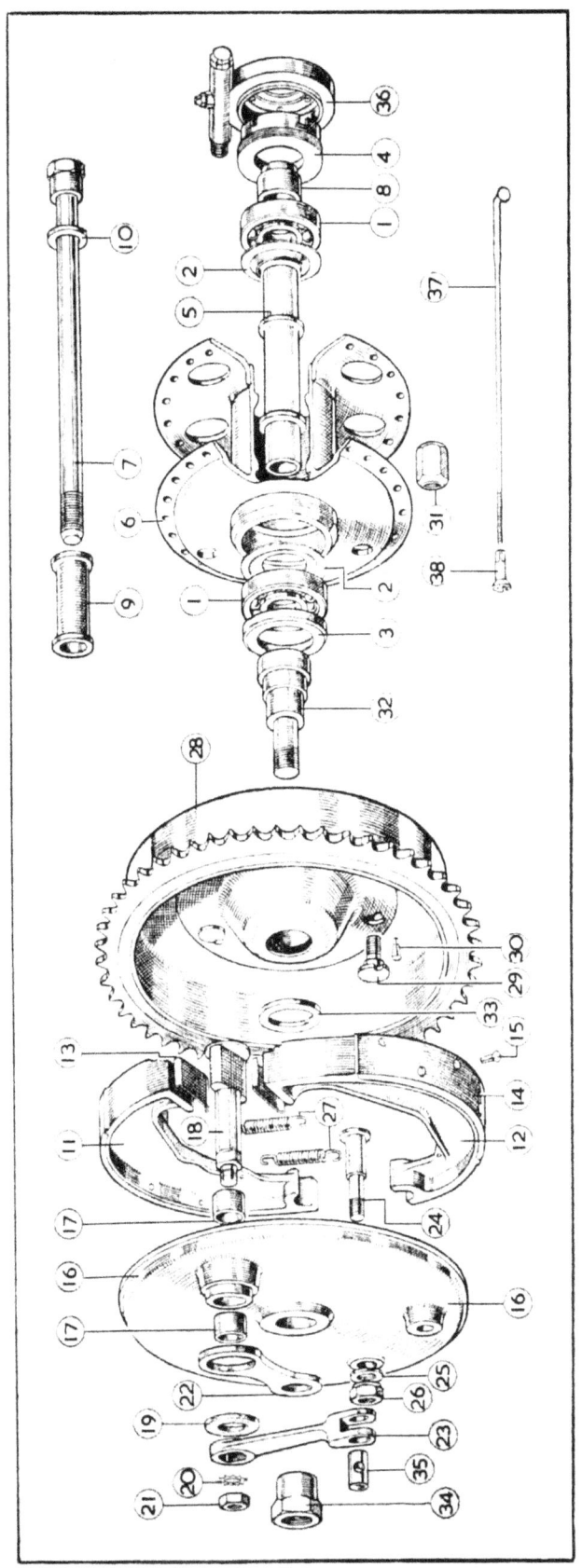

REAR WHEEL AND BRAKE SECTION.
See Illustration "K," page 39.

Note.—Quote Part Numbers when ordering.
NOT Illustration Reference Numbers.

Illus. Ref.	Part No.	Description.	Qty. Off.
1	KS18/3	*Rear hub ball bearing	2
2	KS57/3	*Rear hub grease retainer	2
3	KS11/4	*Rear hub inner dust cap	1
4	KS61/2	*Rear hub retaining ring	1
5	KS8/9	*Rear hub hollow spindle	1
6	MAS83	*Rear hub assembly	1
7	KS8/10	Rear wheel spindle	1
8	KS62/3	Rear hub clamping sleeve	1
9	KS52/4	Rear wheel distance piece	1
10	KS51/2	Rear wheel spindle washer	1
11	MAS75	§Brake shoe assembly—R.H. ⎧Not supplied⎫	1
12	MAS74	§Brake shoe assembly—L.H. ⎩separately⎭	1
13	KS16/2	§Brake shoe slipper. (Included in assemblies MAS74 and MAS75)	2
14	KS19/2	Brake shoe lining. (Included in assemblies MAS74 and MAS75)	2
15	KS31	Brake shoe lining rivet	12
16	MAS81	§Rear brake plate assembly	1
17	S68	§Rear brake plate bush. (Included in assembly MAS81)	2
18	MAS78	§Rear brake cam assembly	1
19	LE106	§Rear brake cam felt washer	1
20	LE369	§Rear brake cam lockwasher, ⅜"	1
21	SL56/8	§Rear brake cam nut, ⅜" 26 T.P.I.	1
22	S41/5	§Rear brake cam steady	1
23	S3/5	§Rear brake lever	1
24	W10/4	§Brake shoe fulcrum pin	1
25	SL6/50	§Brake shoe fulcrum pin washer, ⅜" × ¾" O/D	1
26	SL56/8	§Brake shoe fulcrum pin nut, ⅜" 26 T.P.I.	1
27	S27/2	§Brake shoe spring	2
28	MAS77	Rear brake drum assembly. Includes KS12/4 Stud and KS73 Locking peg	1
29	KS12/4	Rear brake drum driving stud. Included in assembly MAS77	3
30	KS73	Rear brake drum locking peg. Included in in assembly MAS77	3
31	KS60	Rear brake drum stud nut	3
32	S66/3	Rear brake plate locking bolt	1
33	S67	Rear brake plate washer	1
34	W65/2	Rear wheel spindle nut	1
35	FK43/2	Rear brake rod trunnion. Plain hole	1
36	KA272/2	Speedometer drive reduction gearbox	1
37	KA18/25	†Rear wheel spoke, 8/10 S.W.G. × 7⅛" long	40
38	KA19	†Rear wheel spoke nipple, 10 S.W.G.	40
—	A17/7	†Rear wheel rim, WM2 × 19", (40 holes)	1

* These items may be ordered assembled as :
    MAS82   Rear hub assembly.

† These items, together with MAS82 may be ordered assembled as :
    MAS79   Rear wheel assembly.

§ These items may be ordered assembled as :
    MAS80   Brake plate and shoes assembly.

VELOCEPRESS MANUALS – MOTORCYCLE BY MAKE

AJS 1932-1948 SINGLES & TWINS 250cc THRU 1000cc (BOOK OF)
AJS 1945-1960 SINGLES 350cc & 500cc MODELS 16 & 18 (BOOK OF)
AJS 1955-1965 SINGLES 350cc & 500cc (BOOK OF)
AJS 1957-1966 FACTORY WSM - ALL SINGLES & TWINS
AJS 1959-1969 FACTORY WSM G80CS G85CS & P11 OFF ROAD
ARIEL UP TO 1932 (BOOK OF)
ARIEL 1932-1939 PREWAR MODELS (BOOK OF)
ARIEL 1933-1951 (WORKSHOP MANUAL)
ARIEL 1939-1960 4 STROKE SINGLES (BOOK OF)
ARIEL 1958-1964 LEADER & ARROW FACTORY WSM & PARTS LIST
ARIEL 1958-1964 LEADER & ARROW (BOOK OF)
BMW R26 R27 (1956-1967) FACTORY WORKSHOP MANUAL
BMW R50 R50S R60 R69S (1955-1969) FACTORY WORKSHOP MANUAL
BMW R50/5 R60/5 R75/5 (1969-1973) FACTORY WORKSHOP MANUAL
BRIDGESTONE 90 SERIES FACTORY WSM & PARTS CATALOGUE
BRIDGESTONE 175 SERIES FACTORY WSM & PARTS CATALOGUE
BRIDGESTONE 350 SERIES FACTORY WSM & PARTS CATALOGUES
BSA SERVICE SHEETS MASTER CATALOGUE ALL MODELS 1945-1967
BSA BANTAM D1 TO D7 1948-1966 FACTORY SERVICE SHEETS MANUAL
BSA BANTAM ALL MODELS FROM 1948 ONWARDS (BOOK OF)
BSA BANTAM D14 FACTORY SERVICE MANUAL
BSA DANDY FACTORY WORKSHOP MANUAL (COMPILATION)
BSA SINGLES & V-TWINS UP TO 1926 inc. 1927 SUPPLEMENT (BOOK OF)
BSA SINGLES & V-TWINS UP TO 1930 (BOOK OF)
BSA SINGLES & V-TWINS UP TO 1935 (BOOK OF)
BSA SINGLES & V-TWINS 1936-1939 (BOOK OF)
BSA C10, C11 & C12 1945-1958 FACTORY SERVICE SHEETS MANUAL
BSA OHV & SV SINGLES 250-600cc 1945-1959 (BOOK OF)
BSA C15 & B40 1958-1967 FACTORY SERVICE SHEETS MANUAL
BSA OHV & SV SINGLES 250cc (ONLY) 1954-1970 (BOOK OF)
BSA B31, B32, B33 & B34 1945-60 FACTORY SERVICE SHEETS MANUAL
BSA OHV SINGLES 350 & 500cc 1955-1967 (BOOK OF)
BSA M20, M21 & M33 1945-1963 FACTORY SERVICE SHEETS MANUAL
BSA TWINS A7 & A10 1948-1962 FACTORY SERVICE SHEETS MANUAL
BSA TWINS A7 & A10 1948-1962 (BOOK OF)
BSA TWINS A50 & A65 1962-1965 FACTORY WORKSHOP MANUAL
BSA TWINS A50 & A65 1962-1969 (SECOND BOOK OF)
DOUGLAS 1929-1939 PREWAR ALL MODELS (BOOK OF)
DOUGLAS 1948-1957 POSTWAR ALL MODELS FACTORY SHOP MANUAL
DUCATI 160cc, 250cc & 350cc OHC MODELS FACTORY SHOP MANUAL
HONDA 50cc ALL MODELS UP TO 1970 INC MONKEY & TRAIL (BOOK OF)
HONDA 90cc ALL MODELS UP TO 1966 (BOOK OF)
HONDA TWINS & SINGLES 50cc THRU 305cc 1960-1966 (BOOK OF)
HONDA TWINS ALL MODELS 125cc THRU 450cc UP TO 1968 (BOOK OF)
HONDA C100 50cc SUPER CUB O.H.C. 1959-1962 FACTORY WSM
HONDA C110 50cc SPORT CUB O.H.C. 1960-1962 FACTORY WSM
HONDA 50-65-70-90cc O.H.C. SINGLES 1959-1983 WSM
HONDA 100-125cc SINGLES CB/CD/CL/SL/TL 1970-1984 FACTORY WSM
HONDA 125-150cc TWINS C/CS/CB/CA 1959-1966 FACTORY WSM
HONDA 125-160-175-200cc TWINS 1965-1978 WORKSHOP MANUAL
HONDA 250-305cc TWINS C/CS/CB 1961-1968 FACTORY WSM
HOHDA 250-350cc TWINS CB/CL/SL 1968-1973 FACTORY WSM
HONDA 250-360cc TWINS CB/CL/CJ 1974-1977 FACTORY WSM
HONDA 354F & 400F 4-CYLINDER 1972-1977 FACTORY WSM
HONDA 450cc TWINS CB/CL 1965-1974 K0 TO K7 WORKSHOP MANUAL
HONDA 500cc & 550cc 4-CYL 1971-1978 FACTORY WORKSHOP MANUAL
HONDA 750cc SHOC 4-CYL 1969-1978 K0~K8 WORKSHOP MANUAL
INDIAN PONYBIKE, BOY RACER & PAPOOSE ILL PARTS LIST & SALES LIT

J.A.P. ENGINES 1927-1952 & MOTORCYCLES 1934-1952 (BOOK OF)
MATCHLESS 1931-1939 ALL MODELS 250cc THRU 990cc (BOOK OF)
MATCHLESS 1945-1956 350 & 500cc SINGLES (BOOK OF)
MATCHLESS 1955-1966 350 & 500cc SINGLES (BOOK OF)
MATCHLESS 1957-1966 FACTORY WSM - ALL SINGLES & TWINS
NEW IMPERIAL ALL SV & OHV FROM 1935 ONWARDS (BOOK OF)
NORTON 1932-1939 PREWAR MODELS (BOOK OF)
NORTON 1932-1947 (BOOK OF)
NORTON 1938-1956 (BOOK OF)
NORTON 1945-1963 MODELS 16H, Big4, ES2, 19 & 50 WSM'S & PARTS
NORTON 1955-1963 MODELS 19, 50 & ES2 (BOOK OF)
NORTON 1948-1970 DOMINATOR TWINS FACTORY WSM'S & PARTS
NORTON 1955-1965 DOMINATOR TWINS (BOOK OF)
NORTON 1960-1970 TWIN CYLINDER FACTORY WORKSHOP MANUAL
NORTON 1970-1975 COMMANDO 850 & 750cc FACTORY WSM
NORTON 1975-1978 MK 3 COMMANDO 850 cc FACTORY WSM
PANTHER 1932-1958 LIGHTWEIGHT MODELS 250 & 350cc (BOOK OF)
PANTHER 1938-1966 HEAVYWEIGHT MODELS 600 & 650cc (BOOK OF)
PENTON-KTM-SACHS 1968-1975 100cc & 125cc WORKSHOP MANUAL
RALEIGH MOTORCYCLES 1919-1933 (BOOK OF)
ROYAL ENFIELD 1934-1946 SINGLES & V TWINS (BOOK OF)
ROYAL ENFIELD 1937-1953 SINGLES & V TWINS (BOOK OF)
ROYAL ENFIELD 1946-1962 SINGLES (BOOK OF)
ROYAL ENFIELD 1948-1962 350cc & 500cc PRE-UNIT BULLET WSM
ROYAL ENFIELD 1948-1963 500cc TWINS FACTORY WORKSHOP MANUAL
ROYAL ENFIELD 1952-1963 700cc TWINS FACTORY WORKSHOP MANUAL
ROYAL ENFIELD 1956-1966 250cc CRUSADER & 350cc NEW BULLET WSM
ROYAL ENFIELD 1958-1966 250cc & 350cc SINGLES (SECOND BOOK OF)
ROYAL ENFIELD 1962-1970 INTERCEPTOR WSM'S & PARTS (Compilation)
RUDGE 1933-1939 (BOOK OF)
SACHS 1968-1975 100cc & 125cc ENGINES WSM & M/CYCLE PARTS LIST
SUNBEAM 1928-1939 (BOOK OF)
SUNBEAM 1946-1957 S7 & S8 (BOOK OF)
SUZUKI 50cc & 80cc UP TO 1966 (BOOK OF)
SUZUKI T10 1963-1967 FACTORY WORKSHOP MANUAL
SUZUKI T20 & T200 1965-1969 FACTORY WORKSHOP MANUAL
SUZUKI TWINS 1962 ONWARDS 125-500cc WORKSHOP MANUAL
TRIUMPH 1935-1949 SINGLES & TWINS (BOOK OF)
TRIUMPH 1937-1961 SINGLES SV & OHV 250cc-600cc + TERRIER & CUB
TRIUMPH 1945-1955 PRE-UNIT 350cc, 500cc & 650cc TWINS WSM No.11
TRIUMPH 1945-1959 TWINS (BOOK OF)
TRIUMPH 1956-1969 TWINS (BOOK OF)
TRIUMPH 1956-1962 PRE-UNIT 500cc & 650cc TWINS WSM No.17
TRIUMPH 1957-1963 UNIT CONSTRUCTION 350-500cc WSM No.4
TRIUMPH 1963-1974 UNIT CONSTRUCTION 350-500cc FACTORY WSM
TRIUMPH 1963-1970 UNIT CONSTRUCTION 650cc FACTORY WSM
TRIUMPH 1968-1974 TRIDENT T150 & T150V FACTORY WSM
TRIUMPH 1971-1973 650cc OIL-IN-FRAME FACTORY WSM
TRIUMPH 1973-1978 750cc BONNEVILLE & TIGER FACTORY WSM
TRIUMPH 1979-1983 750cc T140, TR7 & TR65 FACTORY WSM
VELOCETTE 1925-1970 ALL SINGLES & TWINS (BOOK OF)
VELOCETTE 1933-1952 MOV-MAC-MSS RIGID FRAME FACTORY WSM
VELOCETTE 1953-1960 MAC SPRING FRAME WSM & ILL PARTS LIST
VELOCETTE 1954-1971 MSS-VENOM-THRUXTON-VIPER FACTORY WSM
VILLIERS ENGINE UP TO 1959 INC. 3 WHEELERS (BOOK OF)
VILLIERS ENGINE UP TO 1969 (BOOK OF)
VINCENT 1935-1955 (WORKSHOP MANUAL)
YAMAHA 1961-1967 YA5 & YA6 (WORKSHOP MANUAL & ILL PARTS LIST)
YAMAHA 1971-1972 JT1& JT2 (WORKSHOP MANUAL & ILL PARTS LIST)

VELOCEPRESS MANUALS – SCOOTERS BY MAKE

BSA SUNBEAM SCOOTER WORKSHOP MANUAL 1959-1965
BSA SUNBEAM SCOOTER 1959-1965 (BOOK OF)
LAMBRETTA 1947-1957 ALL 125 & 150cc MODELS (BOOK OF)
LAMBRETTA 1957-1970 LI & TV MODELS (SECOND BOOK OF)
NSU PRIMA 1956-1964 ALL MODELS (BOOK OF)
TRIUMPH TIGRESS SCOOTER WORKSHOP MANUAL 1959-1965
TRIUMPH TIGRESS SCOOTER (BOOK OF)
VESPA 1951-1961 (BOOK OF)
VESPA 1955-1963 125 & 150cc & GS MODELS (SECOND BOOK OF)
VESPA 1955-1968 GS & SS (BOOK OF)
VESPA 1963-1972 90, 125 & 150cc (THIRD BOOK OF)

VELOCEPRESS MANUALS – MOPEDS & MOTORIZED BICYCLES

CYCLEMOTOR (BOOK OF)
NSU QUICKLY 1953-1963 ALL MODELS (BOOK OF)
PUCH MAXI N & S MAINTENANCE & REPAIR (3 MANUAL COMPILATION)
RALEIGH MOPEDS 1960-1969 (BOOK OF)

VELOCEPRESS MANUALS - THREE WHEELER'S

BOND MINICAR THREE WHEELER 1948-1967 (BOOK OF)
BMW ISETTA FACTORY WORKSHOP MANUAL
BSA THREE WHEELER (BOOK OF)
RELIANT REGAL THREE WHEELER 1952-1973 (BOOK OF)
VINTAGE MORGAN THREE WHEELER (BOOK OF)

VELOCEPRESS TECHNICAL BOOKS – MOTORCYCLE

1930'S BRITISH MOTORCYCLE CARBS & ELEC COMPONENTS (BOOK OF)
1930'S BRITISH MOTORCYCLE ENGINES (OVERHAUL & MAINTENANCE)
1930'S BRITISH MOTORCYCLE GEARBOXES & CLUTCHES (BOOK OF)
CATALOG OF BRITISH MOTORCYCLES (1951 MODELS)
LUCAS ELECTRONICS BRITISH M/CYCLES REPAIR & PARTS (1950-1977)
MOTORCYCLE ENGINEERING (P.E. Irving)
MOTORCYCLE ROAD TESTS 1949-1953 (Motor Cycle Magazine UK)
SPEED AND HOW TO OBTAIN IT (Motor Cycle Magazine UK)
TUNING FOR SPEED (P.E. Irving)
WIPAC (COMBO) MANUAL NUMBER 3 + M/CYCLE & SCOOTER MANUAL

VELOCEPRESS MANUALS – AUTOMOBILE BY MAKE

ALFA ROMEO GIULIA WORKSHOP MANUAL 1300 TO 2000cc 1962-1975
ALFA ROMEO GIULIA TECH MANUAL CARBURETED CARS FROM 1962
ALFA ROMEO GIULIA TECH MANUAL FUEL INJECTED CARS FROM 1969
ALFA ROMEO GIULIETTA & GIULIA 750 & 101 SERIES 1955-1965 WSM
AUSTIN-HEALEY SPRITE & MG MIDGET WORKSHOP MANUAL 1958-1971
BMW 600 LIMOUSINE FACTORY WORKSHOP MANUAL
BMW 600 LIMOUSINE OWNERS HAND BOOK & SERVICE MANUAL
BMW 2000 & 2002 1966-1976 WORKSHOP MANUAL
BMW 2500, 2800, 3.0 & BARVARIA WORKSHOP MANUAL
CORVAIR 1960-1969 WORKSHOP MANUAL
CORVETTE V8 1955-1962 WORKSHOP MANUAL
FERRARI HANDBOOK ROAD & RACE CARS (SERVICE/SPECS) 1948-1958
FERRARI 250GT SERVICE & MAINTENANCE by JIM RIFF 1956-1965
FERRARI 250GT & 250GTE FACTORY PARTS AND REPAIR MANUALS
FIAT 500 FACTORY WORKSHOP MANUAL 1957-1973
FIAT 600, 600D & MULTIPLA FACTORY WORKSHOP MANUAL 1955-1969
JAGUAR E-TYPE 3.8 & 4.2 SERIES 1 & 2 WORKSHOP MANUAL
JAGUAR MK 7, 8, 9 & XK120, 140, 150 WORKSHOP MANUAL 1948-1961
MERCEDES-BENZ 280 SERIES 1968-1972
METROPOLITAN FACTORY WORKSHOP MANUAL
MGA & MGB OWNERS HANDBOOK & WORKSHOP MANUAL
MG MIDGET TC, TD, TF & TF1500 WORKSHOP MANUAL
PORSCHE 356 1948-1965 WORKSHOP MANUAL
PORSCHE 911 2.0, 2.2, 2.4 LITRE 1964-1973 WORKSHOP MANUAL
PORSCHE 911 2.7, 3.0, 3.2 LITRE 1973-1989 WORKSHOP MANUAL
PORSCHE 912 WORKSHOP MANUAL
PORSCHE 914/4 & 914/6 1.7, 1.8, 2.0 LITRE 1970-1976 WSM
TRIUMPH TR2, TR3, TR4 1953-1965 WORKSHOP MANUAL
VOLKSWAGEN TRANSPORTER, TRUCKS & WAGONS 1950-1979 WSM
VOLVO 1944-1968 ALL MODELS WORKSHOP MANUAL

VELOCEPRESS TECHNICAL BOOKS - AUTOMOBILE

HOW TO BUILD A FIBERGLASS CAR
HOW TO BUILD A RACING CAR
HOW TO RESTORE THE MODEL 'A' FORD
MASERATI OWNER'S HANDBOOK
PERFORMANCE TUNING THE SUNBEAM TIGER
SOUPING THE VOLKSWAGEN
SOLEX CARBURETORS (EMPHASIS ON UK & EU AUTOMOBILES)
SU CARBURETORS (EMPHASIS ON UK AUTOMOBILES)
WEBER CARBURETORS (EMPHASIS ON ALFA & FIAT)

VELOCEPRESS BOOKS & GUIDES - AUTOMOBILE

COMPLETE CATALOG OF JAPANESE MOTOR VEHICLES
FERRARI 308 SERIES BUYER'S AND OWNER'S GUIDE
FERRARI BROCHURES AND SALES LITERATURE 1968-1989
FERRARI SERIAL NUMBERS PART I - ODD NUMBERS TO 21399
FERRARI SERIAL NUMBERS PART II - EVEN NUMBERS TO 1050
HENRY'S FABULOUS MODEL "A" FORD
MASERATI BROCHURES AND SALES LITERATURE

VELOCEPRESS BOOKS – AUTO RACING

BOOK OF THE 1950 CARRERA PANAMERICANA - MEXICAN ROAD RACE
DIALED IN - THE JAN OPPERMAN STORY
VEDA ORR'S NEW REVISED HOT ROD PICTORIAL
LIFE OF TED HORN – AMERICAN RACING CHAMPION

www.VelocePress.com